'It's as if fate placed Niamh in the precise place and time to capture this important cover image that tells a thousand words. The decisive moment … indeed, a defining moment in history. We can feel the churn in the water, the triumph through the expression on his face, and the perfect paired offset geometry of the body positions in the frame. It's "the" shot.

However, that's not the half of it … if fate placed Niamh there, it was destiny that guided the story to the pages of this book. And there are so many more than a thousand words to be told. I think it's the relatability of Phil and Paul, and the idea that heroes are among us. What a photo, but what a story behind the it. I couldn't put it down.'

David Evans,
Australian Landscape Photographer of the Year

'A compelling read from an author whose intimate knowledge of the sea and seafaring infuses every page.

A story of extraordinary courage and endurance shot through with the enduring power of ordinary love'

Hilary Fannin,
Irish Times Columnist of the Year and author of
The Weight of Love *and* Hopscotch

Front cover and back photographs by Niamh McAnally

FLARES
UP

FLARES UP

A Story Bigger
Than The Atlantic

Niamh McAnally

First published by Pitch Publishing, 2022

Pitch Publishing
9 Donnington Park,
85 Birdham Road,
Chichester,
West Sussex,
PO20 7AJ
www.pitchpublishing.co.uk
info@pitchpublishing.co.uk

A CIP catalogue record is available for this book
from the British Library.

ISBN 978 1 80150 398 3

Typesetting and origination by Pitch Publishing

For Gary

Foreword

by Jeremy Irons

I first met Niamh McAnally in Colombia, in the jungle, on the arm of her father, the great Irish actor, the late Ray McAnally. It was 1985 and she must have been in her early twenties. We were making a film called *The Mission*, and Niamh was there for the ride.

I suspect 'there for the ride' was not a phrase in her lexicon, since as well as supporting her father, she quickly made herself a valued assistant to the director Roland Joffé, and an enthusiastic member of the stunt team.

Years passed before I heard of her again, and by then she had grown into an ocean traveller, living aboard her now husband's yacht, sailing the seven seas in search of adventure, fuelled by a curiosity for what life had to offer and writing down her experiences for others to share. A person with a lust for life and love who seemed to have learned the lesson that the more you give of yourself, the more life will give you back.

So it came as no surprise that being by chance in Antigua, and witnessing the landfall of two middle-aged Englishmen who had spent 70 days rowing the Atlantic, she should become fascinated enough by their plight to set pen to paper and record why and how two such unlikely heroes came to pit their wits against the fierce Atlantic. She must have recognised them as fellow travellers, determined to make the most of what life has to offer, to test themselves to their limits, becoming an example of what can be achieved when we push ourselves far beyond our comfort zone.

In a world of growing affluence, the majority of such tests of skill, bravery and pure guts are most often facilitated by large corporate back-up, allowing for the latest technology and communications in support.

But the 55-year-old Paul Hopkins and the 65-year-old Phil Pugh, both from Tyneside in the north of England, had little financial support compared to the other competitors in the Talisker Whisky Atlantic Challenge, and had to rely on their second-hand boat, the only wooden boat in that 2019 crossing. The boat was aptly named *Didi – Dream It, Do It*.

Paul, a firefighter, had never rowed a boat before, but in the long hours of training with Phil on the River Tyne and in the North Sea, stroke by stroke, these two middle-aged men grew a mutual trust that was to serve them well during an Atlantic crossing plagued with equipment failure and continual rough weather. But no matter what the sea or news from back home threw at them, they refused to let each other down.

These were the two men Niamh photographed standing in their boat off Nelson's Dockyard in Antigua as they landed amongst flares and strangers, their loved ones absent. And the following pages chart the hopes and the sacrifices that they made to get there.

As one who has learned how hard it can be for those living alongside people who become focused on a particular project, I recognise the many sacrifices that others have to make to allow such dreams to be followed. Niamh does not ignore the downside of such obsession, and the burden carried by those left at home. Neither does she let us forget Paul and Phil's desire to inspire children of all backgrounds to know they can achieve amazing things. Dream It, Do It. And they Did It.

This is an inspirational story for all ages and pockets.

Prologue
20 February 2020

Antigua

The flare set fire to the evening sky. From the same boat, a second one blazed; its red sparks reflected on the dusky waters off the Antiguan coast. Two flares. Normally a sign of distress, a call for help, a plea for rescue, but not these flares, not this time, not this night.

An hour earlier, locals and visitors, cruisers and superyacht staff had begun to gather around a podium at Nelson's Dockyard in English Harbour on the southern end of Antigua. The atmosphere tingled. Word had gone out: 'They're coming!'

Outside the inlet, wind drove white caps on to nearby rocks and pelicans deferred their dives for fish. In the fading light, a dot appeared on the horizon. It disappeared, then reappeared as it rode the swells. The closer it got, the more details emerged — a white boat, maybe 20 feet long, oars dipping in a lumpy sea. Stick figures became the silhouettes of two men slicing their way home. The media and race officials of the Talisker Whisky Atlantic Challenge jumped in powerboats and sped out to sea to guide them in. Only a couple more strokes and these two middle-aged British men would complete their arduous voyage, having rowed 3,000 nautical miles across the Atlantic, from the Canary Islands to the Caribbean.

As the tiny vessel skimmed between the red and green buoys marking the finish line, the cannon fired and the harbour erupted in a cacophony of horns, hooters, ships' bells and whistles. From sailboats to luxury yachts, every deck of every moored boat was laden with mariners applauding their achievement, and along the cliff road citizens and expats waved their national flags.

In keeping with race tradition, the two balding, bearded men stood up in their tiny boat, despite the choppy sea, lit their hand-held flares and raised them to the skies. The red-hot blaze illuminated their weary but elated faces. Smoke snaked its way around their torsos and morphed into clouds of grey against the dark green hills. The media boat circled them, filming their moment of triumph. Race officials in an inflatable dinghy followed their arc. Round and around the rowers they sped, churning up a congratulatory spray. In the centre of the rowboat, still as bronze, stood the two men who had dared to dream.

On the quay, emotion overwhelmed the well-wishers who waited for them to step ashore.

'I'm in bits,' one tourist said, 'and I don't even know them.'

'Me neither,' said a local woman, passing her a tissue. 'I came down because I heard they had no family here to greet them.'

Beside them, a proud father, who'd flown from South Africa, chatted with his 25-year-old son, who'd crossed the finish line the previous week. Four small children with Scottish accents stood next to their mum, anxiously awaiting their dad, who still had six more days to row. This crowd of international strangers had become friends, united in recognition of the potential of the human spirit.

'Ladies and gentlemen,' the Danish race director, Carsten Olsen, announced, 'let's give it up for team Atlantic Dream Challenge.'

Cheers echoed off the harbour walls as the vessel touched the dock. Onlookers found it hard to grasp that this boat — adorned with inspirational stickers, signatures of supporters, and rust stains that dripped from a now defunct solar panel – this small wooden boat, whose only form of propulsion came from the carbon fibre oars and the sheer determination of the men who plied them, had just traversed a tumultuous sea. In homes across the world, devoted followers watched the livestream on the internet as these two stocky, unathletic-looking men posed for photos. Between them they held the official banner which read: *We Rowed the Atlantic.*

'Would you like to see them step ashore?' Carsten asked the crowd.

Another cheer. One after the other, the men set foot on solid ground and swayed. Marine-lagged, their bodies were still tuned to the rhythms of their watery home. They weren't the first to arrive, nor were they the last, but when they took their place on the podium, next to the sign documenting their certified time, they hugged, slapped each other on the back and bellowed a winner's roar. They'd done it. They had damn-well-done-it.

Questions peppered the minds of those who stood in awe. Who were these intrepid characters, Paul Hopkins and Phil Pugh from Newcastle upon Tyne? And *why*? Why did they decide to row across an ocean? Not the prepared why they told the press or the noble why they told their friends, but the real why they told themselves in the dark of night. The why that drove them during the years of preparation and enabled them to say goodbye to loved ones they prayed they would see again. The why that made quitting not an option when they faced storms and equipment failure in the middle of Poseidon's rage, and the why they had yet to discover once they'd stepped on dry land and reflected on who they had become during those 70 days, 9 hours and 11 minutes at sea.

PART ONE

Chapter 1

6 September 2014

PAUL HOPKINS was hungry. Dinner at Byker Community Fire Station was hit or miss, depending on who was cooking. Tonight, thankfully, was a hit. His plate was heaped with piping-hot spaghetti bologese and garlic bread.

'Smells delicious, Andy, thanks.'

'Welcome, gaffer.'

While he waited for the lads to pass around the large bowl of parmesan, Paul crunched into the bread. He loved mealtimes, the bonding, the banter, and for him, a break from the office, the reports, and having to wear reading glasses. His boss, and fellow triathlete, Carl Latimer, was on holiday, which left him in charge as acting watch manager.

Whoop, whoop, whoop …

The siren went off. Spoons clattered; chairs screeched backwards. Within seconds the first person was down the pole. Paul tore the message off the printer. He'd already assigned duties for the evening – Doug would drive, Bill and Maurice would wear the breathing apparatus – now he shouted the address.

When they pulled up at the student accommodation block for one of Newcastle upon Tyne's universities, they found the street littered with teenagers, some dressed for bed, others for a Saturday night on the town. But no sign of a fire. Paul hoped this wasn't another prank call-out, especially since his stomach and dinner had been so rudely separated.

'Anyone know what happened?'

A chap in a dressing gown came forward.

'I think it's my flat.'

'Okay. Let's check it out.'

When Paul and his crew reached the young man's room, they found the detector had been activated, but no sign of any damage.

'What were you doing that might have set this off?'

'My hair.'

'Sorry?'

'I think I used too much cream. My straighteners started smoking.'

'Right.'

After Paul reset the panel, they headed back to base.

'It was a splash of Brut in my day,' said Paul.

'You're only jealous,' Doug said. 'Been a long time since you needed a hairbrush.'

Paul patted his head. 'Sooner have a semi-polished noggin than your ugly mop.'

'At least mine isn't grey,' said Doug.

'I think you'll find my Nicola calls this colour "distinguished".'

'She's biased.'

'Biased wife, happy life.'

Doug laughed. 'This from the man on his third marriage.'

'I'm a slow learner.'

As they drove through town Paul noticed the pubs and restaurants had started to fill. They were in for a busy weekend with all the out-of-towners who had descended on Newcastle for the half-marathon tomorrow. If he wasn't working, he wouldn't mind heading out for a pint or two himself. He loved the pub atmosphere. He'd met almost everyone he'd ever dated in a bar, including Diane, his first wife, and mother of his two older sons, Sean and Jamie, and Vicki, his second wife, too. Well, if he couldn't go out for a beer, the next best thing was a good plate of grub. Fifteen minutes later, he and the crew were once again sitting down to eat. Paul eyed his mountain of food with that heady feeling of love at first sight. He stabbed the pasta with his fork and twirled, scooped the meat sauce on top and shoved the whole lot into his mouth.

'God, this is a feast, Andy.'

Two more mouthfuls. Joy.

Whoop, whoop …

Once again, the turn-out system transformed the crew like a pack of Pavlov's dogs. In rapid succession Paul swallowed, jumped, and slid. He ripped the message off the printer.

Persons reported.

This was the big one. The practice, the drills, all for this — to rescue people from a burning building. There was no banter now, just the echo of Paul's announcement being repeated from one firefighter to the next. Persons reported. Seconds could determine life or death.

Lights flashing, alarm screeching, they left the forecourt and drove up the hill. Paul watched Doug rock back and forth in the driver's seat. His face was taut. This part of the call-out was all on him.

'Clear left,' said Paul.

'Thanks, gaffer.'

Doug took the intersection as fast as he dared, the engine leaning hard over. The fastest route was past the busy bars. Paul scanned the street for idiots. He heard the lads in the back checking their breathing apparatus and in the wing mirror he saw the second fire engine right behind them. Good. Two teams, better chance.

Doug parked the rig as close to the block of flats as possible.

'Let's go.' Even though there was still no sign of a fire, Paul grabbed his kit and ran across the grass. A group of neighbours waved, directing him to the rear of the building.

'Is anyone home?' he asked them.

'Yes, yes,' one of them answered, 'the door is locked.'

As soon as Paul came around the corner, he could see smoke coming out of a flat on the ground floor. The windows were blackened. Paul was glad to see a wooden door, not composite.

'Stand back.'

Paul swung hard and fast with the sledgehammer. He knew breaking the door would add oxygen to the fire, putting his team in more danger, but he had no option but to send them in. He hit the lock full on. The door broke open, wood splinters flew. As the air rushed in, smoke poured out the top of the doorway. Without hesitation Bill and Maurice disappeared into the thick smoke. They were well trained, but, as always, Paul was conscious that he was responsible for whether or not his crew would see their loved ones again. He briefed the second team and sent them in.

Paul radioed Control, letting them know how many people he had committed to the property and the equipment in use. Just after the second crew entered the flat, the first rushed out, Bill carrying a middle-aged woman. He didn't need to call for oxygen. Maurice had the O_2 mask covering her mouth and nose before Bill set her down on the chair a neighbour had brought. Her face was black with soot, but not burned.

'Is there anyone else in there?' Paul asked her.

She coughed, spluttered.

'Anyone else in there?'

Paul knew she needed to take a breath, to replace the toxic smoke clinging to her throat and lungs, but he had to know. If there was someone else, they only had seconds left.

'Anyone else?'

The lady gasped. 'My dogs, save my dogs.'

'Got it, gaffer.' Bill and Maurice went back in.

Paul radioed the second pair.

'How are we doing?'

'Structure's okay. Just got two more hotspots.'

'Okay. Look for dogs.'

'Copy.'

Paul heard the ambulance arrive. The rush of adrenaline that had flooded his body started to fade. Although his teams were trained first-aiders, it was always a relief to see the paramedics arrive on scene. He sent an update to Control. The fire was almost out, the woman's breathing was improving. If they could save her dogs, it would be a bonus.

An older couple approached. Paul was happy to let these neighbours console her. The comfort of familiar faces would do her good.

'Where's John?' the gentleman asked her.

'Who's John?' said Paul.

'Her husband.'

'Where's John?' Paul asked the woman.

She pointed at her flat.

'Where? What room?'

She shook her head.

'One more, lads. A man.'

They'd lost valuable time. What would they find? He didn't want to open that box, the box he kept locked at the back of his mind: images of corpses he'd pulled from burned-out buildings, body parts he'd picked up from railway tracks, human remains he'd cut out of cars. If he let those pictures loose, he would never sleep again.

'Lads, any sign?'

'Coming.'

The second crew came out carrying an unconscious man. The ambulance team went to work, pounding on his chest.

The woman gasped. 'Oh my God, John.'

'Would you mind walking her to the ambulance?' Paul asked the neighbours. Real-life CPR was a lot more physical than in the movies.

As he watched the couple lead her away, he wondered how she could have remembered her dogs before her husband. But then, even though he had been to many fires, he had never been pulled out of one, so who was he to judge? At least he was sure his wife, Nicola, would think of him and their 13-year-old son, James, before their dog, Betty Boo. Wouldn't she?

His radio squawked.

'Gaffer, we have them.'

The first crew emerged, each of them carrying a dog.

Chapter 2

7 September 2014

PHIL PUGH didn't need the alarm. Even though it was Sunday, and he would normally like a bit of a lie-in, his eyes flew open and he jumped out of bed. Race day. The annual Newcastle half-marathon, known as the Great North Run, was a highlight in his family's calendar. For the past seven years, he had run it with his three sons. He and his two younger lads, Rod and Alex, would take turns pushing Tom's wheelchair through the course while collecting money for Tiny Lives, a charity which supports the families, babies and staff on the Neonatal Unit at the Royal Victoria Infirmary, Newcastle upon Tyne.

His wife, Meme, called from the kitchen. 'Morning, Phil. Scrambled?'

'Lovely, thanks. Just going to give Tom a quick call.' He dialled the independent living facility on The Causeway and his son's support worker answered.

'Hi, Mr Pugh.'

'Good morning, Emily, how are you? How's Tom?'

'Excited. He's already talking about his beer at the finish line.'

Phil chuckled.

'Here he is.'

'Hi, Dad.'

'Are you ready, son?'

'Can't wait, Dad.' Tom laughed. The pure joy and innocence that burst out of his eldest was Phil's favourite sound. He wished he could bottle the love and pride he felt when he heard his voice.

'Soon. Emily will bring you.'

'Are Alex and Rod coming?'

'Of course.'

'Will you be there, Dad?'

'Yes, Tom.'

'And Mum?'

'Yes Tom, she'll be there too.'

'Meme?'

'We'll all be there.' Phil heard the doorbell. 'Rod, can you get that? Okay, Tom, sounds like Alex has just arrived. We'll see you at the rendezvous.'

'Where will I see you?'

'Emily knows.'

'Can't wait to see you, Dad, and can't wait for that beer.'

Tom was still laughing when they disconnected. In the kitchen, Meme was setting a platter of sausages and scrambled eggs on the table.

'Thanks, love, looks delicious.'

'Yum,' said Alex, sitting down.

Rod took his leftover pizza out of the fridge and offered it around.

'No thanks,' said Phil. 'I'll stick with protein.'

'Gotta carb up, Dad,' said Rod, 'Tom's chair's not light any more.'

'Oh, did you finish the modifications, Rod?' said Alex. 'How's it going?'

'Great. I've come up with a name for the company. I'm going to call it Adventure Mobility.'

'Cool. Bet Tom's thrilled to have the prototype. How is he?'

'Thirsty,' said Phil.

'Ha, he's been talking about that cold one for weeks.'

Phil smiled. 'Yes, he has.'

'So, Alex, how are things at uni?' asked Meme. 'Did your professor get back?'

'Unfortunately. Eggs are delicious, thanks.'

'I'm so glad to be done with college,' said Rod, his mouth full of pizza crust.

As Phil ate, he couldn't help but feel proud of all three of his boys. They'd only been young teenagers when he and their mum, Debbie, divorced, but they'd got through it, and then later had very generously accepted Meme into their lives. He was enjoying having Rod living with them again while he was working to set up his own business.

'We'd better get a move on,' said Alex, starting to clear the table.

'Don't worry about the dishes,' said Meme. 'I'll get them later, thanks. Would you like me to give you guys a ride down?'

'It'll probably be easier to walk from here, thanks anyway.'

'Better to meet us at the finish line, love.' Phil gave her a kiss.

'You got it.'

As Phil and his sons strolled towards the meeting point, they passed a handful of people, then larger groups, all heading in the same direction. The closer they got, the thicker the crowds, hundreds, then thousands.

The serious athletes, many of whom had come from overseas, were dressed in branded running gear and expensive trainers but there were also plenty of fun runners attired in fancy dress.

'Dad, Dad.'

'There he is.' Phil gave Tom a big wave.

The 26-year-old's excitement was infectious. Dressed as a superhero, Tom sat in the all-terrain wheelchair that Phil had helped Rod adapt for him.

'How's my bestest pal?' Phil bent down to give him a hug. 'Any jokes for me?'

Tom grinned. 'What do you get when you cross a cat with a lemon?'

'I don't know.'

'A sourpuss,' said Tom, laughing in delight.

'Good one,' said Phil. Rod and Alex joined in the merriment which made Tom laugh even more.

'Ladies and gentlemen,' the marshal announced over the PA system, 'the entry gates are now closed.'

The music started. TV cameras rolled. Athletes stretched their quads, shook their shoulders; runners sipped their water, checked their snacks. Phil tucked Tom's diabetic kit into the back of his chair. He was delighted to see even more people in wheelchairs taking part this year.

The starter began the countdown. 'Ten, nine, eight …'

The crowd picked up the chant, 'seven, six …'

'Where's Ant and Dec?' asked Tom, as he did every year since the TV presenting duo had started the 2010 race. He'd loved how they'd high-fived the runners as they'd passed by.

'Someone else this year,' replied Phil as he did every year Tom asked.

'… two, one,' Tom finished.

The pistol fired.

'Let's go, Dad.'

Phil moved into position behind Tom's chair, Rod and Alex flanking him. The Pugh family was ready to run but there was barely enough room to jog. It took 40 minutes for all 57,000 runners to cross the starting line. Once the athletes up front broke away the crowd thinned. Phil pushed while Rod and Alex ran along the edge of the road seeking donations. Spectators dropped coins in the buckets. The first half mile took them beneath the underpass and on to the central motorway. As they approached Tyne Bridge, they spotted people they knew along the route.

'Well done, Tom, keep going.'

Tom laughed and cheered. Just past McDonald's, Phil spotted his ex-wife waving from the sidelines.

'Look, Tom, there's Mum.'

'Hi, Mum.'

'You're doing great, Tom,' called Debbie. 'See you at the finish.'

'That's one mile done, Tom,' said Phil, already sweating in the blazing heat. 'Do you want a drink?'

'Yeah.'

Rod squeezed the water bottle into Tom's mouth but it spattered over his face. Tom coughed and laughed and coughed.

'How much longer?'

'Another couple of hours, mate.'

Runners overtook them, they overtook others. At the seven-mile mark Team Pugh pulled over to the side to check Tom's blood sugar.

'How long till my beer?'

'Another while yet. Time for some food first, but let's keep going.'

Rod took over pushing while Phil ran alongside, breaking a sandwich into bite-size pieces and feeding them to Tom. When they approached the town of South Shields, the punishing incline slowed them to a walk.

'This hill gets harder every year,' said Phil.

'Look, Tom, there's Mo Farah,' said Rod. 'How cool.'

'He's going the wrong way,' said Tom.

Having already won, in a personal best of exactly one hour, the British Olympian waved as he passed.

'It's okay, he's on his way back to Newcastle.'

'Dad?'

'Don't worry, son, we are going back by car.'

Seeing the great athlete inspired their final push up the hill. At the top, they circled the roundabout that marked the last mile. As they took off down the steep gradient Tom chanted: 'Beer, beer, beer.'

Halfway down Phil's left leg cramped, then his right. Both calves knotted tight. He moved to the railing and groaned in pain. Rod looked over his shoulder. 'Dad?'

'Keep going, lads.'

'We'll wait for you.'

'No, don't, get Tom across the line.'

Phil moved his right foot forward, but it was as if it belonged to someone else. He tried to put weight on his left. Same. He put one foot up on the kerb and pushed down through his heel to stretch his calf. The pain was excruciating. His fingers curled around the rail even tighter. He took a deep breath and willed the steel knots to unravel. Then he pushed off the railing and hobbled forward. He had to keep going. He had no choice. He couldn't disappoint Tom, but above all, he still owed God.

Twenty-six years earlier, in Bath General Hospital, Phil and Debbie had kept vigil beside their son's cot. Their first-born had come into the world at 24 weeks and now, two months later, was making his exit. The consultant and nursing staff suggested they call a priest; Tom wouldn't last the night. But Phil and Debbie refused to give up hope. They prayed for a miracle and willed the ventilator to force oxygen into Tom's tiny lungs. As the night progressed, Tom's hold on life slipped further away.

The nurse returned and asked Debbie if she would like to rest.

'No, I don't want to leave him.'

'I'll stay,' said Phil.

'What if—'

'If there's any change I'll come and get you right away.'

Debbie was too tired to yawn and too distraught to argue. 'Promise?'

'I promise.'

She laid her hand on the incubator. 'I love you to the moon and back, Tom. Stay with us, my angel.'

After the nurse led Debbie to a room across the hall, Phil put his head in his hands and cried. He bargained with God. Hour after hour, he begged, he promised. He vowed he would do everything he could to take care of Tom if God would just let him live.

'Are you listening, God? Just give us a chance to love him.'

No matter how hard he prayed, no matter how much he hoped, he could feel Tom leaving. The sun was about to rise on what Phil knew would be the worst day of his life. At 6am the door to the unit opened, and a man in white approached Tom's cot.

'Shall we give him the full amount?'

'Yes, of course.'

Phil watched the syringe, with 100ml of type O positive blood, empty into his tiny son. The doctor smiled and left as calmly as he had arrived.

'Please God, please.'

Then Phil thought he saw something. Not the face of God, but something different on the monitor. Yes, the numbers had changed. The oxygen input into Tom's little body had fallen from 90 per cent to 85. Seconds became minutes, 85 per cent dropped to 80. Was he imagining it, or was Tom taking charge of his own breathing? Phil watched, thrilled with every number his son claimed. 'Yes, Tom, breathe. Keep breathing. I'll be back with your mum.'

Across the hall, Phil put his hand on Debbie's shoulder. She jumped.

'Oh my God. Tom.'

'It's okay, it's okay. Come.' He took her hand and together they crossed to the Special Baby Unit, but before they reached the door, Debbie stopped.

'Look,' she said, pointing down the corridor.

Phil followed her gaze. At the end of the hall, he saw a ball of sunlight. How could that be? There were no windows and no doors to the outside. It grew, expanded outwards and inched up the corridor, lighting everything along the way. When it reached them, it seemed to swirl around their bodies, enveloping them in golden light. A sense of peace embraced them and they held each other close. In that moment they both knew God had granted their miracle.

'Come on, you're almost there.'

Supporters on the sidelines brought Phil back to the race. He moved his right foot in front and pushed down through the heel, trying to keep the scream from reaching his throat. Then, the left. He hobbled forward. He saw his three sons waiting at the finish.

'Come on, Dad,' Rod shouted. 'You've got this.'

His left leg was easing and he used it to limp. Every step seemed to take forever but he focused his eyes on Tom, breathed through the pain and stumbled across the line.

'Well done, Dad.'

'Well done you, Tom,' said Phil. 'Let's go get our medals and tee-shirts.'

'Do you need my chair?'

Oh, how he loved his boy's wicked sense of humour. He kissed the top of Tom's head.

'Now can we have beer?'

'Absolutely, you've earned it.'

The car park was crowded but they manoeuvred their way to the pub where Meme and Debbie were waiting. Debbie gave each of her boys a hug.

'Did you see us running, Mum?' Tom asked.

'I did, my angel,' said Debbie, taking Tom's hand in hers. 'I'm so proud of you.'

'You did great, Tom, you even beat your dad,' said Meme.

Alex battled his way to the bar and returned with a tray of pints. He put the one with the plastic straw down in front of Tom.

'Cheers, everyone,' said Phil. 'Three hours and five minutes. Our fastest time yet.'

Before Phil had taken his first sip, Tom had sucked his glass dry.

Later, the whole family sat together and shared one of Meme's lovely hotpots. By eight o'clock the four grown men were yawning. Debbie and Alex headed back to their respective homes and Rod gave Meme a hand with the clean-up.

'Right, Tom, time to drive you home too.'

Phil loved evenings like this at the care facility when he could relieve Tom's support workers and spend precious time with his son: bathing him, dressing him in his pyjamas, and carrying him to bed.

'God, the weight of you. How many beers did you have?'

Tom giggled.

Phil was strong, but tonight every muscle in his body ached. His calves still stung from the cramps earlier. Lifting Tom was so much easier when they were both younger. But when he carried his son in his arms, Tom's arm around his neck, his head resting on his shoulder, Phil felt energised by the boundless love they had for each other. As he'd aged, he'd become even more determined to stay fit and healthy enough to be able to support Tom's weight and his dreams. This was what he had signed up for, and he could feel God watching, approving.

When he'd turned 60 in June, Phil had committed to undertaking a new and strenuous challenge every year over the next five. Each one, like swimming the English Channel with Alex and Rod earlier that summer, had to be physically demanding and an adventure that Tom would love to do if cerebral palsy didn't confine him to his chair.

'I had a fantastic day, Dad.'

'That makes me so happy,' said Phil, laying him down on the bed.

'Can we do it again next year?'

'Yes, Tom,' Phil said, standing up and arching his back, 'we'll do it all again next year.'

'Thanks.'

Phil pulled the blankets up over his son.

'Hey, Dad, do elephants snore?'
'I don't know, do they?'
'Only when they're asleep.'
'Good one, Tom. Night, night.'
'Goodnight, Dad. Love you.'
'I love you too.'

Chapter 3

6 October 2014

Given the crushing pain at the back of Paul's skull, he couldn't open his eyes, but the antiseptic smell told him where he was. He lay still, listened. *Beep, beep, beep.* Thank God there was more than one, not that continuous tone. But then he wouldn't have been the one hearing it, of course. The tinnitus in his left ear was dialled up to rock-concert level. A puff of air blew across his torso as he heard metal curtain rings scrape aside. He felt a warm breath near his face. A scent of pesto? Or was it perfume?

'Mr Hopkins.' A cool hand touched the middle of his forearm. 'Mr Hopkins, how are you feeling?'

How was he feeling? How was he feeling? He was feeling *what the fuck?*

Hours earlier he'd been training for the next triathlon he and Carl were planning to do together. He'd set up his stationary bike in the garage. No shame there, even the hardiest of athletes trained indoors during the English winter. James was upstairs doing his homework and Nicola was watching TV. Nothing for it but to stick on Queen's *Greatest Hits* and drag himself through an hour of torture.

As usual, the first few minutes crawled until he got into his rhythm. He focused on the long bike rides he and Carl took on the open roads in the summer: the smell of cut grass, the perfume of flowers in bloom, and the sense of accomplishment when they'd crest that final hill. They were often joined by Carl's neighbour, Zoe Neasham, who'd completed her first marathon and was considering a triathlon next. By the time Freddie Mercury was singing that he'd just killed a man, Paul was pushing peak.

BANG.

Something hit him in the head. Hard. He spun around. Nobody there. He felt for blood but found only sweat. No bumps, no contusions. The pain was intense, as though someone had poured acid inside his head. His legs stopped spinning but his heart pumped faster as panic clawed. *Get a grip, Paul, you're a firefighter, you know how to stay in control.* A couple of deep breaths. Right, let's do something constructive. What though? Peas. The freezer was right there. He stepped off the bike and bent down to retrieve the bag from the bottom drawer. Whoa, that did not feel good. He straightened up. Okay, that was better. He held the peas against the base of his skull. His skin cooled but his head still burned. At least he felt in control now, and pain was just pain − something his dad had told him to deal with when no one was watching. After that one time as a 12-year-old kid, when he'd rolled and bawled on the football pitch, Paul never wanted to disappoint his father ever again.

'Run it off, son, run it off.'

Paul got back on the bike and started pedalling. Not too hard, just turning his legs over. It didn't help. Maybe time to take some pills. In the kitchen, he found the medical box and swallowed a couple. Perhaps a lie-down. As he passed through the lounge, Nic looked up from the telly.

'What's up with you?'

'Pain in my head, going to rest till it clears.' He climbed the stairs and stretched out on the bed. He lay there in the semi-darkness. Was it easing? Footsteps on the stairs. Nic at the doorway.

'Paul?'

'My head, it's burning at the back.'

'Change out of that wet kit and come downstairs where I can keep an eye on you,' Nic said in her no-nonsense nurse's voice.

For once, Paul didn't argue. He came down in a clean tee-shirt and shorts and sat on the settee.

'Could you turn the TV down a bit, love?'

'You think it's loud?'

Even the lights seemed too bright to Paul.

'James,' Nic called out.

'No need to bother him.'

James came bounding down from his room.

'What's up?' He looked at his father. 'Dad? Are you okay?'

'Pain in my head, son, but I'm okay.'

'Find your dad's shoes, James. We're going to the hospital.'

'No, I'm fine, it's getting better, honest.'

'You're slurring, love.'

'The pills must be kicking in.'

'Shoes.'

Her change in tone scared Paul and James enough to comply.

At the local hospital, A&E was busy, but at least it was a Monday. He let Nic fill out the forms and answer questions.

'Take a seat, sir, we'll call you.'

Paul sat quietly between Nic and James. The burning had stopped but the pressure felt relentless. Despite all his sporting injuries, he had never passed out; he wished he could do so now. But the trained first-aider part of his brain knew patients with head injuries should not go to sleep. He sat forward on the seat, closed his eyes but willed himself to stay awake. Nearby, the cooling motor for the drinks machine kicked on. He focused on its cycle. On, off. On, off. He had no idea how long he had been sitting there when his stomach churned and saliva filled his mouth.

'Nic, Nic, I'm going to be sick.'

Nic flew to reception and came back with a bowl. Now Paul had two things to focus on – don't throw up and don't fall asleep. The nausea passed. Good. Now he only had to concentrate on staying awake. He interlocked his fingers, squeezed his hands. The more trips Nic made to the counter the more agitated she became with the receptionist.

'Don't worry, love, I'm okay.'

'No, Paul, you're not. And if you are not called in next, I'll have something to say.'

'Mr Hopkins?'

Someone, somewhere, was calling his name. He stood up.

'Would you like me to come in with you?' Nic asked.

'No, love, thanks. Don't worry.'

Paul walked into the office and the questions started again. After a brief survey to check the reaction of his pupils and whether he could lift his arms and squeeze her hand, the doctor declared that Paul seemed fine but ordered a CT scan to be sure. More waiting. He went out to tell Nic.

'Why don't you go on and bring James home, this could take a while.'

'I don't mind, Dad.'

'You've got school in the morning, and your mum's been working all day.'

'Are you sure you don't want us to stay with you?' Nic said.

'I'll be okay, love. Promise. I'll ring when I'm done.'

'Mr Hopkins?' A woman in scrubs waited by the door.

Nic gave him a kiss on the cheek and rubbed his shoulder. 'Come on, James.' She turned away but not before Paul saw the look of worry beneath her calm.

After the scans, he was sent to a ward to lie down and await the results.

He'd lost all sense of time when a different doctor arrived in the ward. 'Mr Hopkins, we've had a look, and can't find anything wrong.'

'Really?' said Paul. 'A pain like this is not nothing.'

'Well, you could have a trapped nerve in your neck. We'll keep you in tonight and do a lumbar puncture test in the morning. If that's clear you can go home.'

'Okay, doc, you're the boss. Whatever you think's best.'

'I'll also send your scan to the Royal Victoria Infirmary and let their neurologist have a look.'

'Thanks.'

Ten minutes later, one of the nurses returned.

'We're transferring you.'

'Oh.' The RVI was 12 kilometres away. 'I'll call my wife, she can come back.'

'No time. You need to see their specialist now.'

'Oh.'

Within minutes two paramedics entered the ward pulling a gurney. Paul sat up.

'No, sir, please lie back. We'll do everything.'

The two chaps log-rolled him on to a spinal board, taped his head down and wheeled him to the ambulance, which drove off, sirens blaring. *Bit of overkill for a trapped nerve in my neck*, thought Paul, *but at least I'm getting my money's worth out of the NHS.*

'Can someone call my wife?'

Although he hadn't slept, it was almost morning when the nurse at the Royal Victoria placed her cool hand on his forearm.

'Mr Hopkins, how are you feeling?' she asked again. He should probably open his eyes. It was the polite thing to do. She was pretty, and pretty young.

'Well, I've been better,' said Paul, 'but I'm okay.'

'Yes. You're doing okay for a man who's had a brain haemorrhage.'

'A what?'

'Oh, sorry, had no one told you yet?'

Chapter 4

8 October 2014

On the second day after his brain had bled, Paul was woken by the noise of the hospital day getting under way. Nurses flitted about, checking vitals and updating charts. He couldn't remember how many times he'd been wheeled in and out of various cold rooms for further scans yesterday, but the headache had persisted throughout. When the consultant was satisfied that he could let Paul go to sleep, he was given medication which had seemed to relax him. Last night, he'd even been allowed to sit up, using only one pillow, mind you. He'd been startled to find himself in a room with four other people wearing post-surgical turban-like bandages. Bloody hell, if these were his wardmates, how dire was his own situation?

The one empty bed beside him had been filled this morning. A nurse was asking the man if he was in pain, to which the patient replied: 'Pink grapefruits.'

'Would you like something for the pain?' the nurse tried again.

'Bicycles.'

'Let me get you a pen and paper.'

Paul thought it was a bit harsh asking the lad to write something down when he could hardly speak. Later, when he asked the nurse, she explained how speech and motor skills were located in different parts of the brain. Paul hadn't thought of that, but he wasn't too hard on himself considering he also had a brain injury.

What he couldn't understand was why it had happened to him. He was only 50 years old. Maybe he was a little stocky, and could afford to lose a kilo or two, but with all his training for the triathlon next spring, he was fitter than he'd been in years. It didn't seem fair. Yet here he was, only one hospital bed away from talking gibberish. He was scared to think about how serious it was. So far, he was deaf in his left ear, his legs felt heavy and every heartbeat made his head throb. How long would it take for him to get better? Was a full recovery even possible? He had to find out.

After all the nurses left, he scanned the ward. Good, no one was watching. Time to see whether he could walk. He slid his right leg out, swivelled, next the left. He pressed both hands on to the bed and pushed himself up into a stance.

'STOP. Get back in that bed.' The nurse rushed towards him. 'Who said you could stand up?'

'Em …'

'The doctor told you these first two weeks are critical. So, back in the bed and wait till we say you can move.'

Red-faced, Paul obeyed, but he felt humiliated and depressed. Was this his new life? Dependent on others to help him walk? What would his dad say? He closed his eyes and drew strength from the man he admired the most. His father had endured more physical pain than any other human he knew: TB as a teenager followed by experimental surgeries to fuse his hip joint, cancer of the eye which left it blind, and a heart bypass in the days when they cut you open from throat to ankle. But his father had never complained. He just got on with it, worked hard to provide for his wife and family. Just recently, a rupture in his colon had released E. coli bacteria into his system, attacking his previously replaced knee. The joint had been removed. Now his 81-year-old dad was housebound, his femur and tibia held together by a surgically implanted bar, until the infection could be controlled. He was dealing with it in the same stoic fashion he had done with everything else life had thrown at him, a trait he had instilled in Paul.

The image of his dad morphed into the prettiness of Nic. How she had looked when he'd first met her almost 14 years ago. He'd been sworn off women, having already been married and divorced twice by the time he was 30, but Nic's confidence and joy had been irresistible.

'Paul.'

He could hear her gentle voice, as he had that first weekend when he'd heard her singing to herself.

'Paul.'

Was he dreaming or was she standing beside his hospital bed? He opened his eyes. As beautiful as she was, she looked like she had aged ten years in the last few days. Stress had stamped out her joy, and her confidence had been replaced by fear. He reached for her.

'I'm okay, love.'

'Oh, Paul.' She took his hand. 'I could have lost you ...'

'You know me, I'm indestructible.'

But Nic didn't laugh. His eyelids dropped. When he opened them again it was dark and the doctor stood in her place.

'What's this I hear about you getting out of bed by yourself, Mr Hopkins?'

'Sorry, doc.'

'Remember, any pressure in your head could cause it to bleed again, and next time you might not be so lucky.'

'Okay. When will I be able to go back to work?'

'Eight weeks at the earliest. What do you do?'

'I'm a firefighter.'

'Oh. Well, that's different. Let's just concentrate on you getting better and then we shall see.'

Paul had stopped listening after he'd heard eight weeks.

That afternoon two physiotherapists arrived to help him exercise. They swivelled his legs to the side and helped him into a sitting position.

'Right, now, up you come.'

Paul pressed down through his legs until he could feel himself straightening up. He felt light-headed.

'We've got you. Okay, are you ready to take a step?'

A step? Paul wanted to stride off into the corridor. His feet could feel the coldness of the floor. A good sign. Ready. He moved his right foot; it slid along the floor. His tried to lift his left, but no, it just slid too.

'You're doing great.'

Great? He was failing at something a two-year-old could do. He was a firefighter, a triathlete. He concentrated, tried again, but his feet never left the floor. Sweat curled under his chin. He had taken a total of six steps.

'Okay, that's enough for now, we'll come back in the morning and try again.'

Paul collapsed on the bed, exhausted. It was distressing to realise he was going to have to learn to walk again.

The following morning, the physios returned and between the three of them they rejoiced when he got one foot in the air, then set it down. Same with the other. He took a total of 12 steps. After lunch, he took 20 and made it all the way to the day room.

'Why don't you sit here for a rest and change of scenery? We'll be back in an hour.'

It seemed to Paul they came back in five minutes but he must have fallen asleep from the effort. Each step was exhausting but he was a Hopkins, and a Hopkins man would push through. No one would dictate what he could or could not do.

The following morning, much to their surprise, he made it to the day room with the therapists only hovering. The day after that he went to the loo by himself. In between bouts of fatigue, the milestones continued. After ten days he was proud to give his progress report to the doctor and asked to go home.

'That's great, Mr Hopkins, but not yet. We need to monitor you for another week or so.'

'My wife is a nurse, she could monitor me,' he said, without thinking about how much extra stress that would put on Nic.

'And clearly a good nurse. If she hadn't brought you in when she did, we might not be having this conversation. Very well then, I'll sort out your discharge papers, but take it easy. If there's any change, we'll need to see you immediately.'

'Thank you, doctor.'

The drive home was disconcerting. In hospital he had felt ready for the world, but sitting in the passenger seat next to Nic, his brain struggled to keep up with the speed of everything happening all around him. He had never been so glad to get out of a car.

Friends and colleagues had called or messaged. He started to reply but Nic took his phone away.

'You need to rest, love.'

She was right. Everything was a struggle. When some of the lads came to visit that afternoon, he tried to focus but after seven or eight minutes he forgot what he was saying. From then on Nic set up a rota for visitors and anyone who called round without an appointment would be sent away. Nic and James helped him up the stairs so he would have quiet. He slept on and off. That night, his legs started moving by themselves as if at a disco, although the only music he heard was the one-pitch tone in his right ear, and nothing in the other. The next morning, he tried to stand but his legs kept jigging and couldn't hold his weight. He was shocked by this new symptom, having thought he was over the worst of it. Knowing his legs could fail at any time shook his confidence. He tackled the stairs as a toddler might, scooting up and down on his bum. He was glad his mum and dad couldn't travel to see him in this state, and grateful to Nic for keeping them informed about his progress.

As the days passed and his legs calmed, he tried walking down the stairs, but still had to keep a tight grip on the banisters. By the end of the first month, he had started to notice his incremental progress, although it never seemed fast enough.

One Saturday afternoon in November, he was settled down in front of the TV, remote in hand, about to watch Sky Sports, when a waterfall cascaded in his left ear. It bubbled and crackled, then stopped.

'Nic, Nic, come here.'

Nic rushed in from the kitchen.

'What's up, are you okay?'

'My left ear just cleared. I can hear.'

'Thank goodness.'

He stood up, raising his arms to the side. 'Look, I can balance.'

The breakthroughs continued. As he approached the two-month mark, he assessed his recovery. He could now stand and walk by himself. He could carry on a conversation. He was sleeping through the night and staying awake during the day. He called the chief to let him know he was ready to come back to work. He could return to normal.

But he also appreciated just how lucky he had been – had Nic not known to bring him to A&E, had the first hospital not referred him to the neurosurgeon, had they not transported him to RVI by ambulance, he would be dead. Returning to *normal* did not seem a fitting response to this second chance at life. It was time to celebrate by doing something extraordinary.

All through his childhood in Nottingham, Paul had been told he was stupid. Bullies would taunt him, calling him *Thick* or *Waste-of-space-Hopkins*. Even his two brothers, Sean and Michael, would argue between themselves as to which of them was their dad's cleverest son. The middle child, Paul, was never once considered in the running. With the exception of his parents, everyone seemed to put him down. Schoolteachers would tell him he'd never amount to anything. *Must try harder* was a common remark on his year-end report, especially in English class. Paul could read, but when it came to writing, somehow the letters somersaulted off his pen and landed wherever they liked. No one in the 70s seemed to understand the intelligence or needs of a dyslexic child.

Paul had learned to cope and work around the disorder but for years he felt everyone was laughing at him. Now was the time to prove to all those naysayers that he was capable of achieving something great. He would challenge himself to accomplish something big. Bigger than running an extended ironman race or into a burning building. Something that would demand every ounce of courage, sweat, and determination he'd ever had to draw on. Something inspiring that would make everyone proud. But what?

Chapter 5

3 December 2014

It was almost 6pm when Phil approached the outskirts of Newcastle.

After the three-and-a-half-hour drive home from Scotland, his back was stiff but his mind was energised. This new client acquisition would keep them busy but still leave him enough time to train for his next challenge.

When he pulled into the car park it looked like most of their employees at Adept Communications & Technology had left for the day, but he was pleased to see Meme's Citroën still there.

Their family dog and office mascot greeted him at the door. 'Hi, Morgan, did you miss me?' he said, rubbing his back. 'C'mon, let's go see Meme.'

'I don't need to ask how it went,' she said, when Phil came bouncing into her office.

'Sorry. I suppose my energy is high.'

'Spiking.'

'Let's go out for dinner.'

'It's only Wednesday.'

'Nothing says we have to wait till date night to celebrate.'

'Okay, but let's drop the cars and Morgan at home so we can walk over to the Mantra from there.'

'Sure,' he said, knowing she sometimes found his excitability overwhelming. 'I could use a chance to stretch my legs.'

Phil loved walking hand in hand with Meme. It reminded him of the first weekend they'd met back in 2005 when he'd been working for a UK company in America. After weeks of getting to know each other online, she'd flown from her home in Las Vegas to meet him in Washington DC. She was even more beautiful in person. They'd toured the sites, sat up half the night talking, making love and discovering how connected they were spiritually. It didn't take Phil long to realise Meme was an exceptional woman. Over the next six months the pair of them racked up more air miles than either of them had in the previous five years. When her nursing schedule would allow, she'd come to DC; when it didn't, Phil would fly to her.

But in April of the following year the intense romance was about to come to an end. He'd been recalled to the UK.

'When do you leave?' she'd asked.

'Next month.'

'That soon?'

'I'm sorry.'

'Well, it doesn't have to be the end of us,' she said.

Phil's smile didn't reach his eyes. It was a lovely idea, but it was one thing to live on the same continent separated by a four-hour plane ride. To be together now, it would take three flights, 12 hours and crossing an ocean eight time zones away. He already knew how difficult it was to maintain a long-distance relationship. It could work initially, as it had for himself and Debbie during his earlier shorter postings in the US back in the 80s, before they had children. But this had been a three-year posting and even though Debbie had brought the family over to visit him on summer and Christmas holidays during the first two years, and he had flown back to England for board meetings once a quarter, their 27-year marriage had not survived. What hope would this burgeoning romance have?

Meme reached over and stroked his arm. She had this uncanny way of reading him. 'If you have to go, then I'll come with you.'

'What? You'd give up everything here to come with me?'

'I love you, so yes.'

'What about your kids?'

'I'll talk to them. Chris would probably love going to an English school. I'm not sure about Brittany, but 18's old enough that I can let her decide whether she wants to come too.'

'Your career? Would your nursing degree be recognised in England?'

'I don't know. Maybe it's time for a change anyway.'

Walking the Newcastle streets with Meme now, nine years later, filled him with so much gratitude for her and everything she had given up to make this second marriage work, especially since Brittany had decided to stay in America with her dad. Meme had embraced the challenge of starting a new life with him in England, including leaving behind what was then a male-dominated medical profession and starting a print business, then the tech company they now ran together. Her commitment had helped grow it into the successful entity it was today, employing nine people, including her son Chris.

When they arrived at the restaurant, he held the door open and ushered her in, out of the December chill. The corner booth was warm and cosy. Phil scanned the menu but ordered his usual favourite — vegetarian biriyani with Punjabi paneer and spinach. Meme chose cubes of chicken in a korma sauce with lightly spiced baby aubergines. When the waitress left, Meme spread her cutlery further apart and leaned in.

'So, tell me about the deal.'

'They've agreed to the monthly service contract, but I'm confident we'll win the bid to replace their desktops too when we bring them on to our cloud solution.'

'Awesome.' Meme thanked the waitress when she set down two glasses of water. 'And it's kinda cool that they're in the care facility business.'

'Yep. But that's enough shop talk, how are you?'

'Good, busy day. Had a nice call from Brittany.'

'How is she?'

'She's good. She misses me and Chris.'

'Are you sure you don't want to come to the States with us? You could visit her and all your friends and then come to meet us when we get to Santa Monica.'

'It's a nice idea but you can't be sure when you'll get there.'

'True.'

For Phil's second of the five annual challenges he was going to cycle Route 66 across America with Alex. They planned to leave Chicago in the first week of June the following year and hoped to get to Los Angeles by early July. However, if they ran into problems with the bikes or weather, there was no guarantee they would be able to maintain 60–70 miles per day.

'Besides,' said Meme, 'one of us has to stay to run the business. It wouldn't be fair to ask Chris to hold the fort that long.'

'How did I get to be so lucky?' he said, taking her hand. 'I couldn't do any of these challenges without your support and help with the fundraising and social media. Thank you.'

'You're welcome, love.'

'What?' He saw that slight shift in her smile.

'Have you given any more thought to the fifth?'

She'd embraced all of his ideas for challenges, including the third, planned for 2016, to kayak from Gibraltar to Morocco and back, and the fourth planned for the year after that, to kayak the English Channel from Dungeness to Boulogne-sur-Mer and cycle through France to the south of Spain. But when it came to his concept for 2018, she had her reservations. He wanted to undertake the longest solo bodyflight in South America. He wasn't sure which part made her most uncomfortable – that he would have to run off a mountain in Peru wearing a wingsuit, fly at terminal velocity of 120mph for four miles over the Amazon or descend by parachute and land on a four-metre diameter target on the back of a moving boat. The idea thrilled him but he didn't want to scare her either.

'Chicken korma?'

'For me, thank you,' said Meme. 'Looks delicious.'

The server set Phil's plate down in front of him. 'Can I get you anything else?'

'No thanks, we're good.'

'Enjoy.'

'The other option for the last challenge,' he said, once their server had left, 'would be to maybe base jump in Austria.'

'Oh, so instead of risking falling into the Amazon River and being eaten by piranhas, crocodiles or whatever other carnivorous creatures swim in those murky waters, you think it's safer to fly down the side of a mountain that is probably already littered with dead skiers?'

'Well, when you put it like that … okay, I'll give it some more thought.' Phil raised his glass. 'I promise.'

She clinked and took a swig. 'Good to know you don't have a death wish.'

Chapter 6

12 March 2015

For the second time in five months, Paul thought he was going to die. But this time, it would be death by PowerPoint. He'd been back at work since mid-December, the minute eight weeks had elapsed. He'd convinced the doctor he was ready to return to active duty – although, looking back, he had to admit it had probably been too soon. Those early shifts had been tough and his reaction times were slower than normal. Today, he felt fine, he was just bored to be stuck in a classroom. Because his station covered the River Tyne, and their rescue boat was licensed to go to sea, he had to complete this sea-survival course at the South Shields Marine training college.

He glanced at Carl, his friend and watch manager, to see if he was equally bored, but Carl was paying attention to the slides demonstrating the correct deployment of a life raft. Paul's stomach rumbled. At least the practical session in the pool should be fun. Supposedly the wave machine could simulate three- to four-metre seas.

Lunchtime finally came. In the canteen, employees from the shipping companies, perfectly turned out in their white shirts with gold trim, all sat together. The fire team took up another table. Paul felt sorry for the one chap sitting by himself and invited him over.

'Hi, I'm Paul, this is Carl.'

'Nice to meet you, I'm Robert.'

'You work on boats?' Carl asked.

'No, I'm a lab technician.'

'Really?' said Paul. 'So why are you taking this course?'

'I am rowing from Newcastle to Amsterdam.'

Paul thought he misheard. 'Rowing?'

'Yes.'

'Across the North Sea?'

'Yes.'

'How far is that?' said Carl.

'About 300 miles.'

Paul gazed at him. 'You know there's an overnight ferry that comes with a bed, a bar and breakfast for around fifty quid?'

The young man smiled. 'It's a growing sport.'

'Have you done a lot of rowing on the open sea?' said Carl.

'Just training rows so far.'

Paul had spent many a miserable winter night shift beneath the Tyne Bridge, waiting to fish someone out of the river if they couldn't be talked down off the ledge. He couldn't imagine what it would be like to be freezing offshore at the mercy of the wind and waves as well. The man was mad.

And yet, as crazy as it was, the notion of rowing a boat across the North Sea was unusual enough to pique Paul's interest. Over the coming days, he couldn't get the idea out of his head. When he googled it, he was amazed to discover the lad was right, it was indeed a growing sport. The more he researched, the more he wondered if he could do something like that.

Paul had grown up in landlocked Nottingham, so apart from paddling along the shore when his parents took them on family holidays to the seaside, he had no experience of the ocean. He hadn't learned to swim properly until he was an adult. Before his first triathlon he had to learn how to put his face in the water. The one time he'd been on a fishing trip he'd been seasick. But, for Paul, this lack of experience made the idea even more appealing. It would be the most challenging thing he'd ever done, a fitting celebration after surviving the brain haemorrhage.

He tucked into the laptop with renewed enthusiasm. What other challenges were out there? Was there anything even bolder than the North Sea? He wanted something that would test his limits, something so tough that it would make his brothers and mates gasp in awe. He typed *the world's toughest row*. Up came four words that would change the rest of his life – Talisker Whisky Atlantic Challenge, or as he would come to know it, TWAC.

More people, he read, have been in space or climbed Mount Everest than have rowed the 3,000 nautical miles across the Atlantic Ocean. Paul absorbed every article, every promotional video, captivated by the audacity of this tiny portion of the world's population who had pushed themselves to overcome all physical and mental obstacles on their journey to the finish line. Plus, each team raised money for their favourite charities. Imagine him being part of such an elite group. No one could call him a waste of space again. Paul closed the laptop. He had found his challenge and he was going to prove every naysayer in his life wrong. He *would* amount to something.

Next on the agenda was to find a team, a boat, learn how to row, and oh, convince Nic it was a great idea.

Carl was an obvious first choice for a team-mate. They'd completed triathlon and ironman races together, and Carl had been equally intrigued by the young man they'd met who planned to row the North Sea. They chatted on and off about the Atlantic idea for a couple of months, and on a slow day like today they watched videos of previous races. While it was referred to as a 'race' and the first boat to arrive in Antigua was the overall winner, and each class had winners, like the fastest team of four, three, pairs or solos, they were pleased to hear most entrants say they were in it for the challenge. Everyone who crossed the finish line was a winner in their own right.

As the pair of them walked out to the car park at the end of their shift Paul said: 'Can you imagine how much money we'd be able to raise for the Fire Fighters Charity?'

'Would be great.'

'Tonight's the night. I'm going to ask Nic. Will you ask Katrina?'

'Yeah, I'll see what she thinks.'

'Brilliant, see you tomorrow.'

On the drive home Paul noticed that the wild daffodils of spring had started their handover to the bluebells of early summer. Only another couple of weeks and the secondary schools would be done till September. He was excited to tell James about the Atlantic Challenge, but first he had to get Nic's blessing. Paul rehearsed what he would say to her. No point in going into too much detail at this stage. Step one was to get a yes. Her car was in the driveway when he arrived. Whichever of them got off work first would start the dinner so he wasn't surprised to hear music coming from the kitchen.

'Hi, love,' she said. 'Do you want a cup of tea?'

'Yes, please.' He gave her a kiss and asked about her day. As a nurse for patients with learning disabilities, her job could be tough but thankfully today seemed to have gone well.

'Could you set the table?'

'Okay.' Paul took the place mats out of the drawer.

'Any incidents today?' she asked.

'No, a light day, thanks.'

Okay, here goes, thought Paul.

'A few of us were watching videos this afternoon about rowing across the Atlantic Ocean.'

'Is that a thing?' she said as she began mashing the potatoes.

'Yeah, it looks amazing. I'd really like to do it, what do you think?'

She turned around. 'You?'

'Yeah.'

'Who else wants to do it?'

'Well, Carl for one.'

'Why am I not surprised,' said Nic, going back to mashing. 'There's no show without Punch.'

She had a point. He and Carl trained together 12 to 16 hours a week before a triathlon, and of course spent another 48 hours in each other's company at work. She often said he spent more time with Carl than with her. But she'd never stopped him from going or doing anything he wanted, nor he her. Apart from one night a week when they volunteered in Tynemouth at a club for people with mild disabilities, they rarely did things together. It was not unusual for her to go away for a few days with her friends and he was free to take off to run his races.

'So, what do you think?'

'Well, if that's what you want, it's okay with me.'

'Thanks love, that's really good of you.'

'Will you call James down? Dinner's ready.'

The next morning, Paul almost took the door off the hinges of Carl's office.

'Nic said yes.'

'Good for you, Hops, that's great. And James?'

'He thought it was cool. What did Katrina say?'

'Sorry mate, it's a no.'

'Oh.'

'Poppy doesn't want me to do it. She feels it is too dangerous.'

Well, that was a definite no. He knew Carl wouldn't do anything to upset his teenage daughter.

'Katrina said I would be away too long.'

Carl's wife's reaction was understandable, but it made Paul feel a little guilty about how easy it had been with Nic. He'd been so desperate to get a yes, he'd been economical with the truth about what was involved. Previously, the longest he had been away was two weeks, to complete his first ironman in

Lanzarote. Rowing the Atlantic could take months and the time of year couldn't be worse. Maybe ...

Carl was saying: 'I'll do whatever I can to help support you. For safety, I think you should consider a team of four.'

'Thanks, mate. Yeah, four would be good.'

Paul put the word out. Responses varied from 'are you completely insane?' to 'it sounds like an amazing adventure, I'd love to', but as soon as he told prospective team-mates the race departed the Canaries in mid-December, the answer was invariably 'sorry, our lass would kill me to be away at Christmas'. Something else he had neglected to tell Nic.

Chapter 7

14 June 2015

Phil was glad he hadn't waited until he was actually 66 to cycle Route 66, although he was only four years shy. Today's ride was tough. Through the haze of rain, he could see Alex on his Trek bike about a mile ahead. His son was faster on the long uphill stretches against the wind, not just because he was 40 years younger, but also because Phil was towing the trailer that carried their tent, sleeping bags, food, drinks, repair kit and spare wheels. The extra weight did give him an advantage going downhill, though.

When they'd left their campsite that morning for their tenth day on the road, the weather forecast had predicted showers and thunderstorms, but, because their progress had been slow so far – sometimes only making 15 miles in a day – they'd decided to press on anyway. They'd already lost half a week in Chicago. No amount of staring at the end of the conveyor belt in O'Hare International Airport had made those black flaps burp out a second bike. Alex had his, but Phil's Giant Hybrid was still in Heathrow. He'd considered renting one instead, so they could make it to Santa Monica by 4 July, but having been assured it was on its way, they'd opted to wait. Now their reward was to cycle through Illinois in the rain. If lightning threatened, they planned to jump off the bikes and run in the direction of the nearest shelter. Not exactly the most scientific emergency plan but better than remaining out in the open.

Phil heard a crack. Not thunder, something on the bike had shifted. He got off to take a look and found the gearing had jammed up against the spokes. He tried to ease it back but it wouldn't budge. He detached the trailer, turned the bike upside down and sat on the hard shoulder to make the repair. Cars and trucks continued to whoosh past him. The rain pelted the sweat off his neck and the sky darkened. He wrestled with the gears, but still no luck.

He saw Alex pedalling towards him. 'You okay, Dad?'

'Yeah, glad you came back though. Can you give me a hand with—'

The sky lit up and thunder clapped three seconds later. The wind began to pull.

'Look, Dad.' To the south-east it seemed as if one black cloud touched the ground. 'Is that a tornado?'

'Could be.'

They were in the middle of the countryside with nowhere to hide. At the side of the road the ditches were already swamped.

'If it comes close,' said Phil, 'we'll take cover down there.'

'Where?'

'In the ditch, under the water.'

'Right.' Alex laughed. 'We're wet anyway.'

The wind grew stronger, louder. Phil's bike seemed to lift inches off the ground before it toppled over. The trailer lurched sideways. Vehicles sped by faster. The black wind was coming their way. Just before they rolled into the ditch, a red pickup truck squealed to a halt beside them, its wipers flinging water with every sweep. Despite the deluge, the well-dressed driver jumped out and yelled at Phil: 'Get in.'

The woman in the passenger seat motioned for them to hurry.

Without ceremony, the man helped them throw all their gear into the open bed of the pickup and shoved Phil and Alex in after it. Then he snapped the tailgate shut, jumped back into the cab and hit the gas. Hard. As the vehicle flew down the two-laned road, Phil and Alex grabbed on to the sides of the truck to stop from bouncing out. If they'd been able to open their eyes against the rain and flying dirt, they'd have seen the funnel cloud ripping across the fields to their right.

A couple of minutes later the driver pulled on to the hard shoulder beneath an underpass and parked tight up against the wall. It was a relief to be out of the rain which had now turned to hail – great big balls of iced water that could dent the roof of a car, or their noggins for that matter, if they'd still been out in the open. And the noise. No sign of railway tracks nearby but the clichés were all true: that tornado sounded like an oncoming train. They watched it tear across the road behind them and then continue through farmland to the north-east. Blue sky followed in its wake.

The driver slid open the rear window in the cabin. 'You guys okay?'

'Yes, sir,' said Phil. 'Thank you so much for your help.'

'It's the Lord you have to thank. We were on our way home from church, trying to outrun the storm like everyone else, when my wife spotted you on the side of the road.'

The woman in the floral dress smiled.

'Thank you, ma'am,' said Alex.

'Where you headed?' said her husband.

'Santa Monica,' said Phil.

'Where?'

'California.'

'Oh, you're some of those crazy Route 66ers, huh? We can drop you in town if that helps.'

'That would be lovely, thanks.'

Twenty minutes down the road, Phil and Alex laughed at the road sign which said: *Welcome to Normal, Illinois.*

After two nights at a Motel 6, and several visits to a bike repair shop in Bloomington, father and son were once again on the road to the west. Over the next two weeks, and through the plains of Missouri, Oklahoma, northern Texas and New Mexico, they picked up the pace, making over 85 miles some days. They camped along the route, often stopping for dinner in eateries Alex liked to call 'Old Man Restaurants'. Every morning, before they set off, Phil would call Tom and tell him where they were and what they'd seen.

When they got to Flagstaff, they made that mandatory detour to check out the Grand Canyon. The air was cooler here, a welcome respite from the heat of the roads. No number of photos or videos could have given either of them the sense of scale they experienced sitting on the top edge of the southern rim. The crevasse was as deep as it was vast. Looking down into the gorge below, Phil felt like he was gazing into Middle-earth. This natural wonder of the world had existed for millions of years before he was born and would likely exist for millions more after he was gone. His aching muscles seemed insignificant and he was reminded how transient his life really was. He vowed to make the most of his remaining days.

As they progressed through Arizona and crossed into California, the old road was broken or badly maintained in several places. Temperatures often touched 38°C, sometimes 40°C, in the middle of the day. They would find shade under a bridge and nap for an hour or so.

On this particular day near the end of June, with Barstow well behind them, they came to a sign that read: *Route 66 Closed.*

Ahead was a cliff leading down to the valley. They'd heard wildfires were moving fast through the California basin, sometimes travelling across the highways at 70 miles per hour. To their right was a dirt track. The sign here read: *Private Property. Trespassers will be shot.*

To their left, an interstate led into Cajon Canyon. It was illegal to cycle on the freeways.

'So, Alex, with these options we could either be gunned down, burned or arrested. I vote for potential jail time, do you concur?'

'I concur,' said Alex, in his best impersonation of Leo DiCaprio portraying Frank Abagnale in the movie *Catch Me If You Can*.

After riding two miles up the steady incline, they paused at the top to check for police vehicles.

'All clear for now,' said Phil, looking at Interstate 15, stretching out before them. 'Once we get going down this hill, they won't be able to stop us for at least 36 miles. As for what happens at the bottom, who knows.'

Phil took off first with the trailer. The hard shoulder was littered with shards of old tyres, odd engine parts, and bits of rubbish he had to dodge. In less than ten minutes, he was clocking 40mph. Trucks squealed next to him, drivers pushing on their brakes in an attempt to slow their descent. Many waved and honked. Further down, open grids, designed to allow for water run-off, punctuated the middle of the shoulder. As they were only a foot wide, Phil was able to ride to one side, but after a couple of miles they increased to almost the width of the entire shoulder. At these speeds it took every ounce of concentration for Phil to weave across them on an angle to avoid getting a tyre stuck, and hoping he would not jackknife the trailer. He didn't dare look over his shoulder to check on Alex. He flew past a group of roadworkers who seemed utterly shocked to see a bicycle hurtling down the canyon. Two of them had to jump out of his way.

Thirty-something miles and about 5,000 rapid heartbeats later, the road levelled somewhat, and he pulled over on to a turn-off lane. He hid behind a large road sign and waited for Alex. And waited. Traffic noise disappeared and all he could hear was Debbie's voice warning him to take care of their son. She'd gone so far as to say if he lost him, Phil needn't bother coming back to the UK. He tried Alex's mobile. Straight to voicemail. He waited some more.

The sun was starting to settle in the west. Phil peered up the hill and thought he saw a dot at the side of the highway.

As the seconds passed it grew into Alex. Thank God. When his youngest pulled up beside him they clapped each other on the back and rejoiced in the knowledge that taking the canyon had probably saved them about three days.

A siren interrupted their celebrations.

'Cyclists, proceed to the next exit and get off the freeway.' The booming voice came from a megaphone mounted on the California Highway Patrol car that had pulled up behind them.

'I suppose they mean us, Dad.'

'Yep.'

Phil and Alex pedalled towards the next exit. As they took the off-ramp, they saw another black-and-white car waiting.

The police officer who stepped out was bigger than any American football linebacker Phil had ever seen. The cop gave them a right telling-off, particularly Phil for being an irresponsible father and putting them both in danger. Phil explained their predicament and thankfully the officer didn't charge them but let them go with a warning that if they were ever caught on one of California's freeways again, they would be enjoying some sightseeing on the inside of a cell. Suitably chastised, Phil thanked him and promised to obey the law from here on out.

Thirty days after they'd left Chicago, they approached the outskirts of Santa Monica. The air had a coolness to it and as they cycled towards the coast, they could smell the sea. It was too soon to relax though, they still had to navigate their way around parked cars, bus lanes and the busy city streets. But at the bottom of Colorado Avenue, they crested the humpback bridge over the Pacific Coast Highway and freewheeled down onto the famous Santa Monica pier. With great pride, the two of them stepped off their bikes and posed for photos beneath the blue-and-white signpost that read: *Santa Monica, 66, End of the Trail*.

They wheeled their bikes further down the pier, past the solar-powered Ferris wheel, the souvenir shops, and the tourists sitting for caricature artists. Seagulls circled as fishermen cast their lines, and pelicans perched themselves on white-stained pylons, ready to dive. At the end of the pier, beneath the two-storey restaurant, they sat on one of the wooden benches facing out over the ocean. Just like the canyon, it seemed vast and endless, holding mysteries and wonders of its own.

The bench was hard. Phil could feel every one of those 2,458 miles in his backside and legs, but the sense of accomplishment soothed the soreness. He was 62 years old and he had just cycled almost the whole width of America. He remembered the days when the sun shone on country roads and the traffic was so light he felt like a settler from a time long gone making his way on a wagon trail heading west. Still, cycling through cities and his daily phone calls with Tom back home reminded him he was very much part of a modern era. He'd enjoyed pitching their tent in campsites along the route and drying out in motels when the weather turned bad. Some beds were comfortable, others felt like sleeping on cement floors.

So many kind strangers had helped them along the way. Somewhere near Albuquerque, shortly after Phil had crashed into Alex and bloodied his knee, the tyre on the trailer had blown. He'd lain down on the ground to attempt the repair. Within minutes three black Lincoln Town Cars had surrounded them. Men in suits stepped out and stopped traffic to keep them safe. It felt like he and Alex had somehow stumbled on to a movie set filming a scene about the CIA.

Then there was that bizarre afternoon when they'd come across a strange burned-out bar miles from anywhere. The landlady had served them a couple of cold beers on the house. Phil chuckled when he remembered that two miles down the road he'd collapsed from dehydration and slept it off in a gulley.

This, his second of the five-year challenges, had been one to remember and what better way to experience it than with one of his sons. Beside him, Alex was quiet too, lost in his own replay. They still had to cycle another day or two south to where they'd planned a holiday with Meme's relatives, but for now it felt wonderful to just relax and stare out at the vast Pacific Ocean. Almost an hour passed before either of them spoke. Then, Alex said: 'What are you thinking about, Dad?'

'Oh, just wondering if you want to join me on next year's challenge, to kayak from Gibraltar to Morocco and back.'

Chapter 8

6 July 2015

It took Paul six weeks to find a bloke who was as excited about rowing the Atlantic as he was – an ex-forces firefighter from another station. Now there was two of them, all they had to do was to recruit two more.

The next hurdle was to get the time off. Given his finances, he could not afford to take unpaid leave, and even if he could, what employer would give someone three months off and still hold their job? He secured a meeting with the deputy chief of Tyne and Wear Fire and Rescue Service, a keen sportsman who loved boxing and keeping fit.

'Paul, come in, what can I do for you today?'

'I'm glad you asked.'

Paul described the challenge and the philanthropic angle.

'I've got to stop you there, Paul. You don't think I want to do it?'

'No sir. But now that you mention it, I'm still looking for two more people ...'

'Not in a million years. When I first heard about it, I thought you were mad. Listening to you now, I know you're mad.'

Paul grinned.

'So, what else can I help with?'

'Well sir, I need time off.'

The deputy chief relaxed back in his chair. 'How much do you need?'

'That's the thing, I'm not sure.'

'Let me guess, it depends on how fast you can row.'

'Kind of. I was thinking if I took all my annual leave for 2017 in December, and took the 2018 leave in January, I could ask some of the lads to cover any shifts I might miss in February.'

'That's fine, Paul,' said Chris as he stood up. 'You can make up whatever days you are short when you come back.'

'Thanks, sir.'

'*If* you come back.'

'If I don't come back, sir, no need to worry about making up the time, huh?'

He laughed. 'True enough. If you need any help from the brigade, tell whoever it is that they have my authorisation to help you.'

'Thank you so much, sir, I appreciate it.'

Armed with the support of the deputy chief, he headed straight for the media department.

Samantha and Steve were happy to help. They took several head shots and recorded a video for Paul to send to potential sponsors.

'How about a logo?' said Steve.

'Never thought of that.'

'It will give you a visual presence. What's your team name?'

'Eh …'

'Let's think about what you are doing,' said Samantha. 'You are rowing the Atlantic.'

'That's the plan.'

'Why are you doing it, is it a dream?'

'Sort of.'

'How about Atlantic Dream?'

'Sounds like a cruise ship,' said Paul. 'This will be no cushy cruise. It's a challenge.'

'How about Atlantic Dream Challenge?' Samantha suggested.

'Kind of says it all,' said Steve.

'Atlantic Dream Challenge?' Paul said, taking the name for a test drive around his mind. 'I think you're right, it does say it all.'

Paul left HQ, pleased with his progress. He had his yes from Nic, he had the blessing from work, and he had a team-mate.

When he'd visited his parents for his dad's birthday in May, he'd taken his mother aside and told her about the row. She was nervous for his safety but also incredibly proud of him for undertaking such a challenge. But she said it was better not to tell his father, given the state of his health. Paul agreed. He worried about him; he'd noticed a tremor in his dad's left hand, but more disturbing, he'd found a note his father had written, which read: glasses, watch, wallet, cap, as if he was reminding himself what he would need to gather before leaving the house for a medical appointment. Paul also knew his dad believed a husband and father's place was at home with his family, doing jobs around the house, and tending to the garden. So, yes, it was best not to tell him. Still, Paul hoped that if his dad did know, he would be proud of him too.

Anyways, no need to dwell on that now, it was time to commit. He called Atlantic Campaigns and paid the £1,000 deposit to officially enter the race, departing in December 2017.

Now it was real.

That evening James was off playing video games at a friend's house. He and Nic had the place to themselves. Paul was so excited about the challenge he couldn't help talking about it during dinner. Nic asked about the training and what the boats looked like. He was happy she seemed to be taking more of an interest until she asked: 'How long does it take?'

He almost choked. He'd known he'd have to be honest with her sooner or later, but since it was still two and a half years away, he'd hoped it would have been later.

'Em ... depends on how many on the team and how fast you row.'

'Roughly?'

He had no choice but to come clean. 'Could take a couple of months.'

'Months? You never said you'd be away that long.'

'You never asked,' he said, immediately regretting it. He knew he was in the wrong but he wasn't going to own up to it.

She stared at him, then her eyes blinked rapidly, calculating. He saw the exact moment she realised the full implication.

'That means you'll be gone over Christmas.'

He waited.

'Christmas! Paul.' She threw down her serviette and pushed back from the table. 'You should have told me.'

'Let's not go down this route. It's a ways off, Nic. It might not even happen.'

She got up and put her plate in the sink. 'I'm taking Betty out for a walk.'

'Nic.'

'Enjoy the rest of your dinner.'

Alone in the kitchen, Paul put down his fork. He wished he could have explained to her why he'd been afraid to tell her the whole truth. He could have died last year. Everything had changed since then. He knew she would probably never understand, but he simply had to do this. They'd always said yes to each other but he'd been afraid this time she would've said no.

He cleared the table and went through to the lounge. He knew he'd overstepped and the conversation wasn't over, but for now, he had a bit of peace and quiet, so he settled in to watch the telly.

The quiet continued well into the next day. He knew she was a thinker and needed time to process. It wasn't her style to get angry, she was more likely to say she was disappointed in him. And she did. But once she said it, she started to come around. She had given her permission and wouldn't go back on her word. She still didn't like it but because she knew it was something he really wanted, and she never wanted to be that woman who curtailed her husband, she said she'd support him in any way she could.

By the weekend they were back to their usual easy pattern of conversation.

During that summer, his father's behaviour became erratic. With his mum's help, Paul convinced him to get checked at the hospital.

While they waited to be seen, his mum went to get them some tea, and Paul sat with his dad. For the first time, he saw his father's stoicism waver.

'Paul, I don't want to do this.'

'Do what, Dad?'

'If it is bad news, I need you to finish me off.'

'What?'

'I mean it, Paul, I don't want to rot away.'

Paul couldn't speak. Had his dad just asked him to kill him? The man who rarely took a paracetamol because he could tough it out, the man who had been his rock throughout his life, had inspired him to never quit, the man he could never disappoint, had just asked him to finish him off. What was he supposed to do with that?

'Paul?'

'Dad, stop.'

'I'm serious.'

Paul didn't know what to say, but he didn't want to let him down.

'Dad … okay, Dad, if that is what you want, I will help you, but let's get the scans and results first, okay?'

Driving home, Paul was still in a state of shock at what he'd promised. It only took Nic a few minutes to knock some sense into him.

'Are you out of your mind? You can't do that.'

'I didn't know what to say, I never want to let him down.'

'Paul, they would send you to prison. You have to think about your own family, about me, about James. You have a responsibility to us.'

'I know, I know.'

'Plus, it is morally wrong. You can't just take someone's life, even if they ask you to.'

Nic was right. He couldn't. Wouldn't. But what was he going to say to his dad?

On the day of his father's follow-up appointment with the consultant, Paul was working but he drove down to his parents' house in Nottingham that evening. Both his brothers' cars were parked outside.

His younger brother opened the door.

'Hey, Sean, didn't expect to see you.'

'Well ... you know.'

'Yeah. Where's Dad?'

'Upstairs. Mum's in the kitchen making tea.'

'How is she?'

'Come in. Michael and I are in the lounge.'

The three grown sons sat together in their childhood home, chatting about football, work, and whatever other small talk they could stumble on.

Paul's mother arrived with the tea tray. No one spoke while she poured. As soon as she settled on the settee, she looked straight at Paul and announced: 'Paul, you can't kill your dad.'

'I never said I was going to kill him.'

'That's not what he thinks,' said Michael. 'I was with him and Mum today when the consultant confirmed Dad has Lewy body dementia. He said it was advanced and that's what's causing the problems with his thinking and behaviour. He said there was little they could do for him.'

'And instead of being upset like the rest of us,' his mum said, 'your dad turns around and says, "No bother, that's all sorted."'

'Then,' said Michael, 'the doctor asks him what he meant by "sorted" and Dad says, "I've asked our Paul to finish me off."'

Paul sat in silence, isolated, as three pairs of eyes glared at him. Did they really believe he could actually kill his own father? *Wow.* How could he convince them that he was trying to appease his dad? But as he looked at his mum and his brothers, he saw what they saw in him – someone who could do whatever was needed to be done, no matter the cost. His dad had taught him that.

By the time autumn had stripped the trees, Paul's father was suffering from hallucinations and paranoia. One night, he thought the burglar alarm was a bomb so he dragged Paul's mum out into the garden where he thought it would be safe. The problem was, he grabbed a knife from the kitchen en route.

How could this be? His dad had been the kindest man he knew, the type of man friends and neighbours referred to as the salt of the earth. Yet here he was, a danger to himself and his adoring wife. His mum had been so frightened that the doctors admitted him to a cognitive facility for assessment. Over time, the doctors stabilised him enough with medication that he could be discharged to a care facility but Paul's 80-year-old mother was having none of that. She said she had stood on that altar and vowed to take care of her husband in sickness and in health. She insisted he be brought home.

Meanwhile, when Paul wasn't at work, or helping out with his dad, he focused on the challenge. In October, he managed to recruit two more firefighters and his team began training in the gym. The dream was on. But it didn't take Paul long to realise the cost to play in this rich man's sport could turn it into a nightmare. When he sat down and researched how much money he'd need, he was dismayed to discover that boats were priced anywhere between £35,000 and £85,000, depending on size and age. Equipment and supplies ran from £25,000 to £35,000. The entry fee, payable in euros, was €24,500 for a four-man crew. Then there was the matter of £5,000 to ship the boat to the Canaries and, presuming they did row her all the way to Antigua, an additional £6,500 to bring her back. No matter what way he added it all up it looked like he would need the best part of a hundred grand.

All through that winter he sought corporate sponsorship from various companies in the North East but the biggest donation he received was a whopping £25. He also hosted his first fundraiser – a music night in his local pub. Although Nic was a superstar, selling more raffle tickets than anyone else, the money they collected would barely buy a set of oars.

When he spoke to anyone who had completed the row, they told him the same thing – the hardest part was getting to the starting line. In addition to the costs, his team would have to be certified in First Aid at Sea, Essential Navigation & Seamanship and Sea Survival, and hold VHF Short Range radio licences. Many warned he might not make it. They didn't know Paul. He had announced he was going to row the Atlantic, and that was that.

The first thing he needed was a boat. And soon. It would help donors see the vision but, more importantly, they had to start training on the water. Another entry prerequisite was for each team to have rowed, at a very minimum, 120 hours, 24 of them in darkness, in the same boat they would use to make the crossing. More hours would be better. He scoured the internet for second-hand boats.

On a rainy Saturday morning in March 2016, Paul climbed into a red Vauxhall Corsa belonging to the station and drove five hours south to Henley-on-Thames, where the Armed Forces charity had a second-hand boat for sale. An Aston Martin pulled in beside him and a gentleman with a double-barrelled name and a polite accent stepped out. He was delighted to show Paul the rowboat that had already carried four men across the Atlantic. It was in fair condition, but because it had been stripped down and would require thousands of pounds' worth of upgrading, the owner agreed to reduce the price to £15,000. He even offered Paul the option of three £5,000 payments over 12 months. What could be better? It would give them time to raise more money, and get them on the water now.

Too excited to stop for a wee, Paul drove straight back to Newcastle to give his crew the good news. But not all his teammates shared his enthusiasm. The time they were having to commit to training and the reality of the financial obligations had begun to hit home. Before Paul had a chance to sign the contract, two of the lads dropped out. He called the boat owner to give him the bad news.

Since quitting was not an option Paul could entertain, he then called Atlantic Campaigns and asked the event manager, Nikki Holt, to switch his entry from a four-man crew to a pair instead.

On the bright side – he hadn't forked out for a four-man boat, and a two-man vessel would cost less.

Chapter 9

4 April 2016

Since returning from cycling Route 66, Phil had shifted the focus of his training from legs to back and shoulders. With only two months to go before he would attempt his third challenge – to kayak from Gibraltar to Morocco and back – he was spending four or five evenings a week at the gym. Aside from buffed biceps, the increase in his upper body strength had made lifting Tom out of his chair a lot easier. Phil was looking forward to spending another Monday evening with him. He stopped by Meme's office on the way out.

'Are you sure you don't mind taking this meeting?' he said. 'We could reschedule if you like?'

'No bother,' said Meme. 'Although maybe you could drop Morgan at home in case it runs late.'

Phil checked his watch. 'Sure. Come here, buddy, come here.' Morgan scrambled up from under Meme's desk. 'Wanna come for a fast ride in the car?'

'Phil.'

'Okay, buddy, listen to your mama. You have to drive slow.'

'Thanks. Give Tom a hug from me.'

'Will do.'

He drove fast, helped by a run of green lights. As he entered his apartment building the lift door opened and one of the new tenants, a Chinese woman, rushed out, clearly distressed.

'What's the matter?'

'Water, water,' she said, pointing to the ceiling.

'Your flat?'

She nodded.

'Come on,' Phil said, escorting her back into the lift. 'I'll take a look.'

When they reached her apartment on the fifth floor Phil turned to Morgan: 'Stay.'

The greyhound sat. Phil followed the lady in. Water was pouring down the walls and the carpet squelched under his feet. This was not a leak from someone leaving a shower running upstairs. He pushed aside some of the ceiling tiles and found the source – a large crack in a plastic pipe. Good luck trying to find a plumber at this hour. He called the fire brigade.

The lady watched him closely.

'I'm sorry, I have to go now. Help is coming.'

She nodded.

'Stay here. Leave the door open.'

He took the lift up to the seventh floor, dashed into his flat, filled Morgan's bowl and ran back to the lift, but it had already descended. He opted for the stairwell and was almost down to the second floor when he met two fully kitted firemen making their way up. One of them appeared to be limping.

'Hello, sir,' the firefighter said. 'Is it your flat?'

'No, two below, on the fifth floor.'

'Do you know if it is occupied?'

'Yes.' Phil reached in his wallet. 'The lady doesn't speak much English but here's the management company's card if that helps. Sorry, I've got to run.'

'That's great, thank you.'

Phil jumped in the car. This time almost every light was red. He phoned Tom. Thankfully Emily was still there and said she could wait for him.

Paul cursed every step in the cement stairwell. His big toe throbbed. One thing he knew for sure, anyone who laughed at gout never suffered from it. His right foot was so swollen it wouldn't fit in his size-eight safety shoe and fire boot. Anyone else would have called in sick but not Paul, he hated to be off work. He'd taken a couple of painkillers and borrowed a size twelve from one of the lads instead. With two odd boots, he was only short of a red ball for his nose to complete the clown effect.

Some might have taken the lift but he preferred to survey the building on the way up. When he and Billy reached the flat, he knocked on the open door, thankful he wouldn't have to break it down and deal with all that paperwork. The lady was spreading buckets and towels on the floor, but until they shut off the water it was pointless.

Paul asked her where the stopcock was. The man on the stairs had been right, she had very little English. He mimed turning off a tap but she shook her head. He and Billy looked in all the usual places but could find nothing. The water continued to pour. Paul radioed Doug in the fire truck.

'Can you contact the management company?'

'A mate of mine used to live in this building, might be faster?'

'Go ahead.'

Minutes later, Doug said: 'It's in the ceiling outside the front door.'

Sure enough, there it was. A few turns and the water stopped. Before Paul knew what was happening the tiny lady had grabbed him in a hug as fierce as any bear's. He'd had less thanks from some people he'd pulled out of fires. She seemed so helpless that they stayed a while to help her clean up as best they could.

On the drive back to the station, Paul wondered how Nic would cope if she had a problem while he was away at sea. She was far more self-reliant but was it fair to put her in that position? She'd been doing her best to support him but he could tell she was starting to get fed up with the project. Between work and training, and helping his mum take care of his dad, he was rarely home. There was nothing he could do for now but plough on. As soon as it was all over, he promised himself he would make it up to her.

Chapter 10

10 June 2016

Phil counted to ten before exhaling. He sucked in the next breath through his mouth and tried to hold it for longer. The stench of raw sewage was making him gag. At 7am, he and Alex had put their double kayak in the water at the port of La Línea de la Concepción – the last Spanish town before the border with Gibraltar – and set off on his third annual challenge.

And challenging it was. Albert, the Spaniard from Neptune Marine who was operating their cover boat, a twin-engine Catapult Catamaran, had explained how the Mediterranean Sea, en route to the Atlantic, squeezed its way up into the Bay of Gibraltar and bounced off the coast, adding turbulent waters to the already busy shipping route. Alex sat in the bow, Phil in the stern. Having trained in the North Sea, Phil felt confident that they would handle the rough conditions fairly well, but nothing could have prepared him for this brown patch of water off Europa Point. Since there were no sanitation plants on the Rock, Gibraltar pumped its effluent directly into the sea.

'Whose bright idea was this, Dad?' said Alex, as his paddle caught a lump of sodden toilet paper which then careered over Phil's head and into the back of the kayak.

Phil didn't answer; he was too busy trying to place his blades in between chunks of floating excrement. As he dipped one side in and then the other, dribbles of disgusting water dripped on to his boat and arms. It would've been bad enough if it was a millpond out here, but now that they were out in the straits proper, the waves smashed up against each other and spewed the filth up on top of them. Phil jammed his feet into the footrests and braced his knees against the lip of the open-deck kayak to keep as balanced as possible. Capsizing in this cesspit was not an option. On the plus side, the powerboats and motor yachts were able to go around this area, so at least he and Alex were spared some additional rocky wakes for now. Albert had told them that the size of the slick varied from day to day but this one was particularly bad. Ideally, Phil would have chosen a different day but they had already spent two days driving through France and Spain to get here, and another day resting up.

At 5am on the morning they'd planned to depart, Phil had pulled the flap back on their tent and knew something was wrong. The wind had died and the ground was saturated. When he stuck his arm out, his hand disappeared into the dense fog. He called Albert.

'Not today, Señor Phil. Maybe tomorrow.'

But the next day had been socked in, and the day after that too. As with all his challenges, Phil had thoroughly researched all elements and had allowed for some weather delay but the fog that had descended was here to stay. And stay.

So, unfortunately, today was the first, and last, opportunity they'd have to complete the challenge; they still had to drive to northern Spain and catch the Santander to Plymouth ferry on Sunday evening.

Fifteen long minutes later, they were out the other side of the murk. Phil didn't need to rely on his degree in virology to know that remaining covered in E. coli bacteria could be detrimental to their health. They regrouped with Albert, who helped pour fresh water on the kayak and themselves.

'Surely pumping raw sewage into the sea is against environmental laws?' said Phil.

'Yes,' said Albert. 'Your countrymen talk about building a plant for years, but still nothing.'

'Maybe,' said Alex, 'the government needs a "show and tell" day.'

'Eh?' said Albert.

'The politicians should be forced to come out here and paddle through this shit themselves.'

'Not a bad idea,' said Phil, 'but hey, let's keep going, we really need to make it there and back before it gets too dark, or the fog descends again.'

Kayaking the distance between Europe and Africa was not where the challenge lay, it was in navigating this narrow stretch of water where the Mediterranean Sea meets the Atlantic Ocean and creates unusual wave patterns and tidal flow. For the next two hours, they put their heads down and paddled in unison.

It had been five days since the new moon, so the tides were transitioning from spring to neap. Beneath them, the denser, saltier outgoing waters of the Med sank beneath the incoming colder, less saline waters of the Atlantic, and with the typical increase in wind mid-afternoon, the sea was becoming even more confused.

Large container ships passed in front of them and behind, adding to the washing-machine effect. Only every third or fourth stroke yielded any forward momentum – the rest were about keeping the kayak stable. Rather than stop for food and be tossed about, they snacked on protein bars on the go.

They were almost across the 16-nautical-mile stretch when Alex said: 'Check out that ship, Dad.'

Phil recognised Morocco's national flag – red with a green star – on the stern of a grey patrol frigate. Since the straits were notoriously traversed by smugglers and traffickers, it wasn't surprising to see large guns mounted on the bow.

They had planned to head to Ceuta, the autonomous Spanish city on the African coast, but having been pushed to the east, they were now more likely to arrive near Benzú. Albert came alongside.

'We don't have permission to land in Morocco,' he said. 'When you get 500 metres from shore, time to turn around. Okay?'

'No worries,' said Phil.

Only it became a worry.

As they approached the coastline and started to make the turn, it was as if Moby Dick had tied a line to their keel and began swimming to shore with them in tow.

'Dig and pull, Alex, dig.'

'I am.'

The patrol boat shifted course and headed their way.

'We need to get out of here,' said Phil, paddling as hard as he could. With all the training he'd done to swim the English Channel, he was familiar with dangerous rip currents that would pull you out to sea, but this seemed to be doing the exact opposite. They were being pushed even closer to shore and were soon caught in the breaking surf. They lost control and then the tide, quite illegally, tossed them ashore.

'Eh, Dad, did you pack our passports?'

'Somehow, I don't think we'll be getting a stamp.' Phil watched the patrol vessel approach their cover boat. 'We'll let Albert sort it out. He runs these straits every day, so I am sure they know him.'

Within ten minutes the patrol boat veered off and Albert came as close to shore as he could without getting beached, and yelled across: 'Sorry, my friends, you have to leave Morocco, otherwise they say they ...' Albert gestured a big explosion and mimed pieces of debris floating back to earth.

Phil was quite sure something had been lost in translation and that the Royal Moroccan Navy hadn't intended to blow up two Brits in a plastic kayak. Nonetheless, he grabbed a hold of the line Albert threw to them and accepted the tow back across the surf.

When they'd paddled to the middle of the straits again, and the sun started sinking in the sky, they finally paused for a drink of water. Another challenge almost completed. He was halfway through the five-year plan and feeling grateful to everyone who supported him logistically and financially on these wild events.

'Is this not a great day, Alex? Can't wait to tell Tom all about it.'

'Yeah, it is, but aren't you forgetting something?'

'What?'

'It's almost dinner time.'

'You starving?'

'No, just worried about getting back to Spain before the people of Gibraltar start flushing their toilets again.'

Chapter 11

24 August 2016

Paul fuelled up the borrowed van. This was it. It had taken a year to find a pairs boat that he could afford. Since signing up for the race he'd organised all sorts of events including music nights, booze cruises and special evenings with footballers Malcolm Macdonald and John Beresford, but he'd still been short on cash. With Nic's blessing, he cleared out his savings account. He even applied to the Bank of Mum and Dad, an embarrassing request for a man in his fifties, especially while his dad's health was failing, and had eventually come up with £10,000. He knew nothing about assessing boats, but the one he was going to see today had already crossed the Atlantic three times without capsizing, something that could not be said for the more expensive lighter vessels. As far as Paul was concerned, unless she had a *Titanic*-size hole in the side of her, she was coming home with him today.

When he arrived at the address in Coventry, Paul was surprised to find himself on a street of Victorian houses. So where was the boat? The seller, Martin, who had returned from Antigua in March having completed the 2015 race, invited him in for a spot of tea.

'She's a wonderful boat, strong. She'll take great care of you.'

Paul noticed how Martin talked about her as if she was a real person. 'How old is she?'

'She was built in 2008 by Roger Haines. You know the race used to be called the Woodvale Challenge?'

'Yeah, I heard.'

'Back then you had to build the boat yourself from a kit of laser-cut marine plywood.'

'Really? You'd better be confident in your woodworking skills.'

'No kidding. In 2009, Roger was the first man to row her across. Then he sold her to a couple who rowed it in 2011, who sold her to me and my team-mate, Adrian.'

Paul's foot had started to tap.

'I suppose you want to see her?'

'Yes, mate.'

As he followed Martin out the back door, Paul tried to figure out how he'd got a boat into the pretty walled garden. Passing shrubs, flower beds and several trees, they kept walking, but there was still no sign of a vessel.

'Through here,' Martin said, shifting dense foliage to one side.

When Paul entered the lane via the hidden gate it was as if he had stepped through a wardrobe and entered Narnia. There she was, stranded on a galvanised trailer, miles from her ocean home. She was about 20 feet long with an open rowing deck. Tracks ran along the centre to facilitate the two seats that would slide back and forth with each stroke. To the right and left of the tracks, watertight lids covered storage cubbyholes below. The compartment at the bow was large enough to house bulky items like a life raft and anchors, but not humans. Theirs would be the 6ft-by-6ft cabin at the stern, which was accessible through a sealable hatch.

She would hardly win top prize in a boat parade: her orange paint was blistered and peeling, her hatches were scratched from wear, and her rails and oarlocks were in need of major repair. Paul was underwhelmed by the state of her, but when he ran his hand along her bow he felt a pull. It was as if her soul reached out to him and said: *Rescue me and I will save you.*

Martin didn't need to say a thing. Paul was already handing over his wad of cash, all ten grand.

Right before Paul drove off, Martin said: 'By the way, don't change her name. It's bad luck.'

Paul had heard that before, from almost every boat owner he'd ever met. But he also needed money. He planned to offer three sponsorship packages ranging from £5,000 to £10,000. The most expensive would come with naming rights. Unlucky or not, Paul reckoned if he could get someone to fork out that much money, they could call the boat whatever they liked.

'I'll try, but I can't promise.'

'Seriously,' said Martin, 'it's really bad luck and you're going to need every bit.'

On the way home, Paul grinned every time he checked his rear-view mirror. He had a boat. He drove straight to Byker Fire Station, where he'd been granted permission to store her until he could find a mooring. Before locking up, he paused at the door for one last look. Painted along the side of the hull was her name: *Dream It, Do It.* He felt that spark, the one that would ignite on a promising first date, but he had no idea he was about to embark on a four-year love affair that might cost him everything.

A week after Paul had purchased *Didi*, as she was nicknamed, and after a preliminary fix of the oarlocks, he and his last remaining team-mate got their chance to put her in the water. It was a day of firsts: first time reversing a trailer down a slip, first attempt at getting her off said trailer, which turned out to be a lot more difficult than they'd thought, especially if they wanted to keep their feet dry, and the first time they rowed her on the Tyne.

Four miles upstream from Newcastle's city centre, they shoved off on their maiden voyage. While they had both trained on an indoor rowing machine, this was their first time in the same boat, literally. Their first attempts bore a closer resemblance to Laurel and Hardy, oars clashing clumsily, than to the sort of smooth synchronicity you might expect from an Oxford or Cambridge pairs team at the Henley Regatta.

But after a mile or so, their oars plied the waters in harmony more often than the mid-air combat from earlier. Boats usually seen on the river were either pleasure craft with engines or the more familiar racing rowboats. The closer *Didi* got to town the more people stopped to watch this unfamiliar-looking rowing vessel with cabins on either end. Paul felt like quite the celebrity and the pair of them put on a good show.

They rowed under the Gateshead Millennium Bridge, or the Blinking Eye as it had been nicknamed, because of how it tilted to allow tall vessels to pass, and arrived at the iconic Tyne Bridge in just under an hour. This meant they had been cruising at four knots, the equivalent of almost 7.5km per hour, which was a welcome boost to their confidence. Paul started to calculate how long it would take to cross the Atlantic at that speed. Forty-two days, he reckoned, although he knew that wasn't realistic, considering that one of them would probably be resting while the other rowed and a forward speed on the ocean was more likely to be one and a half to two knots.

That notion was further debunked when it came time to turn around on the river. Paul quickly realised that most of their speed had been thanks to the current. Pulling against the outgoing tide now was hard work, but with all the onlookers still gawking at them, pride had him pulling even harder. It felt like every muscle was forced to work: his back, his legs, his shoulders. It took twice as long to return to the slipway. Paul's hands were cramping and the first indications of blisters were beginning to show. If these were the physical demands on his body after only a three-hour stint in flat conditions, imagine what reserves he'd need to manage the suggested shift rotation of rowing for two hours, followed by two hours' rest, around the clock seven days a week, for weeks on end. He would have to up his game.

Getting the boat off the trailer had been difficult, but they soon learned that getting her back on was even tougher. After several attempts, and the occasional curse, *Didi* was once more riding her aluminium horse, en route back to her land home at the fire station. When they were sure she'd been safely manoeuvred into place, his team-mate left. Paul stayed a while longer, tinkering. Many of the brigade came over to check out the boat, and when they saw Paul drying her with a cloth, one of the lads piped up: 'Aw, Hops, you tucking her in for the night?'

Later that evening, another firefighter phoned him at home.

'Just saw your boat. Tell me you're not going to sea in that thing, are you?'

'What do you mean?'

'The state of it.'

Paul could feel his fist curl. 'She's fantastic, she just needs a lick of paint.'

'And maybe a little makeover?'

'Listen, if you want to remain friends, don't speak about *Didi* like that.'

'Sorry mate, didn't mean anything by it.'

'Yeah, well, goodnight.' Paul hung up.

'Who was that?' Nic asked, putting her TV show on pause.

'Oh, just one of the blokes at work.'

'And what has you all riled up?'

'He was insulting *Didi*.'

Nic looked at her husband. 'It's just a boat, Paul.'

'You're right.' Paul cleared his throat. 'Would you like a cup of tea?'

'Love one, thanks.'

Paul went through to the kitchen. He put the kettle on and stood staring at it, waiting for it to boil. What had just happened? He'd jumped to defend *Didi* as though she was a girlfriend. It felt both weird and natural. After being with her on the water today he'd felt their relationship grow. He only hoped it wasn't going to turn out to be one-sided.

Paul planned to train on the river for the rest of that autumn and winter but as his father's health continued to deteriorate, he spent more and more time in Nottingham. On New Year's Eve, a night considered to be the gateway from old to new, his father passed away. January came and went in a blur of disbelief. His dad was gone. But Paul couldn't dwell on it. He dried his tears and locked them away in the box at the back of his mind. He would follow in his dad's footsteps and just get on with it.

He needed to get *Didi* checked out like he would a car, but hadn't a clue where to start. It seemed every time someone posed a question about rowing, or the boat, he had to learn something new.

In February, he found someone at a boatyard who declared her seaworthy. As Paul was hitching her up to take her home again, a chap who was detailing another boat on site wandered over. Enchanted by Paul's story about the challenge, and in the spirit of helping the cause, he offered to paint her for free in his spare time so long as Paul supplied the paint and did all the prep. Never afraid of hard work, Paul gladly accepted his offer. Even better, the lad's workshop was only ten minutes from his house.

Didi began her transformation in March. Over the following weeks, Paul spent hours before and after his shifts sanding her down to her essence. As he did so, he could see the details of her construction emerge, the sturdy lumber that was clear of knots and the joints that had been glued tight. Roger had indeed built a strong and stable vessel. Paul was confident she'd make it across the Atlantic a fourth time. He just hoped he could live up to her expectations too.

In the meantime, he secured a mooring at St Peter's Marina. Paul was grateful to the owner for the hefty discount he gave him in recognition of the fire brigade's previous efforts to keep another vessel afloat when it had sprung a leak and the on-board pumps could not keep up.

On 15 July 2017, *Didi* was wheeled out of the workshop into the sunlight. Gone was the ugly duckling orange and now here was a beautiful swan, a red swan, fire engine red. If Paul had been falling for *Didi* before, he was head over heels now.

Chapter 12

17 July 2017

Two days later, with only six months to go before the race was due to start, Paul watched his last team-mate get off the boat and drive away. After a disagreement on the water, he too had quit. Maybe the lad was right. Maybe Paul was too stubborn and demanded too much. But if they couldn't survive one afternoon in rough conditions on the North Sea without having words, what hope did they have of staying strong and working together as a team when things got tough on the ocean? The two of them would have to rely on their wits and each other. Better to find out now that they weren't compatible because it was unlikely Paul's personality was going to change much before December. He locked the hatches, secured *Didi*'s lines, and headed home, deflated.

'You're back early,' said Nic.

'Yeah.' Paul explained what happened. 'Now it's just me, I'll have to do it by myself.'

'No.'

'Lots of people row it solo.'

'You still want to do that race, fine,' said Nic, 'but not by yourself.'

'But——'

'No, Paul. I can't … I almost lost you once. This is where I draw the line.'

As though returning to the womb, Paul drove back to the mooring, climbed into the cabin and lay down on the cushioned pad that was designed to serve as his ocean bed. He stared at the roof 12 inches above his head and felt the first tear slide out of the side of his eye. It wasn't fair. He'd overcome so many obstacles in the last two years, but now he was even further away from the starting line. First he had a team and no boat; now he had a boat and no team. In his mind he believed he could do it by himself if he had to, but Nic was adamant. She'd said yes easily when he'd first asked — probably because he'd omitted certain facts to get that yes — but today her no was firm. He would have to respect her wishes.

But what should he do? Even if he could find a team, money was still an issue. He'd been hopeful the local medical and safety technology corporation that made the breathing apparatus they used to fight fires would avail of the opportunity to sponsor him. He'd visualised the poster campaign: his firefighting team would stand next to the boat, wearing the company's kit. One of them would be holding his baby, who had been saved by one of the corporation's incubators. Paul had thought it was a marketing dream; the company, unfortunately, had not. Sporting events did not qualify for their sponsorship programmes.

Then he'd tried The Emergency Services Show at the National Exhibition Centre in Birmingham, confident he would find support there. Over a two-day period, he'd stood next to *Didi*, talked to hundreds of people, given away countless wristbands, but received not a single donation. Everything he'd already raised had been spent on buying the boat. He would still need to come up with another £20,000 to pay off the balance due on the entry fee and probably at least £30,000 to purchase equipment and supplies. After that, he would need to find the money to have the boat shipped to the Canaries, not to mention fundraising for his chosen charity.

The dream was falling apart. Maybe he should just sell the boat and be done with the madness. If he did, it would make those he loved happy, especially Nic. But then he imagined the faces of all those who'd called him a waste of space, how they would delight in his failure, saying *I told you so*. Their glee would be unbearable. No, he could not give them the satisfaction. He picked up his mobile.

'Atlantic Campaigns.'

'May I speak to Nikki please?' She had been so sweet when he'd needed to swap from a four-man team to a pair. Hopefully she could help him now.

'Speaking.'

'Hi, it's Paul Hopkins.'

'Hi, Paul, how are you getting along?'

He wished he felt as cheery as she sounded. 'Had another lad drop out. I don't think I can make the start.'

'Oh, I'm sorry to hear that.'

'Is it possible to transfer my entry to the 2018 race?'

'Of course. Better to be fully ready.'

'Thank you, Nikki. I'll be there.'

The momentary relief he felt when he hung up was soon replaced by the burden of the next task. He still had to find someone who was as passionate as he was, someone brave and daring, a man who stood by his word and believed life was an adventure to be lived. But he had exhausted all his contacts in the fire service. Who else was there?

Chapter 13

20 October 2017

Phil's phone vibrated. Right in the middle of date night with Meme. The cinema was almost full, but the movie hadn't yet started. He sneaked a peek. A text from his cycling buddy, Zoe.

Would you be interested in rowing the Atlantic with a friend of mine? Race starts December 2018.

Phil read it again, and a third time. A vision of a rolling ocean and a sense of fun flooded his mind. He loved being on the water, but so far, his kayak passages had been day trips — 11 hours in the Gibraltar Straits, and it had taken only eight hours to cross the English Channel this past June. The idea of being at sea in the dark of night would be an exciting new experience. Meme was still not happy about the bodysuit flight over the Amazon he'd planned for next year. He'd been looking for alternatives. Maybe this might be more to her liking? He turned to his wife and whispered: 'How would you feel if I rowed the Atlantic with a friend of Zoe's?'

Meme looked at the text: 'Sounds intense. But at least you'd be starting *in* the boat instead of trying to land on one.'

'True. So, what do you think?'

'If you want to, okay.'

'Great, thanks.' With one finger Phil typed: *I'm in.*

As the movie began, Phil sat back in the red velvet chair, but he couldn't concentrate on the screen. To row the Atlantic — now that was a challenge to beat all the rest, a perfect finale to his five-year plan. What would Tom say? Phil thought about the night he'd bargained with God for Tom's life, and how the promises he'd made had determined the purpose of his own. Each challenge had been designed with two core requirements: to push himself physically in honour of his son, and to go where Tom wasn't able. He was sure Tom would be excited, he always loved the stories Phil had to tell him on his return from these challenges. But he also knew it would be difficult for him to grasp the enormity of this latest idea. Tom liked routine. The most important thing for Tom was the daily phone calls when his dad was away on a challenge. Phil started to make mental notes of questions to ask Zoe's friend – how long would it take, what were the costs, could he be guaranteed ship-to-shore communications and could he raise money for Tiny Lives?

The movie he was supposed to be watching was about a family road trip. Phil thought about Rod and Alex. He'd been thrilled to have swum the English Channel with both of them. Rod would have loved to be on all the challenges but once he'd started work after college, he no longer had enough time off. But he still supported them in every way he could. Alex, on the other hand, had been with him on all four. How would he feel about missing out on this final one? Still, they always had the Great North Run, the perfect family challenge.

He wondered what Debbie would think. He was blessed they had remained friends. She was a good woman and a wonderful mother to their boys. If he was being honest with himself, the breakdown of his marriage to Debbie was not really a result of living in two separate countries – if anything, it probably prolonged it. It had been strained before he left. And maybe that was why he *had* left. Regardless, he felt very lucky that their partnership had produced three fine young men. He hoped they'd inherited only their parents' better traits.

Meme put her hand on his arm. 'Shush, I can hear you thinking from here.'

Phil mimed 'sorry'; he knew she wasn't joking. He considered himself a good judge of character and could read people's energy but nothing like how she was able to read his. He still hadn't mastered any technique to calm himself when his excitability was too much for her, although he tried.

Yet, it was her empathy that he found endearing. She understood him, anticipated his needs and supported him in all his endeavours. He loved how she connected with those around her, how she always seemed to recognise when someone needed help. She was in tune with the natural world and cared about all living creatures. One day while they were driving in America, she'd made him stop the car so she could get out and help a fallen bird. She'd taken it home and nursed it back to health. Phil understood her nature was to nurture and saying goodbye to her animals in the US had been hard on her. Shortly after she arrived in the UK, he took her to the local dog shelter. She'd gravitated to Morgan at the end of the long line of kennels. He stood tall, his paws resting on the crossbars, clearly waiting for her. And what a fabulous addition he was to their family.

As the credits rolled at the end of the movie he hadn't watched, his phone buzzed again: *Meet him tomorrow at noon? Perfect.*

It was fate. He'd been looking for something new and now God had delivered his fifth and final challenge — to get in a small boat with someone he had yet to meet, and row it across the Atlantic Ocean. What could possibly go wrong?

Chapter 14

21 October 2017

To everyone else it was an ordinary Saturday in October. To Paul it felt like that first day at school or Christmas morning, but he went about breakfast with Nic as usual, chatting, watching the news.

'Well, are you excited?' Nic asked when the ads came on.

'About what?'

Paul knew exactly what she meant but couldn't share how he felt. It was too personal. Ever since the last firefighter had quit the team three months earlier, it had been hard to stay motivated. He'd kept hunting for that elusive partner, asking anyone and everyone he knew if they'd join his team: paramedics, police, triathletes and cyclists, anyone who was into outdoor sports and had courage. But no one said yes. He'd started to doubt he could do it at all, but he was afraid to confide in anyone because he knew he was vulnerable. On a bad day, any one of them might persuade him to give up. If that person was Nic, he knew it would come back to haunt every future argument they might ever have.

'Aren't you meeting Zoe's friend today,' she said, 'the one in her spin class or whatever?'

Paul nodded but kept his grin on the inside. He was glad Nic seemed interested, and today could be the day, but he didn't want to jinx it. Trust Zoe to come through for him though. She'd become such a good mate since she'd started cycling with him and Carl.

As he drove along the quayside to the café, Paul thought about meeting Phil. He wasn't a firefighter or ex-service, but Zoe had told him about Phil's yearly challenges. Even though rowing the Atlantic would be bigger than anything else Phil had done, he still had more experience at sea than Paul. The text Zoe had forwarded had given him hope but Paul couldn't wait to look him in the eye, to see who Phil really was and what he was about. Probably not the most scientific way to assess his capabilities, but it would give him some measure of the man.

He paid for parking and displayed the ticket in the windscreen, but instead of walking into the café, Paul sat back in the car to gather himself and run the conversation in his head one last time. He felt like he was going on a first date. He didn't want to appear too needy, nor too arrogant, but wanted to pitch it just right. He thumbed through the documents he'd brought, including the report on the death of one ocean rower back in 2015. He didn't want to frighten Phil, but he wanted to make sure he gave him all the facts. He didn't need an Olympic athlete, but he needed to know he could depend on that person to show up for training, help with fundraising, make it to the starting line and try his very best out on the ocean. Okay, deep breath, time to go in.

Paul scanned the restaurant; nobody matched the description Zoe had given him.

'Excuse me,' he said to the young lady at the counter, 'I'm meeting a bloke called Phil Pugh, do you know him?'

'Phil? Yeah. Haven't seen him today yet. Would you like something to drink while you wait?'

Decisions. What to drink? Perhaps he would have a beer. Wait, no, might look bad to be drinking at lunchtime. Coffee? No, he was too perked up already.

'Tea, please, a pot of tea.'

'Sure. Have a seat.'

More decisions. High chairs? No, he would fidget on a high chair. Dining table would feel too formal. Had to be the leather sofas. Sorted. Paul had only just settled in when he heard a voice behind him.

'Hi Paul, I'm Phil.'

Paul stood up and spun around. Zoe's description was spot on but Paul was still surprised to see a mirror image of himself. Phil was about 5ft 9in, a muscular, stocky man, like a well-built, pocket-sized Hercules. They even had matching male pattern baldness.

'Hi, great to meet you.' Paul offered his hand and noted Phil's honourable grip, not so tight as to dominate, nor limp like overcooked pasta, but firm, capable of holding an oar hour after hour. Phil's big wide smile put Paul further at ease.

'Have you ordered?'

'I have tea on the way.'

'Suits me too, let me order a coffee for Meme, she just popped into the ladies.'

'Oh, okay.' He hadn't realised Phil's wife was coming. It hadn't dawned on him to invite Nic. She probably wouldn't have been interested anyway. They did most things separately, that was just their style.

'Be right back.'

Paul watched Phil stride to the counter, pleased to notice he carried a proper bound diary, old school – another good omen for compatibility. He looked fit and healthy, maybe five or ten years older than Paul. Phil's exchange with the server also told Paul he was a man of integrity, with a smile for everyone. So far, it was looking good – this might be the one who could help him get the project back on course.

As Phil came back with the coffee, Meme arrived.

'Hi, Paul, nice to meet you,' she said in a soft American accent, clearly diluted by years in the UK. Paul wondered if he should hug her or give her a kiss on the cheek, but settled for the safer handshake instead. Once they all sat down and the pleasantries were over, there was a pause in the conversation.

'Right,' said Paul. 'I suppose I should tell you what's what.'

As Paul outlined the costs, the prerequisites, the ten days they'd need to spend in La Gomera in the Canaries before the race, the approximate time frame it would take to complete the 3,000 miles to Antigua, and the debriefing they would need to go through once there, Phil and Meme listened intently. Now it was time to hit them with the fact that he could also lose his life out there. Paul showed them the 2015 report.

Phil considered it for a moment. 'If we follow the safety measures, could we ensure it did not happen to us?'

'Yes, as long as we're harnessed to the boat, we shouldn't get washed away if we capsize.'

Meme didn't say anything, but Paul could tell she would have questions for Phil once they were alone.

'Is there a safety boat?' asked Phil.

'Yes, but it's not going to save you. It could be a couple of days away.'

'Satphone, VHF radio?'

'Yes.'

'Life raft?'

'Yes, here's a full list of the safety kit we have to carry,' said Paul, feeling a little more relaxed that the conversation was going well.

'What about the money, where are you at with all that?'

And here it comes, Paul thought. Probably where Phil is going to bolt. 'Well, I have the boat and some of the kit, but need to raise a lot more money.'

'Wow, that's fantastic, Paul. Having the boat already will make a massive difference when we are trying to get sponsorship.'

Did Paul hear him right, did he just say 'we'? Could this be the team-mate he'd been desperate to find? The excitement he'd kept bottled tried to bubble up, but he had to quash it:

'Well, Phil, what do you think? Are you up for it?'

Paul saw a glint of a smile starting in Phil's eyes and thought, *I'm back on track, I'm going to row the Atlantic after all. Come on, Phil, get those words out, or at least one good one starting with a capital Y.* He knew Phil wanted to, he could feel it, but the words didn't come. Phil looked down and then at Meme. In Paul's excitement he had almost forgotten she was there. Meme had that concerned look, the same one Nic wore more often than not these days. His hopes dropped like a 40-pound anchor.

'Meme ...?' Phil asked.

She paused. It wasn't an outright no, but it wasn't a yes. Paul imagined her brain computing everything she had just learned. *So, you want my husband to spend the next year training with you, organising fundraising events, flying to the Canaries and then getting in a 20-foot boat, just the two of you, and rowing it across the Atlantic. For what? For a challenge that has left a wife widowed and children fatherless?* He could almost agree with her. But then she looked at Phil.

'If you want to, then it's fine by me. I'm not going to stop you.'

Phil's grin cracked wide open. He stood up and put out his hand.

'I am in, skipper.'

Paul jumped up too. This was too big for a handshake. He threw his arms around Phil and gave him a hug.

'Welcome aboard, mate, welcome aboard.'

The two of them sat down, smiling so hard they could barely drink their tea.

After agreeing to a planning meeting for the following week, Paul bade farewell to his new team-mate and sat in his car to let the emotion roll over him like a giant Atlantic wave he'd been so looking forward to tackling. Relief flowed out as he sucked excitement back in. It was intoxicating. He grabbed his phone and pinged a message first to Zoe, and then Carl. They would be so happy for him. Then he called Nic, even though he knew she was at work and couldn't answer but he just had to let her know.

As Paul drove home, his mind raced faster than his car. Lists upon lists wrote themselves in his head. Nic rang back. He pulled over.

'Well, what did you think of him? What is he like? Do you think you will get on? Was he nice?'

Paul had never heard Nic as excited about the race before.

'It went really well, he's dead keen. Seemed impressed at how much I've already got sorted. He brought his wife, Meme.'

'Oh … and?'

'She seemed a little cautious, but she said yes.'

'Well, I'm not that keen on it either, but you want to do it, so it is okay with me.'

Paul didn't want to dwell on the fact that he had heard Nic say this before. 'Okay, love, I'll let you get back to work. We can talk about it some more when you get home.'

'Okay. I'm happy for you.'

'I love you.'

Phil took Meme's hand in his on their walk home. 'Well, what do you think?'

'This is bigger than anything else you've done, isn't it?'

'Sure is. What did you think of Paul?'

'He's got a great background. If he's anything like the firefighters I met when I worked in the ER back home, he should be rock-solid.'

'Did you like him?'

'Yes, he seems like an honest guy, very sincere.'

'Very.'

'You two come from different backgrounds, but you also have a lot in common.'

'How so?'

'You're both adventurous, and determined. But you have different skill sets so you should be able to complement each other's weaknesses.'

'I have a weakness?'

Meme laughed. 'Maybe some of Paul's calm demeanour will rub off on you, although he seems pretty passionate about this. It's a huge undertaking but I believe the two of you will do it.'

Phil stopped walking, took her in his arms and kissed her. 'That makes me feel good. Thank you.'

It was getting cooler, so they picked up the pace.

'What about you though, Meme? It's going to require a lot more fundraising effort and social media updates than the previous challenges. Are you up for that?'

'I'll do my best. You know I always support you.'

When they reached the apartment, Meme fed Morgan while Phil boiled the kettle. This challenge would be time-consuming, both in preparation and execution. What about their company? Was it fair to leave her without a business partner or a husband for so long?

'We could be gone for almost three months, Meme.'

'Morgan will keep me company, won't you, Morgan?' she said, giving the dog his after-dinner treat. 'Do you think Tom will be able to cope?'

'Good question. I hope so. I don't think we should tell him yet. It's still over a year away. Maybe ease him into the idea a couple of months before.'

'We'll all be here for him – Debbie, me, the boys. I'm sure Rod and Alex will visit as often as they can, and they'll phone him.'

'What about the business?'

'I'll be fine.'

'Are you sure?'

'Didn't I run it without any problems when you were away on all your other challenges?'

'This is a lot longer.'

'I can manage.'

'What did I do to get so lucky to have you?'

As they settled down for the evening, their conversation wandered from family to business to social engagements that weekend but it always circled back to the row. Phil downloaded videos of previous races from the TWAC website. The first clip showed a boat riding up a vertical wave.

'Whoa,' they both said.

The next, the sudden rush of water against the on-board camera as the boat capsized.

'Wow.'

'How big are those waves, Phil?'

'I don't know. Bigger than anything I've ever seen in the Med or the North Sea. They must be at least 12–15 metres?'

The images alternated between exciting Phil and scaring the crap out of him. What had he let himself in for?

Chapter 15

6 January 2018

Paul had always thought of himself as an easy-going person, but maybe his dogged determination about this race might have been what put his previous team-mates off. He had a good feeling about Phil, though, felt he was a man of integrity and understood what it meant to make a commitment to something or someone. So far, they were getting along very well. Phil and Meme had far more experience fundraising than Paul. They also seemed to have a lot more contacts and connections. Where Paul had struggled to find help setting up fundraising events, Phil had pulled together a group of volunteers in a matter of days. Paul was mechanically inclined and had a more flexible schedule to tend to what needed fixing on the boat while Phil had to concentrate on his business.

As they'd both been busy on the run-up to Christmas, they'd agreed to wait until after New Year to get on the water. In the meantime, they trained together two or three times a week at Martin Whitaker's gym, spotting each other on the bench press, and relying on their combined strength to flip a 17-stone tyre. Although they had yet to train on *Didi*, they already felt like a team.

On an icy January afternoon, clad in hats, jumpers, gloves and scarves, they got their chance.

'Where shall we row, towards the bridges?' asked Phil, after they had floated her off the trailer.

'No, tide is coming in. We'll go downstream first, against the current,' said Paul. He wasn't going to make that mistake twice.

They pushed off the pontoon and headed towards the piers.

'Sorry,' said Phil, every time he bumped oars with Paul.

'No bother, we'll find our rhythm.'

It didn't take long to figure out their different stroke rates and with Phil in front Paul was able to match his pull. As they made their way towards the mouth of the river they chatted about Phil's earlier challenges, about his sons, especially Tom.

'He sounds like a great kid,' said Paul.

'He's amazing. I wish I could swap with him sometimes, though, you know, give him my body so he could be the one out here rowing. I'm sure he would adore it.'

Paul could only see Phil's back, but he could feel his smile and the love.

'But I don't think I would do half as good a job as he does living in his body. He is so upbeat, so cheerful, and has a brilliant sense of humour. It's humbling. How about you? What does your son think of this challenge?'

'James thinks it's great. My older boys, Sean and Jamie, probably think it's daft.'

'Oh, I didn't realise you had two more, where are they?'

'Nottingham. They stayed with Diane, my first wife.'

'I take it James is a family name?'

'James Edward, after my dad and Nic's. Diane chose Jamie.'

'How often do you see them?'

'Not as often as I should.' Paul didn't like to think about how he'd flitted in and out of Sean and Jamie's lives since his first divorce and all through his marriage to Vicki. It wasn't until he had moved to Newcastle to be with Nic and their new baby that he realised how little he had been there for them.

'Must be tough.'

'Yeah. I have Diane to thank for how they turned out, she did a wonderful job raising them, and now they have kids of their own.'

'You're a grandfather? Wow. I can't wait for that.'

The two men rowed on, both lost in their own thoughts about their families. When the conversation resumed it turned to the challenge and money.

'So, what do we get for our 20 grand entrance fee?' asked Phil.

'Mostly support. First, there is the sailing vessel.'

'The one that could be two or three days away?'

'Yes, but we will be tracked on GPS. Our families will be able to see where we are and watch our progress. Plus, it's supposed to be easier to get sponsorship with a recognised event. How are your hands doing?'

'Good,' said Phil, 'gloves make a difference. You?'

'Okay.'

'I think one of the reasons we haven't managed to get a major sponsor yet,' said Phil, 'is because the big boys can't see a return on their advertising investment. It's not like it's an Olympic sport or a televised race.'

'You're probably right.'

'If we don't raise enough money, then what? We go by ourselves? We already have the boat.'

'Believe me, the thought has crossed my mind,' said Paul. 'I mentioned the possibility to Nic, but she was not in favour of the idea. Most of my mates agree with her. They say it's dangerous enough even with TWAC support, never mind going without any back-up at all.'

'Yeah, I suppose Meme wouldn't fancy it either.'

'She probably wants you back alive too.'

'No kidding.'

'How does she like living in the UK?'

'She enjoys it. Misses her daughter though. But we plan to sell the apartment and the business in the next couple of years and retire in the States.'

'Oh. Whereabouts?'

'Las Vegas. She has lots of friends there.'

'Never been. I was in Florida a couple of years ago. Brought James to Universal Studios shortly after I signed up for the row. You'll never guess who I bumped into at the top of the water slide – James Cracknell.'

'The Olympic rower?'

'Yes, he was there with his son too. I had about ten seconds and I told him I'd entered the Atlantic Challenge and asked if he had any advice. He said, "Yeah, learn to fix everything on the boat", and *whoosh*, off he went down the slide.'

'Wow, how cool was that.'

'Speaking of cool, ready to head back?'

'Sure. It's not getting any warmer,' said Phil.

'Yes, and better to turn before the tide does.'

'How do you want to do it, skipper?'

'How about we pull on the right oar only until we pivot.'

Although the current was in their favour it had started to slacken a little. The pair of them fell into a comfortable silence as they rowed together, with only the occasional mis-stroke. By the time they arrived alongside the pontoon the winter sun was hiding behind the clouds and keeping any heat to itself.

'Okay. Let's get sorted before it gets too dark.'

'What would you like me to do?' said Phil.

'If you could wait here on the boat while I get the trailer,' Paul said. He walked up to the car and reversed down the muddy slipway until the trailer's wheels were in the water. He'd found that the best way to gain enough traction to pull *Didi* up the ramp was to unhook the trailer, move the car further up the slip, then tie a long rope between the two. After he repositioned the car, he tied one end to the tow-hitch and began walking down the slip.

'What the …?' The trailer was gone.

Phil, still in the boat, was plunging one oar in and out of the water.

'Sorry, skipper, I was trying to row her on to it.'

Paul could see it now – somehow Phil had accidentally knocked the brake off. The trailer had rolled backwards and was submerged. Phil continued to prod the water but without success. Paul waded in up to his knees and began a side-to-side search pattern. Still no sign.

'God, that's cold,' he said as the water covered his nether regions. All the way up to his chest now. He could feel the mud squelching over his ankles. 'And it stinks.'

'Where could it be?' asked Phil.

'Not here anyway. Nothing for it but to wait for low tide. Let's tie *Didi* to the pontoon for now.'

Together they secured the boat and headed up the slip.

'What time do we need to come back?'

Paul checked the tide tables. 'Low's just after one in the morning.'

'Okay, I'll meet you back here then.'

'No point in both of us getting up, I can manage.'

'But it's my—'

'Let's agree on one thing. No matter what happens on this challenge, it's not important who or what's to blame. Let's concentrate on finding the solution instead of focusing on the problem.'

'Agreed, but are you sure?' said Phil.

'No bother. If I need help, I'll call you.'

'Please do.'

Trying not to wake Nic, Paul snuck out of the house shortly after midnight. When he arrived at the river, he shone his headlights down the slip. The trailer was now visible but stuck in the mud. He reversed, got out and ran the rope between it and the car. There. The trailer was going nowhere. Neither was *Didi*, though. Paul still needed to wait until mid-tide before he could float her on. Another three hours should do it. Probably not worth going home. He bumped up the heat in the car and settled in.

It had been a great first day. He enjoyed Phil's company and conversation was easy, which was surprising since Paul didn't have many friends who wore suits and ties to work. Considering they were both into sports, triathlons and cycling, it was a wonder they'd never met before. Thank goodness for Zoe. The more Paul got to know Phil, the more he liked him. There was no shouting, no cross words, no pointing the finger, they just got on with it. Maybe it wouldn't always be like that but ...

Paul awoke mid-snore. Dawn. He checked his mirror and cursed. The trailer had once again disappeared, fully engulfed by the high tide.

Two naps and one alarm call on his mobile later, he pulled *Didi* and her chariot back on to dry land. Another lesson learned.

Chapter 16

16 March 2018

Three hundred pairs of eyes stared up at Paul and Phil, but neither of them was nervous. It wasn't like giving a presentation to possible sponsors. These five- to eleven-year-olds of Hadrian Primary School were eager to watch the video of an ocean rowing boat being thrown about on massive waves.

In addition to fundraising, Paul and Phil wanted to give back to the local community and had reached out to the schools and colleges to teach them about the expedition and show what anyone from Newcastle could do if they put their minds to something. When the film clip was over and Paul invited questions, about 70 small hands flew into the air.

'What about your dinner, won't you get hungry?'

'We'll bring it with us, in a packet,' said Phil.

'I hope you're bringing more than one, Phil,' said Paul.

'You look like you've already had yours today,' said Phil, poking Paul in the belly.

The kids giggled.

'What if it rains?'

'Well, it'll be my turn to nap in the cabin and Phil's turn to row the boat,' said Paul, getting his own back.

'How heavy are the oars?'

'Where do you sleep on a boat?'

'What if you get lost?'

Paul and Phil kept up the banter and took turns firing back answers as fast as the questions kept coming.

'Alright,' the teacher said, 'last question before you all go to your classrooms.' She pointed to a boy near the back. 'Peter, go ahead.'

'What will you miss the most?'

'Easy one,' said Phil. 'My family.'

'Me too,' said Paul.

'What else?'

Paul stood there, stumped. What else would he miss apart from his family? He'd been so focused on getting to the starting line it had never entered his mind to think about what he would miss. 'Great question, Peter. I love watching sports on TV. Until you asked, I hadn't realised how much I will miss football and the Premier League. What would you all miss?'

Peter's question seemed to have resonated. The children were keen to share what they would miss. For the younger ones it was their parents, their brothers, their sisters, their hamsters, their cats, their dogs and one or two would miss their goldfish. The older students had noticed the race started in December and said they wouldn't want to miss Christmas.

'Alright, children, time to go back to class. Say goodbye to Paul and Phil.'

'Bye, Paul, bye, Phil,' they all shouted together.

Paul and Phil waved as the children filed out, class by class. The teacher thanked them for their presentation and invited them to come back again before their trip.

'That went well,' said Paul as they walked out to the car park.

'Yeah, it was fun. You hungry?'

'Funny man.'

'No, seriously, I'm meeting Meme for lunch, and Tom's coming too. Would you like to meet him?'

Paul had things to do, but he knew how important Tom was to Phil.

'I'd love to, thanks.'

Meme was already at the restaurant when they arrived. Phil spent some time choosing a table, one large enough for everyone but also wheelchair accessible. He moved one of the chairs to the side. The server brought waters and menus.

'Here they are,' said Phil, pointing at a car driving in. He was up and out the door like an excited kid.

Paul was surprised to find he was nervous. He wanted Tom to like him, but he also had to remember not to talk about why he and his dad were friends. Phil still hadn't told Tom about the challenge.

'Looks like Emily is his carer today,' said Meme. 'He likes her a lot.'

As they approached, Paul noticed how Tom was able to manoeuvre his electric wheelchair to the table. Phil was giving him directions which Tom was choosing to ignore.

'Tom, this is my friend Paul.'

'Hi, Tom.'

Tom took his time, formed the words and said: 'I'm Tom. This is Em.'

'Emily, really,' said Phil.

Tom wasn't going to be corrected by his dad. 'I call her Em.'

'Nice to meet you,' said Paul, diplomatically avoiding using either name.

'You too, Paul.'

'What would you like to drink, Tom?' said Phil.

Again, it took a moment for him to articulate. Paul noticed how no one prompted or answered for him. They were all comfortable waiting.

'Pint,' he said.

'Okay, Foster's coming up.'

It was obviously a game they played. Phil already knew exactly what Tom would want.

'I'll have one too, then,' said Paul. 'I mean, if Tom is having one it would be rude not to join him, right, Tom?'

Tom chuckled.

When Phil left for the bar, Meme asked: 'What have you been up to this week, Tom?'

This time the pauses were longer and Paul could see he was concentrating hard.

'I've ... been out ... for a ... few beers.'

A man after my own heart, thought Paul.

When Phil came back, he sat beside Tom and helped him drink his pint through a straw. Paul hadn't known quite what to expect, but he was surprised how acute Tom's disability actually was. Then he felt disappointed in himself for even thinking like that. He hoped it didn't show on his face. The only experience he had was volunteering at the social evening for some of Nic's patients with learning disabilities, but few of them had physical challenges.

Phil was teasing Tom about being a ladies' man, as he nodded towards Emily. She smiled, seemingly used to this playfulness. Through the warmth she had for him, Paul was able to see past Tom's health problems and realise there was a special person there.

'Tom, who looks older, me or Paul?'

It was a question Phil loved to ask because he thought he looked like the one who was ten years younger, although most people didn't agree. Tom gazed at Paul, then at his dad, then at Paul.

'He does.'

Paul laughed out loud.

'See how smart my son is, Paul?'

'Can't argue there, Phil.'

'Another beer, Dad?'

'Maybe we should order some food first, Tom,' said Emily. 'It's been a while since breakfast.'

'Emily's right,' said Phil, pleased with how vigilant she was about Tom's diabetes. He beckoned the server.

After the food arrived, Paul noticed how Phil ignored his own plate while he fed Tom. The box at the back of Paul's mind, where he kept all the things he didn't want to think about, cracked open and first out was a feeling of guilt. He had three healthy sons and he had taken that for granted. Worse, he was ashamed to admit he had been a poor father to Sean and Jamie. It was too late to redeem himself with them, but when Nic had become pregnant, he'd made a conscious decision to be a better dad and be a constant in his youngest son's life. He'd taught James how to ride a bike, play sports, and he would stand in a goal for hours while his son blasted a football at him, even letting the occasional one in. He'd been to his school plays, was there to change the batteries in his toys and help him write his letter to Santa. His son knew he could come to him for anything. Paul felt proud to finally be a proper dad, but seeing this bond between Phil and Tom … well, their relationship was on a whole different level.

As he drove away from the restaurant, Paul thought about how the afternoon had given him a deeper look into what kind of man Phil really was, and he liked what he saw. If Phil showed a fraction of the dedication he had for Tom when it came to rowing the Atlantic, they were going to do just fine.

Chapter 17

26 April 2018

Paul, Phil and Meme worked together to plan many fundraising events, including dinner cruises, beach parties, spinathons, and dragon boat races on the Tyne — something they hoped could benefit the city by becoming an annual event. Entry fees supported their Atlantic project, while donations from the public were dedicated to their chosen charities: the Fire Fighters Charity and Tiny Lives.

Today, they were going to repeat one of the more successful events Paul had run before Phil joined the team — to row a million metres non-stop on a Concept2 rowing machine. To be eligible for a world record, as Paul and his friends had achieved last July, they had to form a mixed team which had to include ten people, a third of whom had to be women, over 30 years old and weigh more than 70 kilos. They would do it in shifts, one person rowing at a time. Phil set up a rota based on everyone's availability, leaving him and Paul to cover all the gaps. When the machine logged a million metres it would generate a verification code to validate their time.

Since the weather was lousy, Paul was glad they were set up on the indoor stage of the Gate shopping mall in Newcastle. By 8.55am he and Phil had the banners hung and donation buckets ready. With the local media covering the event, they were hopeful of attracting a major sponsor.

At 9am the countdown clock started. Phil took the first shift, popped in his earbuds and started to pull.

'Well done, mate,' said Paul. 'Only 999,999 more strokes to go. See ya.'

Phil laughed. 'Your turn next, skipper.'

The early shoppers had started to arrive, Paul chatted with a few and the coins started to drop in the buckets. One of the women nodded towards Phil and asked Paul: 'Are you going to have to listen to that the whole away across the Atlantic?'

'I certainly hope not,' said Paul, unable to figure out the song Phil was trying to sing along to. It bore no resemblance to music.

It was amazing to Paul how quickly an hour passed while Phil was on the machine and how long the next one dragged while he was rowing.

'What time's your friend McGarvie coming?' he asked.

Phil consulted the list of volunteers he had pulled together, '4pm. You and I can switch off every hour until I have to leave for the office. You okay with a two-hour row before he gets here?'

'Sure,' said Paul, 'have to get used to it sometime.' It was one thing to do it on an indoor machine for four days, another to keep it up 24 hours a day for a couple of months.

Julia Turner, the manager of the Gate, stopped by. 'How's it going, lads? Need anything?'

'My head examined?' said Paul, sweat rolling from his temples.

'You're probably right. Anyway, just wanted to let you know that Steve will be along later.'

'Brilliant.' Julia's husband, Steve, was their star rower – young, fit, strong as an ox.

Just before 6pm Zoe arrived to take her shift on the machine.

'What have you got there?' said Paul. Looks like you are packed for crossing the Atlantic.

'Just some snacks and drinks. Here, take one. I know what you're like when you get hungry.'

'Aw, thanks,' said Paul, tearing into the protein bar.

'Okay, Zoe, ready?' said Phil.

'Ready.'

The clock was ticking, they couldn't afford to miss a beat. Phil passed the rowing handle to Paul who kept the motion going while Phil and Zoe swapped places.

Later, when the crowd thinned, and the shopping centre closed, Paul collected the buckets and put them aside till morning. Only the cleaners were left to wave at the volunteers who'd agreed to row during the night. He was thankful not to be on the rota that night, but felt honour-bound to stay the entire weekend and keep the volunteer rowers company. Nic brought him refreshments, and Zoe left him her kit bag with the rest of the food and drink in case he ran out. He sorted himself a chair, and at 2am, when he could no longer keep his eyes open, he put his hooded jacket on back to front and snuggled in for a snooze.

By Saturday night, they were on target to break their previous record. Steve Turner had racked up 15,000 metres in a single hour. Martin, their tyre-tossing gym mentor, had smashed it, so too had Lynsey, Paul Rea, himself and Phil. Zoe and McGarvie had completed several shifts and had kept pace with the best of them.

But when Paul got on for his next shift, something looked off with the countdown monitor.

'Hey, Phil, can you take a look?'

Phil prised open his magnetic reading glasses, which were hanging around his neck, and snapped them together on the bridge of his nose. He tried to look closely at the monitor without getting smacked by Paul's head as he whizzed back and forth.

'I'm not sure, let me google it.'

Paul kept rowing.

'Hmm, says here it might be a software problem.'

'Well, we'll just keep going, seems to be counting down okay now.'

'Great,' said Phil. 'Place is filling up again.'

Newcastle United had lost their Premier League match against West Bromwich Albion. Fans strolled the mall. The later it got, the more rowdy the passers-by became.

'Hey, thought you said you were rowing the Atlantic.'

'We are.'

'Don't you need water?'

'Are you not cold?' Paul asked some of the young ones in skimpy clothes. 'Where are your coats?'

'At home. They charge too much to leave them in the cloakrooms.'

And yet, Paul noticed, these youngsters were happy to make donations, especially the girls who enjoyed flirting with a couple of his firefighter buddies shaking the buckets.

One lad sauntered along and gave Paul £20.

'Are you sure?'

'Yeah, mate, fair play to you. I'm off to the casino. If I win more, I'll bring some back.'

As the mall began to close, a ruckus started outside. It looked like a war zone, with people passed out on the street after spending the weekend drinking through the pain of their football team's loss. Police and ambulances started to cart people away. The distraction kept Paul, Phil and Zoe entertained during their final night of rowing.

On Sunday afternoon, Paul sat into the machine for the final 10,000 metres. As tired as he was, the team encouraged him through to the finish and cheered when they beat their previous record. Just. But the monitor had indeed failed and never produced a code to verify their time.

It had been an exhausting four days and seemed like an interminable distance. It had taken ten of them on a stable indoor machine to row a million metres. It wasn't even 20 per cent of the distance Paul and Phil would have to row across the Atlantic.

Chapter 18

5 May 2018

While Phil waited for Paul to arrive, he began getting *Didi* set up for their training session on the river. A young couple ambled down to the pontoon and asked the same question everyone kept asking. Could they hitch a ride to Antigua? It didn't matter where Phil went, kids and adults alike all fancied a holiday in the Caribbean. What better way to go, they thought, than by sea?

Their naivety made Phil smile, but he always gave the same polite answer.

'Sorry, as you can see there's barely enough room for myself and Paul, never mind anyone else.'

'We just got married,' the man said. 'I need to give her a honeymoon.'

As proof, the woman thrust her ring finger under Phil's nose.

'Congratulations, very pretty,' Phil said, throwing his dry-bag on to the boat, 'but as you can see it's too small for passengers.'

'Nonsense, look at us, we're tiny. You won't even know we're here.' The man jumped on board. 'Come on Julie, hop on.'

'Wait a minute—'

'Hey, Phil, Phil.'

Phil turned and saw a teenager running towards him.

'You're that guy that was on the radio.'

'That's right.'

'Heard you saying you're going to row across the Atlantic.'

'Yes. Please don't touch that,' Phil said to the woman, Julie, who was sliding the rowing seat back and forth.

'I want to come too,' the teenager said and climbed aboard.

'Sorry, I don't mean to be rude but can you all please step off.'

'Wait for us,' said another voice as a family with three small children clad in life jackets arrived.

Then a double decker pulled in. Phil watched in disbelief as a dozen people descended the ramp and jumped on. The waterline along *Didi*'s hull rose.

'Stop,' he yelled. 'You have to get off.'

A boy in a red woolly hat waved a pound at him. 'I can pay you.'

'Me too,' said an older gentleman, 'I can give you a fiver.'

Ten more appeared from nowhere. 'Take us with you.'

Phil looked up the slipway, still no sign of Paul. Instead, he saw Tom sitting in the car park.

'Dad, Dad, how many Geordies can you fit on a rowboat?'

'I don't know, Tom.'

'Three thousand, Dad, one per mile.' Tom laughed as he spun doughnuts on the tarmac, chanting, 'One per mile.'

Phil turned back to the river. Men, women and children had started rocking the boat. Waves slapped at her sides and spilled over the gunwales.

'NO ...'

Didi was sinking.

He started grabbing hands, arms, legs, anything he could get a hold of, trying to pull people off.

'Help,' he cried, 'help me.'

Now they were rocking him.

'Phil, it's okay. Phil.'

Who was calling him? Rocking him? Phil opened his eyes and saw his hands clawing the air.

'It's okay, honey, shush, it's okay.'

He could feel Meme's hand laying on his chest, sweat trickling down the side of his neck.

'*Didi?*'

'It's okay.'

As the day wore on, the dream hung on Phil's shoulders. What did it mean? Was this a warning about *Didi*? Was a fourth crossing too much to ask of her? If she sank at sea, how long could he and Paul survive? Meme could probably interpret the significance, but he didn't want to scare her. Maybe it wasn't about the boat at all, maybe it was the business. Was it fair to leave her to run it by herself while he was gone?

Phil was naturally prone to optimism, so he grappled for another explanation. What about all the people, was there a message there? The boy in the red hat floated across his mind, then Tom's voice … 'One per mile, Dad, one per mile.' Oh, wow. That was it!

What time was it? He dialled Paul.

'Hi, Phil, I'm just about to head in for the night shift, what's up?'

'I've had an idea how we can raise more money.'

'Great.'

'But the question is, are you open to repainting the boat?'

Chapter 19

14 May 2018

When *Didi* wasn't on the water, she was locked up for her own protection. Rowers, Paul had learned, could be replaced, but if anything happened to the boat it would be game over before it began.

It was still dark when he pulled into the yard at Byker Fire Station. He opened the garage bay and flicked on the fluorescents.

Some days, like today, she looked so tiny. How were he and Phil going to cope living together in that small space for the best part of three months? He backed the car up and pulled the trailer to the tow-hitch. What was he thinking? She was not a tiny vessel; she was a wooden monster. With a clunk, she settled on his car and Paul straightened up.

'Well, girl, are you ready to be accessorised?'

Gone was her fire-engine red coat. The last nod to his old team. Thanks to Phil's idea, she was now painted a virginal white. No matter how hard they'd tried, they still hadn't managed to secure a major sponsor to help fund the project and raise capital for their chosen charities. But locals were supportive and crowdfunding made sense. For a £3 donation people could sign the boat and their signatures would cross the ocean. Their goal was to collect 3,000 – one for every mile they would row.

The traffic on the way into Newcastle this early was light. Permission to display the boat and collect money on the street required arriving downtown before the business day began and leaving after it ended.

Once in position, Paul blocked the trailer's wheels. Town was quiet, still waking up. The smell of freshly brewed coffee enticed him across the street for a takeaway. Oh, that tasted good. He placed his cup on the bow and set out the permanent markers and donation buckets, placing the sign for Tiny Lives front and centre. Apart from the week of the horrific Grenfell Tower fire, when people gladly donated to the Fire Fighters Charity, Tiny Lives was usually the bigger draw. Paul was hoping for a big donation day for the charities; maybe they could raise as much as £500. Next week, they would collect for the project.

A strong smell of alcohol wafted in his direction.

'Hey, mister, can I sign your boat?'

Paul looked at the man. His face was cut above his left eye, and his cheeks, reddened by broken capillaries, had collapsed long ago. There was a time when Paul would have wondered why such a man couldn't quit drinking, get a job, and contribute to society. But, having pulled bodies from the river beneath the Tyne Bridge over the years, he knew life was not that simple, that everyone was doing the best they could, and that if his own life had not been blessed with opportunity, it could just as easily have been him.

'The idea is to donate.'

'I know. I don't have any money, but I'd like to sign the boat.'

'Okay, sure.' He led him to the stern and handed him a pen. The man wrote his name.

'If I had any money, I would put it in the bucket, honest.'

'Yes, mate, I know you would.' Feeling bad for him, Paul offered him his coffee. Then regretted it as soon as the man wandered down the road with his caffeine. Still, at least it saved him having to go to the loo before Phil arrived.

Minutes later he heard another two men fighting. The smaller of the two had found a half-eaten sandwich in a bin but was unwilling to share it. The big one shoved him to the ground and snatched the food, the little one tried to grab it back.

'Okay, lads,' Paul stepped in. 'You,' he said to the big guy, 'take it, and off with you. Leave this lad alone.'

Happy with his spoils, the man swaggered off.

'Here, give me your hand,' Paul said to the man on the ground.

'What about my food? I found it.'

'Come on.' Paul helped him up and walked him across the street where he bought him a freshly made chicken-and-lettuce wrap.

Well, not exactly the best start to his fundraising. So far Paul was down £8.99 and a cup of coffee. But the morning soon started to pick up. Early shoppers stopped to chat about the challenge, donated to the cause and signed their names. Around 10am, Phil rang.

'Sorry, I'm running a bit late, but I'm on my way, need anything?'

Paul was thinking Phil was the one needing something – like a three-day notice for his own funeral, otherwise he was probably going to be late for that too. In fairness, when he did show up, he always worked hard, and fortunately there'd be no traffic from the cabin to the deck while they were at sea. 'Coffee would be great, thanks.'

'You've got it.'

Paul was chatting with an older gentleman, who had crossed the Atlantic many times during his years in the navy, when a police car slowed to a stop. Paul tapped his pocket to make sure his permits were handy. The officer approached.

'Did you witness two men fighting?'

'Yes. I split them up. Why?'

'Okay, sir, we're going to need your statement. One of them is pressing charges.'

Paul was recounting the event when Phil arrived with the coffee.

'Maybe being questioned by the police is not quite the image that will attract donors,' Phil said after the officer left.

'What a morning. Thanks.' Paul sipped his coffee. Once again, he was overcome with the smell of stale beer.

'Hey mister, can my mate sign the boat too?'

'Yes, of course.'

Phil rattled the bucket, but Paul gave him a nod.

'I suppose he has no money either.'

'Nope.'

'That's okay,' said Paul and directed him to the back of the boat. 'He can sign right next to your name.'

The man stood for a moment. Then he leaned forward. It seemed like he was writing a lot more than his name. When he finished, he handed back the pen and said: 'Good luck, hope you don't drown.'

With that, the two of them strolled off. Paul hoped the lad hadn't written something profane. He and Phil walked around the stern to check. But there, in neat, cursive writing were the words: *Godspeed and may the children's love guide you on your way.*

'Huh,' said Phil, 'you just never know about people, do you?'

'You sure don't.' Paul had no clue what these men's hopes and dreams had once been, but he felt glad he could take them into the wild Atlantic.

For the rest of the day the sun shone, and Paul and Phil enjoyed the banter with the crowds.

'Does your family think you are mad?'

'Only on Tuesdays.'

'What happens if you run out of food?' schoolkids asked.

'No bother,' Paul would say. 'I can eat Phil.'

And then the other classic, 'Where do you go to the toilet?'

'See those two buckets, mate?'

'Yeah?'

'We'll take them with us. The orange one is for washing, and the black one is for the other.'

'Eeuuw.'

'What if you see a shark?'

'Well, then it's Phil's turn to clean the bottom of the boat.'

'Excuse me, are you collecting for Tiny Lives?' asked a well-dressed lady in her early forties.

'Yes, ma'am, would you like to sign?'

She reached into her purse and pulled out a £50 note. 'Where can I write a message?'

Surprised by her generous donation, Paul scanned the vessel and found an unmarked panel near the bow. 'How about here?'

Paul and Phil watched her write: *RIP sweetheart as you sleep with the angels, Love Mum.*

Around the inscription she drew a heart. Paul's eyes welled up. Phil reached out and held her hand in both of his.

'We are so sorry for your loss.'

'My son was born at 28 weeks and weighed less than two pounds. I wasn't allowed to hold him, to comfort him like a mother should.'

Street sounds fell away as Paul and Phil listened to the lady recalling her sorrow.

'He was so pale, tubes everywhere. I prayed for a miracle. I wanted him to survive, promised to love him every day.'

Paul looked at Phil's face, knowing the story was bringing him back to Tom's birth. How was he feeling listening to this woman, knowing his child survived and hers had not?

'I wanted so much to hear his first words, watch his first steps. I envisioned him growing up to be a kind man, bringing his first girlfriend home to meet me, getting married, making me a grandmother. I stayed with him every minute, not knowing those six days would turn out to be his whole life on earth.'

Phil wiped a tear.

'I am so grateful to Tiny Lives,' she said. 'They helped me in ways you can't imagine. I will always support them in any way I can.' She brought two fingers to her lips, kissed them and placed the kiss on the message she had written. 'Well done, lads, I hope you raise lots of money. Be safe.'

Paul and Phil watched her walk away and disappear into the afternoon crowd. They didn't have to look at each other to know that they would do everything in their power to take her message across the ocean.

Paul picked up his phone. He owed his Sean and Jamie a call.

Chapter 20

20 May 2018

Phil had kayaked out the River Tyne and on to the North Sea
plenty of times, but today would be his first time rowing. From
a distance, *Didi* had started to look like a dalmatian dog who'd
been put through a poorly functioning car wash; one side of her
was white, the other spotted with black signatures. By Phil's
count they had about a thousand, almost a third of the way to
their goal, with five months left till she had to be shipped to
the Canaries.

It was a lovely day. He and Paul were in good spirits when
they left the confines of the river, rowed out past the piers and
into the waves. *Didi* was riding them well.

'She's a beaut,' said Phil.

'Yeah,' said Paul, 'she can cut through these like butter.'

They'd only gone about a mile or two up the coast when
the wind picked up.

'These conditions would be good for the south route,
wouldn't they?' said Phil.

'Yes,' said Paul, 'if we were not in a little wooden boat.'

Several weeks earlier, they'd attended the prerequisite
training courses in Exeter, to qualify for their Royal Yachting
Association certifications in sea survival, first aid, VHF
licensure, and navigation. In the session on chart plotting,
three possible routes across the Atlantic had been suggested:
the shorter northern course had a risk of more adverse weather,

the middle was slightly longer but should have more favourable sea conditions, and vessels taking the southern route would likely benefit from the stronger trade winds moving from east to west.

Of the 28 teams entered in the race, 17 of which were British, only a dozen or so rowers were taking the certification courses this particular week. Many were super-fit ex-forces, or current military and much more experienced rowers than either of them. Standing next to the Dutch Atlantic Four, Phil and Paul felt like *The Borrowers* – that four-inch-tall family from children's storybooks. But since the courses were mostly theory, they managed not to disgrace themselves and, in some classes, held their own. Phil felt sorry for the first aid instructor. Like Paul, most of the 'students' had more practical experience dealing with casualties that he did.

'I reckon a lot of those teams in newer boats will take the south route,' said Phil. 'They'll practically be blown across.'

'Don't forget, those lighter boats are more likely to capsize than we are.'

'So, which one do you think we should choose, Goldilocks?'

'I vote for the middle route. You?'

'Agreed,' said Phil. 'What do you say, *Didi*?'

'Ah, if only she could talk.'

'That Danish lad, Lars, from the Wolfpack team doesn't talk a lot either, does he?'

'No,' said Paul, 'but he is a very interesting character. He's done several tours in Afghanistan. I promised to have a beer with him in La Gomera.'

'Can't wait.' Normally it would only be a few weeks till Phil's yearly challenge. He liked staging them around his birthday in June, so December felt like a long way off. But he consoled himself with the knowledge that this mammoth challenge would be worth the wait.

While they'd been chatting, conditions had deteriorated. It felt to Phil like the sea had changed her mind and was no longer welcoming small craft. Clouds were picking up speed, scudding across the sky at an alarming rate, and fishing boats were making their way back to harbour.

'Which way, skipper?'

'This is probably kindergarten compared to the Atlantic,' said Paul, 'but since it's only supposed to be an afternoon row, we should probably start heading in.'

'Okay.'

Executing the turn in the sea was a lot tougher than on the river. Both men pulled hard. Once they were pointed towards the piers, Phil looked off to his left at the beach and the string of lamp-posts that stretched for miles along the coast road. As he and Paul pulled together, he began lining up a post with a house behind it to see if they were making any progress. It took at least 20 strokes for the post to look like it was moving. For the next hour, neither of them spoke, just pulled. It was a silent test. Phil knew it was the first time Paul had been on the North Sea since his last team-mate had quit and was probably wondering if he would let him down too.

Heading against the wind and outgoing tide caused the waves to crash over the bow, run along the cabin top and into the bottom of the boat. Salt spray chilled their ears. Paul and Phil rowed hard, despite the constant wetting.

'Want to stop for a drink?' said Paul.

'Go ahead, you first.' Phil kept rowing. He watched a lamp-post against his latest house. It didn't move, which meant they weren't moving either, but at least they weren't losing headway.

'Thanks,' said Paul, 'your turn.'

Phil drank half his bottle while Paul rowed, then tucked it behind his seat. He picked up his oars again: 'Okay, Paul, let's do this.'

After another hour of pulling together, the team made it past St Mary's Lighthouse and into calm water.

Chapter 21

21 July 2018

Paul was getting stronger, as close to peak fitness as he had been in his entire adult life. He could bench press one and a half times his body weight, had mastered the chin-up, and his shirts were getting tight around his chest and shoulders. Just yesterday he had achieved his goal of picking up that enormous tractor tyre by himself and carrying it for 50 metres. As tough and monotonous as the gym workouts were, he was happy with how much more power he had when he pulled on the oars.

For a change of scenery, when the weather was good, he enjoyed exercising outdoors, especially cycling on country roads. One sunny Saturday, he called Zoe.

'Fancy a bike ride?'

'Yes, but Paul, shouldn't you and Phil be out on the water, training?'

'We were on the river yesterday.'

'But what about the North Sea? You're not going to get the experience you need on the Tyne.'

'But the North Sea isn't like the Atlantic either. Out there we'll have the wind and waves coming behind us, and we won't have to turn around and head into it.'

'But it would be better to be over-prepared than under.'

Because Zoe ran a health and safety company, Paul knew she was hardwired to sniff out the danger in every situation and figure out ways to reduce the risk.

'Seriously, Paul, I'm worried about you. You're trying to do everything on a shoestring. The equipment is old, you still haven't got everything you need, and in my opinion, you're not training nearly enough. It makes me nervous.'

'Don't be. Tell you what, why don't we agree not to talk about the row and just enjoy the afternoon in the fresh air?'

They met outside a quaint country pub and set out on a 50-mile ride. The first 46 were wonderful, a gentle summer breeze keeping them cool. Towards the end, they picked up the pace, ready for the final climb over the hill and down to the pub to enjoy a fine lunch. Paul was looking forward to eating his fill at the buffet. He had the perfect excuse – he would need extra stores of fat to prevent his body consuming muscle during the row. Paul had trained hard in that department and had put on eight kilos and a considerable belly. Cycling an incline was challenging. He was halfway up the hill when a sharp burning pain stabbed his right knee. At 20 miles per hour, he struggled to maintain control, but managed to get to the side of the road. He swung his leg over the crossbar and tried to put some weight on it. Apparently not a good idea. His knee locked up.

Minutes later he saw Zoe riding back to find him.

'What's up?'

'My knee. I can't bend it at all.'

'I'll get the car.'

While he waited, Paul cursed all the injuries his right leg had endured, starting with a football match in his youth.

As a 17-year-old kid, his first job had been on building sites, shovelling cement and carrying bricks to the tradesmen. It was physically exhausting, but he did what he was told for fear of getting a thick ear. Whatever he lacked in skill, he made up for with hard work, a trait he inherited from his dad, and one everybody seemed to admire. On the weekends, he no longer felt like a lackey and stood toe to toe with the men. Football was his chance to shine and be an accepted member of the team. He even fantasised about maybe someday becoming a professional player. On Saturdays he played full out. Sunday games with his mates and the locals were for fun. The downside was the sorry standard of football and a couple of ageing dinosaurs nicknamed Clogger because of their unscrupulous delight in kicking people.

One particular Sunday, Paul made a fool out of one especially grumpy guy. As the man approached, Paul knocked the ball through his legs, collected it the other side of him and ran off down the pitch laughing.

'Do that again, you little prick, and I will snap you in half.'

Paul smirked. There was no way the old man could catch him, and being a teenager, the next time he got the opportunity he repeated the trick. Mistake. Clogger was not going to be fooled a third time. At the very next tackle Paul found himself airborne, unaware his right tibia had been snapped in two places before he hit the ground.

The orthopaedic surgeon was surprised to see his patient in a muddy football kit.

'This injury is more like what I would see if you'd crashed a motorbike at 30mph. Twelve weeks in a cast for you, young man.'

Paul's chance of a dream career in football was over and three months later he walked with his right leg shorter than his left.

Those doctor's words turned out to be prophetic. In 2013, he crashed into a lorry at 30mph. The only difference was that he was on a bicycle rather than a motorbike at the time. He and Carl had been training for a long-distance triathlon, and just like today, all was going well until they'd crested this same hill. Paul had been speeding down the steep descent when a horse transporter had pulled out of a field and blocked the road. Paul hit the brakes hard, and the lorry even harder. His bike buckled, somersaulted over his head and landed in a ditch.

At the hospital, the consultant had reviewed his X-rays.

'Good news, Paul. No broken bones. You have serious tissue damage, though, but it should heal in a month or two.'

'Thanks doc, but that's not going to work for me. I have a triathlon in three weeks.'

The consultant laughed. Paul didn't.

'You're not joking, are you?'

'What are my chances, doc?'

'You would be mad to attempt it.'

'Will I do any more damage?'

'Quite possibly. I wouldn't do it.'

'You're not me.'

The consultant stood up and showed Paul the door. 'Good luck with that.'

To Paul it was simple, he just had to find a way to speed up his recovery. Didn't they give football players an injection or something so they could keep on playing? He called in favours and landed an appointment with a chap from Newcastle United. Excellent. One jab and he'd be on his way.

The medic listened to Paul's story.

'This is not the 80s. We're dealing with players who are worth millions. We do not stick needles in them. We treat them and let them heal.'

'But—'

'We wouldn't even let them do light training for at least four weeks and you want to swim, bike and run a marathon? You'll never complete it.'

'I've done these events before.'

'Here's a bit of free advice.'

'Yes?'

'Don't.'

Paul had left with only one thought on his mind – he couldn't quit. He completed the triathlon, but two years later he required knee surgery. He found a new consultant who agreed to do a minimally invasive procedure in the hope that the inevitable joint replacement could be postponed for several years. In the meantime, Paul required medication and regular injections to manage the chronic ache.

Today's pain felt different, though. He tried shaking his knee to see if he could work it loose. Nothing budged. Great. This was going to mess up his training schedule for next week. What if it took longer than a week though? What would that mean for the row? *Get a grip, Paul, it will be fine.* He remembered reading about a team of military amputees who'd completed the 2015 race. If the four of them had rowed with prosthetics, surely he could make it across with one and a half good legs? But doubt niggled. Was this another sign that it was time to call it off? Fortunately, he saw Zoe's car coming over the hill before he had enough time to answer that annoying question.

When he hobbled in the door, Nic rushed to help him. Between her comments, and the bruising and swelling that showed up the next day, Paul realised he couldn't risk setting off across the Atlantic without knowing if his knee was likely to lock up again. He agreed to get it checked out.

It took a week to get an appointment, by which time the swelling had eased and he could bend it again. He listened to the consultant explain the two X-rays which hung on a light box.

'The one on the left is from 2015. Can you see the difference?'

Paul nodded.

'Today's shows you've worn away the bone, plus you have a build-up of calcium. This is only going to get worse.'

'What can I do?'

'I'll have to do a complete replacement as soon as possible.'

It was July. Paul's brain started to calculate recovery times. If it was done immediately, he could probably still make the starting line in December. As though he could read Paul's mind, the consultant looked him in the eye and said: 'You'll have to put that rowing race off until next year.'

Paul slumped in the chair. No. Not again. Why was this happening? He stared at the light box, wishing that was someone else's knee up there. But on the top right-hand corner of the film, in white capital letters, was the name Paul Christopher Hopkins and his date of birth.

Paul left the surgeon's office feeling like he'd been kicked in the stomach. He drove aimlessly for a while and found himself parking out by Sea Banks in North Shields. The tide was out. He walked along the disused Tynemouth Outdoor Pool, feeling as drained and empty as it was. At the end of the walkway, he sat on the cement wall and looked out at the North Sea. Three years. He'd spent the past three years of his life dedicated to this one challenge. Was there no end to the obstacles he had to overcome? It had taken months to find a team, only to have to replace them, and a year and a half to find a cheap boat. Lack of money was a constant stress. Between work, training and fundraising, he rarely spent any time with James or Nic. When was the last time he'd been down to Nottingham to see his mother? And now this. What would people say if he put it off for another year? They were already making jokes about all the delays, saying that the premature babies they were trying to help via Tiny Lives would be teenagers before he crossed.

But what were his choices: hope his knee would hold up another few months and go ahead with the race, postpone till next year, or cancel altogether? Well, that narrowed it down to two: cancelling was spelled with a Q for quitting, so that was a non-runner. If he went ahead, and his knee crapped out in the middle of the ocean and he had to be rescued, he could never live with the shame. That left him staring at the obvious. No matter how demoralising it was, postponing again seemed his only option.

What about Phil, though? This was to be his fifth and final annual challenge. Would he want to wait or would he find something else to do instead? If he did, Paul would be back to square one. Again.

But first things first: he had to talk to Nic. She'd put her life on hold for three years, would she agree to a fourth? It was already causing a strain on their marriage. He walked back to the car and headed home.

On the way, it occurred to him that the obstacles wouldn't end there. He'd still have to renegotiate time off work. When he'd pulled out of the 2017 race and asked the fire department for the same time off for 2018, his employers seemed a little less accommodating. In Paul's opinion, he'd already been overlooked for a busy station posting because of it. He missed the buzz of frequently flying out the door, sirens blaring. This time, he was doubtful they would grant it at all. Of course, there was one other solution, but it would need Nic's blessing.

'What did the doc say?' she asked when they sat down to eat.

'Says I can't wait. Full knee replacement.'

'Amazing you've lasted this long.'

'He says I won't be recovered in time to row in December.'

'So now what?'

'I know I said I wouldn't ask again, but how would you feel if we put it off another year?'

Nic sighed. 'Do I have a choice?'

'I'd be home for Christmas.'

'This year.'

Paul cut into the chicken, wondering if he should have led with his other idea. 'What if I took early retirement in May?'

'At 55?'

'I'd still qualify for the pension and we'd get the lump sum. We could pay everything off.'

'That would be nice.'

'And I wouldn't have to ask for time off. What do you say?'

Nic pulled the tea-cosy off the teapot and gave it a stir. 'You're determined to do this race, so ...' She began to pour. 'Okay.'

'Thanks, love.' Paul came over and gave her a hug. 'I'll make it up to you, I promise.'

'Yeah. I'm just glad you are getting your knee fixed.'

One down, one to go, thought Paul. After dinner, he called Phil.

'How was it?' Phil asked.

'Not good, mate.'

'I figured as much. Surgery?'

'Yes. I'm so sorry to let you down.'

'No worries,' said Phil. 'Thing is, number one, you need to get it fixed at some point, and number two, better to be in top shape for when we row next year.'

'Thanks, mate, thanks for sticking with me.'

Until that moment Paul hadn't even thought about the idea that Phil could have decided to stay in the 2018 race and row with someone else, or even solo. After all, he had much more experience on the water in a small boat than Paul had.

'Team Atlantic Dream Challenge, baby.' Phil laughed. 'Plus, it will give us time to raise more money.'

Chapter 22

15 November 2018

While Paul recuperated from surgery, Phil continued to train, fundraise, and give presentations to the local community, including several schools. This morning he was addressing Excelsior Academy. The students filtered into the auditorium and filled the tiered seats at the back of the room.

'Hello. Welcome. Come on up front,' said Phil. He knew a few of them already. The school focused on project-based learning and over the years he had offered work placements at his company. In typical teenage fashion the kids grunted and stayed where they were. Phil was not bothered. He was fairly sure the high-octane video of past ocean rowing races would spark their interest. At the end of the presentation, he asked: 'Any questions?'

Silence. It wasn't until Phil invited them to see the boat that they mustered any enthusiasm. Outside, they gathered around *Didi*.

'It's so small,' one young lad said.

'Twenty feet,' said Phil.

'How much is that?'

'About six metres.'

Others asked about how it was powered.

'You mean apart from our backs and shoulders?' Phil grinned. 'We have two batteries inside the cabin that will be charged by these solar panels.'

'Can I see?'

'Sure. Anyone else want to see inside?'

Now they were all interested in seeing the coffin-like cabin.

'Will two of you even fit in there?' asked a young girl.

'We'll have to.'

'How big will the waves be?'

'Ten, fifteen metres, maybe bigger.' Phil remembered the first video he'd watched with Meme, when that visual scared the crap out of them, but judging by the students' lack of reaction, they couldn't relate.

'See your sports hall over there? Imagine if that was a wall of water coming at you.'

'Serious?'

'Wow.'

Now he had them. The video might not have grasped their attention but now that they'd seen the boat in relation to their surroundings and what that might look like on the ocean, their interest exploded. When Phil finished answering the rapid-fire questions he asked: 'So, do you think you guys will enjoy this project? You'll learn about weather affecting the ocean, geography, nutrition and calorie consumption, and then you can track us.'

'Yeah, mate,' said one of the taller lads, 'sounds great.'

'You'll be our "dot watchers".'

'What's that?'

'You're familiar with GPS?'

'Of course.'

'Once the race starts, we'll have a GPS tracker on board which will relay our longitude and latitude co-ordinates to the software on the website and *Didi* will show up like a dot in the ocean. You'll be able to watch the dot and see where we are and how far we have to go.'

'Cool. Are you scared?'

'No,' said Phil. Well, he hadn't been until two minutes ago when he looked at the 15-metre building in front of him and thought: *that's one hell of a lot of water.* 'Paul and I make a good team. We'll take care of each other out there.' Who was he trying to convince?

'Okay, time's up,' said their teacher. 'You'll have plenty of time to ask more questions before they depart.' As the students wandered back inside, she turned to Phil.

'That was wonderful, thank you.'

'You're welcome, they're good kids.'

'Some of them have never asked a question in class before. You'll never know how much you have inspired them. Even the staff. We'll all be following your tracks on the internet.'

Chapter 23

12 December 2018

365 days to the start of the race

Paul's knee surgery, which had needed to be done 'as soon as possible', happened in October, ten weeks after the consultation, which was pretty speedy by NHS standards. Unlike his hospital stay after the brain bleed, Paul was encouraged to get up and walk, albeit on crutches, within two hours of the operation. As he clunked through the corridor, he prayed this would be his last time looking at these walls and inhaling these antiseptic smells.

He wasn't due back to work until February of the following year, but not one to sit idle, he made recovery his full-time job. A week after the operation he was walking around the house without a cane. A fortnight later, he was riding a mobility scooter to the gym to continue his rehab and exercising on the stationary bike. As always, Nic supported him, managed his medication in the early days, and drove him to follow-up appointments.

He hated to be a burden on her and wished he could get back to work sooner, especially since he was still planning to retire in May, but as he looked around the lounge, already decked with holly and tinsel, lights twinkling on the tree, he was glad he could guarantee that, at least for this year, he would spend the entire Christmas holidays with her.

He'd done his physio for the day and had settled himself in his favourite chair, propped his leg up on two cushions and had just fired up the laptop when the doorbell rang.

'I'll get it,' Nic called from the hall.

Paul hoped it was one of her friends, and they would go through to the kitchen to natter over a cuppa so he could have some peace and quiet. Instead, the lounge door opened and Nic came in.

'You've a visitor.'

'Hey,' said Paul, 'what are you doing here – shouldn't you be at work?'

'Boss gave me the morning off.'

'That Meme, she's a good egg. Come in, sit down.'

'I couldn't let you watch the start without me,' said Phil. 'We're a team, remember?'

'Yes, we are.'

'I'm off to the shops,' said Nic. 'Would you lads like tea before I go?'

'Ah, that's kind of you, Nic, but I've just had one, thanks.'

'Paul?'

'Still drinking this one, love, thanks.'

'Right, I'm off then.'

Phil settled in on the settee next to Paul. 'Let's have a look, then.'

There was a wide shot of the marina in La Gomera and then this bright, bubbly young lady called Charlotte appeared on the screen.

'Good morning, everyone, and welcome to the start of the 2018 Talisker Whisky Atlantic Challenge. We're so happy you can join this livestream. It's been a busy week for the crews with lots of last-minute preparations, but today is the day. As the rowers make their way down the pontoon, let me introduce you to Carsten Olsen, the race organiser.'

'Morning, everybody,' Carsten said directly into the camera.

'So, how was the mood in the tent this morning?'

'Excited, as you can imagine, Charlotte. These teams have been training for a year or more …'

'Try three years,' Paul shouted at the laptop.

'… and all their hard work has paid off, and they are about to experience a life-changing voyage.'

'We know you're from Denmark, Carsten, but you're not a rower yourself,' said Charlotte.

'No, I'm a long-distance runner, but many of our staff have rowed the Atlantic, Ian Couch, our safety officer, Fraser, Laura, Ros, all of them have a unique understanding of what the teams are going through.'

'So can you tell everyone how you became involved?'

'Sure. I was here in 2009 to support my brother who was rowing, and also in Antigua to greet him when he arrived. I could see all these incredible, inspirational people crossing an ocean but there was something missing. I felt there was so much that could be done, so many stories that could be told. And in 2012, I founded the company – Atlantic Campaigns – bought the race, moved here and learned Spanish.'

'And the rest, as they say, is history,' said Charlotte. 'Thanks so much, Carsten, I know you need to get down there, so we'll let you go.'

The camera panned off Charlotte's face to the pontoon where the boats were lined up and rowers were stepping aboard.

'I'm getting chills from here,' Phil said to Paul. 'Such a buzz. Can you imagine what it must feel like to be there right now?'

'Yeah,' said Paul. 'Should have been us.' In the last three years he had watched every clip, every interview and every piece of footage Atlantic Campaigns had published but this was the first time he'd been watching it live.

'Don't worry,' said Phil, 'this time next year it will be.'

Paul looked at his leg, still swollen. 'You're right, and I'll be the one with the bionic knee.'

'Ya see?' said Phil. 'It will have been worth the wait. Wow, would you look at those boats.'

'Yeah, bet none of those cost ten grand. See any wooden ones?'

'No. Oh, look, there's your friend Lars.'

'Go Lars,' said Paul.

Lars and his team-mate were climbing on to their very sleek-looking two-man boat. The camera panned down. In white letters against a dark hull was the name: Wolfpack Gym powered by Garmin.

'Now, that's what I call corporate sponsorship,' said Paul.

'Makes me think we should change the name of ours.'

'To what?'

'Dream It, Do It, powered by Paul and Phil.'

It was the best belly laugh Paul had had in months.

Chapter 24

5 April 2019

251 days to go

Wheel bearings. What the hell did Paul know about wheel bearings, or disintegrated trailer brakes for that matter? Nothing. Until six weeks ago. Since signing up for the Atlantic Challenge, he'd learned lots of new skills, like fundraising, event management, applying for city permits, and had taken on many roles, the most recent being team mechanic. With all the postponements, *Didi*'s trailer had been in and out of the river an extra year and the bearings had to be replaced. With money so tight, he had no choice but to learn how to do it himself.

Getting the wheel off had been the easy bit. Once he'd opened the hub, the brakes had fallen into a disintegrated jigsaw on the floor with the wheel bearings landing on top of them. After a day and a half running back and forth to the dealer and emitting some muffled curses while using some of the fire station's heavy equipment, he'd managed to put everything back in place. When he was removing the jack one of the lads from the brigade had sauntered over.

'You doing the other wheel next, Hops?'

'Are you having a laugh?'

'You should, you know.'

Paul wished he had listened. Sure enough, today, it had become almost impossible to push the trailer in and out of the garage. The other wheel needed doing. This time though, he was ready for the task, and photographed every part before dismantling anything. See, he was learning. He whipped the old bearings off and had the new ones on in half the time. It was 5.30pm. He checked the weather, then called Phil.

'We're still on, mate.'

'Great, I'm just packing the cooler. I'll meet you at the slip.'

Paul was looking forward to spending their first overnight on the boat. He pulled out of the station and checked the rear-view mirror. The trailer was riding fine. All good through the next few junctions. As he approached the bottom of Allendale hill he checked again. There seemed to be something stuck to the wheel arch. Once he got through the roundabout he pulled over.

Shit. The plastic wheel arch itself had melted because the outer wheel bearing was gone. Who knew it was supposed to be installed facing inwards? He'd been so concerned about installing the brakes, he'd taken it for granted he knew what he was doing with the bearings. Seems he'd just been lucky the first time. The whole wheel could have fallen off. The shops were closed. The trailer couldn't be moved. This wasn't a part of town where he wanted to leave the boat unattended overnight.

Now what? Nothing for it but to camp out and wait. Phil came to check which parts to get in the morning and Nic arrived with a flask of coffee and sandwiches. Paul sat in his car in the dark and listened to the radio. At around 11pm his rear-view mirror lit up. He waited for the vehicle to pass, but it didn't. Just what he needed. A ticket for parking at the side of the road. As he was about to reach for his driving licence, the mirror returned to black and his driver's wing mirror lit up. Ever so slowly a panel van drove alongside, then passed. Paul relaxed. But then, 50 metres ahead, it pulled over and stopped. It sat there.

He slunk down in his seat. He watched, waited. A couple of minutes later, both driver and passenger doors opened and

146

two figures started walking to the rear of the van. One of them opened the back doors and the other got something out. Paul couldn't see what it was. They started walking towards him. He wasn't sure what they were up to but they certainly weren't from the AA, ready to offer roadside assistance. What to do? He flicked on his headlights. The two blokes stopped mid-stride. One of them was carrying a crowbar. *Shit.* Could he get out of the car and grab something from the boat in time? Should he call it in first? He reached for his phone. Before he could dial 999 the two of them turned, ran back to the van and drove off.

With the excitement over, Paul got out, locked the car and got on the boat. He climbed into the sleeping bag in the cabin and settled in. It was cosy and not as cramped as it would be if Phil was in there with him. It seemed fitting that he would spend his first night on board alone, but so much for lapping waves to lull him to sleep. He yawned, expelling the last of the adrenaline. He could hear voices outside as people walked home from the pub. Thankfully none of them seemed bothered by a boat at the side of the road two miles from the water. Paul nodded off.

He dreamed he was rowing on the river, coming to the mouth of the harbour and then out into the North Sea. The waves picked up; he could feel the boat rocking. Side to side. He woke up. The boat was still rocking. Had the guys from the van come back? He opened the hatch a hair then thrust it wide open. Paul wasn't sure who got the bigger fright. The young lad standing on the deck yelled at him: 'What are you doing here?'

What was *Paul* doing there? It was his boat! What was this idiot doing here? But quick as a flash he said: 'I'm waiting for the tide to come in.'

'Really? I didn't know the tide came in this far.'

'No, you idiot, the trailer is broken.'

'Oh.'

'Would you mind getting off my boat?'

147

'Oh, sorry, mate. Yeah, sorry.' With 20 more apologies the young drunk managed to slither over the side and stumble up the street.

After a fun-filled day of repairs, Paul and Phil launched *Didi* around 6pm and rowed down the wide but twisty river. With Paul on the oars and Phil steering, they made good time and soon left the city lights behind. It had been five months since surgery and his new knee was holding up just fine, almost back to the full range of motion. It was the other one that was doing most of the creaking. Passing Wallsend, he thought of Nic, only a mile inland. She was probably curled up in front of the TV with a glass of wine and here he was heading out to sea in a little white boat.

Before they rounded the next bend, Paul announced their presence on the VHF. Colliding with one of the large vessels or car carriers operating out of the Port of Tyne would be less than ideal. The harbour master responded with an all-clear. The next section was slow going. They had come past these houses on the riverbanks every time they'd gone out training but the contrast of the lit footpaths against the black water affected their night vision.

'Almost there, skipper,' said Phil. 'I can see the lighthouses at the end of the piers.'

The minute they cleared the mouth of the river Paul could feel the change. The North Sea was wide awake.

'Right, Phil, let's set a course.' It was one of the skills they had to log as part of their pre-race competency.

'Where shall we go?'

'Let's head north.'

Music drifted over the water from the pubs and restaurants on the shore, but the sing-song Paul was most happy to hear was the little beeps from the GPS as they moved along the plotted course. The autohelm played its part, keeping the rudder aligned with their heading. Phil sat into the second rowing position and the two of them pulled together, chatting as they went.

'So, have you told Tom about the race yet?'

'No. His short-term memory is not the best. It's better to wait.'

'How do you think he's going to take it?'

'I think he'll be okay. I'll just mention it first, give him time to get used to it. When it gets closer, I'll tell him more.'

'Makes sense. Poor James has heard me banging on about it for the past four years.'

'Long time for a teenager.'

'Yeah, he's cool, though. Bit sad that I won't be there for Christmas, but I think taking him out on the river last week really brought it to life for him.'

The conversation then wandered from family to football to triathlons and back to the race. The sea was lively enough to test their skills but kind enough not to stress them. It was almost four in the morning when Paul checked his watch.

'How about we get some rest?'

'Suits me,' said Phil.

They listened to the anchor chain going over the side, pleased that they'd remembered to tie one end to the boat before they hurled it over.

'How deep do you think it is here?'

The chain stopped; the anchor had hit bottom.

'I suppose about that deep,' Paul laughed.

'Right. So how do you want to sleep?'

They'd tried various ways of squeezing into the cabin together before, but had yet to try sleeping overnight.

'How about we top and tail? If you go in head first, I'll slide in after. That should give us each a bit more room.'

Once they were tucked up inside, they closed the cabin hatch.

'Well, this is snug,' said Phil.

'Yes, mate, although I didn't think it would be this noisy.'

Every wave smacked the side of the boat on its way to shore, but after a long day on the roadside and eight hours of rowing in the dark they both fell asleep.

Sometime after dawn Paul woke up. Where was he? It didn't feel like his bed. He opened his eyes and saw Phil's feet. Oh, right, they were at sea. Then he heard voices. Odd. Even the local drunks couldn't have swum out this far.

'Phil, can you hear anything?' But Phil was sound asleep. Paul heard a bark. That was definitely a dog. Paul opened the hatch. Bloody hell. 'Phil, Phil, wake up.'

'Whaa …?'

'Quick, get up,' Paul shouted as he climbed out on deck.

Didi was only three boat lengths away from riding the surf ashore. The anchor must have dragged when the tide changed. Another rookie mistake. Paul hauled it in as fast as he could. He was not ready for the headline: Atlantic Rowers Run Aground on Local Beach. As soon as the anchor was on deck, he joined Phil on the oars and they rowed out to sea as fast as Popeye escaping the U-boat.

'Well, that was a good pre-breakfast workout,' said Phil, once they were far enough out.

'Too right, I'm starving.'

'Shall we give the anchor another try?'

This time they made sure it was dug in before they set about making food. Phil busied himself with his flask of tea. Paul pulled out his self-heating 'all-day breakfast'. The picture on the box looked appetising, although it bore no resemblance to the contents of the packet. After bobbing around for 15 minutes, waiting for it to warm up, Paul felt a little queasy but still hungry enough to eat the cardboard.

'How's breakfast, skipper?'

'Not as bad as it looks.'

Paul had eaten half but, oh my, that half was about to …

saliva pooled in his mouth. Quick. He grabbed the handrail, stood up and threw up over the side.

'Sorry, mate.'

'No bother. Want some water?'

'Thanks.'

He felt disgusted. How was he going to cope in proper big seas if he was seasick just offshore? Phil was supposed to be the one with the weak stomach. He rinsed his mouth. The last thing he wanted to do now was eat but he was hungry. He could feel Phil watching him as he forced down the second half. Phil continued to sip his tea, one eyebrow raised. The wind picked up.

'Should we get going, skip?'

Both of them knew the struggle of having to row against the wind and tide.

'Good idea. Wait.' Paul grabbed the railings again. The packet had said 'all-day breakfast' but the contents hadn't lasted five minutes in his stomach.

Once they started rowing and the boat made forward motion his tummy settled. But the wind had strengthened significantly, blowing them towards the rocks outside the long harbour wall. They fought to stay off.

Plop.

'What was that?' said Paul.

'One of those fishermen.'

Paul looked up at the top of the pier. Another line whizzed through the air and hit the water right by their bow.

'Those bastards are using us for target practice.'

Nothing they could do but row harder to get away from the rocks and the assault team. They'd been blown so far off course that the GPS squawked like a budgie on speed. No time to stop and reset it, or take a drink, or even a wee, which was tough for men of their age. They kept rowing. It took three more hours before the beeps became occasional.

'Look Paul, a seal.'

The black head disappeared and then reappeared closer to *Didi*.

151

'Wow,' said Paul, 'it's looking right at us.'

'Probably wondering who the two nutters are out on a day like this.'

Whatever the seal thought about them, it seemed to enjoy their company because it swam around and under *Didi* like she was some kind of play date.

During the afternoon the wind relaxed but the temperature started to drop. So did their energy.

'Let's clear the piers before dark.'

'Happy to, skipper.'

When they reached the calm water inside the mouth of the river, Paul took a moment to roll his shoulders. Another milestone. No matter what problem they'd faced out there, not a cross word had been uttered between them. They'd survived their first full 24 hours at sea. A fantastic achievement. Nothing and no one was going to stop them now.

Chapter 25

28 May 2019

198 days to go

At ten to six in the evening Paul arrived at work for his final shift. In 15 hours, his firefighting career would be over. Ten months ago, the decision to take early retirement had seemed like a good idea. The lump sum would help pay off all his debts, buy a nice car for Nic, and free him up to concentrate on *Didi* and the row. But now that it was real, he wondered if he'd made a mistake.

Barring a career as a professional footballer, nothing could have come closer to a dream job than being a firefighter. He remembered the struggle it had taken to pass the entry exams, how he'd sat in that sports hall along with dozens of hopefuls, answering maths quizzes and solving problems. He'd made it all the way to the third and final test – to write an English essay about himself. Given his dyslexia, that should have been the end of the line. As others had bent their heads and scribbled away, he'd looked around the room, desperate for inspiration. Then he'd smiled; the solution had been written on the walls. Posters. Posters about sports. Nothing in the rules said he couldn't copy down the spellings.

My name is Paul and I love soccer, hiking, kayaking and keeping fit …

Had that really been 30 years ago? He remembered his first day on the job, how the old hands had poked fun at the new boy. But he'd survived 15 weeks of training, and the wrath of the instructor who'd made him his pet project and constantly picked on him for the slightest thing. Paul had loved it. Not the usual response. At his exit interview, the instructor had said: 'Of the 12 recruits on this course, 11 did what they were told, but you have done as you please. When we put you under pressure you seemed to keep laughing. When you leave here you can be one of two things — a big fat lazy useless piece of shit, or you can be a good firefighter. It's up to you.'

Paul loved the job so much he proved himself to be the latter. Nothing made him or Nic prouder than to say he was a firefighter. It didn't matter whether it was a Friday night or a holiday, he loved going to work. Through the years, he earned every promotion and was honoured to finish his career as a watch manager.

He locked the car and headed in. It was a slow Tuesday night, only a couple of turn-outs — a small kitchen fire, and a false alarm. When he returned from the last one, he spotted a few more cars parked in the courtyard. The canteen was filled with old faces and off-duty lads who'd come to say goodbye and wish him well. Grant, his old boss from Colby Court station who had coached him for his interview for watch manager had also come. He and Carl sat at the table, and even Zoe had slipped in.

'Couldn't let the occasion go unmarked,' Zoe said, presenting him with a cake.

Happy Retirement Paul.

They all sat around and reminisced about the old days and how much tougher it was back then. The equipment was heavier and their suits less protective, making the fires seem hotter. In some of the stories, they regaled Paul as the hero, and in others he was the butt of the joke. When the cake was devoured and the party broke up, they all slapped Paul on the back and wished him the best. He was a barrel of mixed emotions. These people were family. He was going to miss this camaraderie, but it was all for a good cause — the row.

Carl lingered a while longer.

'So, what do you think about the middle route?' said Paul. Carl and Zoe's husband, Jeff, had agreed to support them from home with navigational assistance once they were under way, a safeguard in case they made poor decisions as a result of sleep deprivation.

'I think it's probably a wise choice,' said Carl. 'How are you feeling?'

'Can't believe it's my last night.'

'Yeah. I can't believe you're going to row the Atlantic, but I do.'

'Thanks, Carl.'

'I best be off, leave you to wrap things up.'

'Give my love to Katrina and Poppy.'

The rest of the night was quiet and Paul spent his time completing all his paperwork to ensure a smooth transition for the next watch manager. Once it was finished, he had nothing to do but wait out the clock. The last hour dragged but then, right at 8.30am: *Whoop, whoop, whoop …*

It was his birthday. He was going to get one final call-out after all. He jumped up, slid down the pole and waited for the message to appear. What would this last one be? Just when he thought the printer was stuck, he felt it. His heart almost stopped as the bucket of iced water was dumped on his head from above. He laughed. Standard farewell procedure; how had he forgotten?

At 9am, wearing his sodden clothes with pride, he drove off the courtyard aged 55, no longer a firefighter. He would never again fly around Newcastle in a fire engine, lights flashing, sirens wailing, his heart racing. He'd been kidding himself that it wouldn't matter. He wasn't leaving a job; he was leaving a way of life. Nic had said she was happy if he was happy, but she worried how he would cope without the job that made him who he was. He'd given it all up because he'd wanted to row an ocean. But what would happen after that? How was he ever going to get that buzz again in normal life?

Chapter 26

13 July 2019

152 days to go

After a 90-mile drive from Newcastle to the Army Foundation College in Harrogate, with the boat in tow, Paul and Phil were about to meet the god of rowing, Ian Couch. They understood it to be an advisory meeting. What they didn't realise was that this meeting was an advisory *inspection* and, as head safety officer, Ian had the power to sign off on whether they and *Didi* could enter the race – or not.

When they arrived, Ian was in a lively discussion with a team of four really fit ex-military men they would come to know as the Mavericks.

'Hi, guys,' Paul greeted the group.

'Hi, I'm Ian. Nice to meet you.'

'Likewise.'

'Go ahead and line up your gear like this,' said Ian, 'and I'll be with you when I'm done here.'

Paul stared at all of the Mavericks' kit which was spread out on a tarp, military style. They already had so much stuff, probably everything on the list. 'Sure, mate, Phil and I will get started.'

Paul climbed on to *Didi* and began handing gear down to Phil.

'How long was Ian in the army?' Phil asked.

'Eighteen years, I think.'

'Looks too young to have retired.'

'I saw one of his interviews, he said he turned in his notice the day after he got back from rowing the Atlantic,' said Paul, passing their life jackets and tethers to Phil.

'Really?'

'Yeah, it says on the website that he set five Guinness World Records.'

'Good for him. Well, I bet he'll have some good advice for us,' said Phil.

'Here, watch out, it's heavy.'

'You're telling me.' Phil lowered the life raft on to the ground. 'Let's hope we never have to use it.'

'Wow, look at that,' said Paul, 'where's my sunglasses?'

A brand-new Audi Q7 towing an equally brand-new boat pulled into the hangar. Paul recognised the Rannoch-built R25 designed for a pairs team like themselves. He'd seen the technical specifications online as well as the starting price tag of at least £65,000. The two lads that climbed out of the car looked younger than Paul's ancient BMW Estate, which he'd acquired to tow the boat. He was always careful not to lean on the bonnet lest he put his hand through it, there was so much rust. Next, the two lads started unloading boxes — more brand-new gear they hadn't even unwrapped yet. Compared to these other teams, Paul felt like he had come to a black-tie ball in ratty jeans and a frayed tee-shirt. How nice it would be to have a shiny new boat and expensive equipment, but considering what he had to work with, he was proud of what they had and was confident they would find a way to make do.

After Ian finished up with the Mavericks, he walked over, clipboard in hand.

'Right, lads, let's have a look.'

Ian was thorough, and found more than a few faults with the boat. He started with the towing eye.

'This is loose,' he said, and made a note on his sheet.

Paul couldn't see how it was loose considering the boat had moved on the trailer when Ian tugged on it.

When he checked the para-anchor, the large parachute which could be used underwater to hold the boat in position in unfavourable conditions at sea, he asked about the length of the buoyant retrieval line.

'Not sure,' said Phil.

'You'll need to measure it. Has to be at least 25 metres longer than the para-anchor line.'

Then he moved to the electrics and shook his head. He pulled on a wire that led nowhere. 'What does this one go to?'

'Honestly, I'm not sure,' said Paul.

'Uh-huh. This whole system will need urgent attention, and will probably need to be completely rewired.' Another note went on the sheet.

'Okay.'

'These grab lines are not adequately fixed to the hull, see here. But not a show-stopper. You're missing the reflective tape and before any more people sign your boat make sure you leave enough room for the race logos which need to be adhered to the sides.'

Paul went to the car to get pen and paper. When he got back, Ian was telling Phil that the batteries needed to be replaced. Paul started to make a list.

'Don't worry,' said Ian, 'you'll get a report in a day or two of what needs to be done.'

After a couple of hours of answering questions about their training schedule and watching Ian dissect every last item of their kit, Paul's head was spinning.

'Well, lads, that's it for today. You do have some issues to take care of, but we'll send you the list. Attention to detail is what's going to keep you safe out there.'

'Great, thanks.'

On the car ride home, Phil asked: 'Well, what did you think?'

'I think it went okay, we're one step closer. You?'

'Yeah, he seems to know what he's talking about.'

'We should probably look for a marine electrician first. In the meantime, we can get started on some of the other stuff,' said Paul. 'How's next weekend?'

Four days later, Paul received an email from the event manager, Nikki Holt, with Ian's report attached. Lucky for Ian, Paul didn't know where he lived. Paul rang Phil.

'You are not going to believe this.'

'What's up?'

'Fucking Ian.'

'What does it say?'

'It's four fucking pages. Listen to this. "The boat is old and not well maintained. I have significant concerns at this stage" … blah, blah, blah … "there are a number of 'show-stoppers' but in reality, every point not resolved is a show-stopper and there is no flexibility on those. Without sign-off, the boat should not be shipped to La Gomera."'

'Okay, Paul, take a breath.'

'Bastard didn't have the balls to say it to my face. How many times did he say "this is not a show-stopper"?'

'I hear you.'

'If you have a problem with me, you tell it to my face. Don't tell me one thing and then send me a report saying different four days later.'

'Yeah, you're right, but let's see what we can do.'

'Listen to this: "I would also require the crew to both demonstrate a greater knowledge of the items they have and the requirements of the rules."'

'Well,' said Phil, 'it is his job to make sure we are safe.'

'I've a good mind to—'

'I know, Paul, but remember, we said no matter what, we were going to focus on the solution, not the problem.'

'Yes, but—'

'Why don't you email it to me and we can take a look together.'

It took Paul almost a week to calm down. His anger was probably a shock to Phil, but he was so pissed off. After everything he had gone through, including quitting his career for this, now they only had six weeks to fix every fault on the boat or they were out of the race before it started. Even though he was retired, Paul wasn't sure he had enough time.

Paul's good friend, station manager Dave Linsley, came to the rescue and allowed them to bring *Didi* back to Byker Fire Station and work on her in one of the bays.

The next six weeks were intense. Paul was so fired up to get the boat ready that he rarely saw Nic or James, and when he did he was exhausted. Every spare moment was spent on the boat. The four-page list seemed like Mount Everest. Some days they got one or two things finished, some days none. A major score was finding a marine electrician who advised them to install separate switches so that the two batteries could work independently of each other. But then there was the expense; they had so much more kit they had to source. They begged, they borrowed, but they drew the line at stealing.

A few days before the deadline, Paul emailed Ian to ask how he wanted to conduct what they now knew was an inspection. In the email Paul said he was looking forward to showing how far they'd come with his list of requirements. It almost killed him to be polite, but their hopes of the challenge were on the line. The response was short and to the point: 'I use WhatsApp or FaceTime.'

Paul and Phil felt confident they had done as much as they could in the time but were still anxious to know if it was enough to pass. Paul had a nagging suspicion that he and Phil and *Didi* didn't fit the profile the race officials were looking for. They weren't supported by a major sponsor; they didn't have one of the new lightweight modern boats decked out in decals. They were just two middle-aged men in an old wooden boat scrawled with signatures, who had barely scraped enough money together to even enter the race.

The inspection was scheduled for midday, or High Noon as Phil had dubbed it. What if they failed? Would they lose their £20,000 entrance fee? They couldn't postpone again. Meme had been supporting this project for over a year now, Nic almost four. They simply had to pass.

By 11.55am they had all the kit laid out in the correct position as per the inspection plan and had a printout of the infamous report at the ready. Nothing left but to dial the number and get the video conference under way.

Ian answered and got straight to business. The first item was the towing eye on the bow. Paul climbed on to the boat with the phone to show Ian how they'd secured the backing plate and that the eye was solid enough to take the pressure of a tow-rope should the need arise.

'Good,' said Ian. 'Okay, next.'

Paul moved down the boat to the rowing gate which held the oar in place.

'Here's how we fixed the gate.'

'No, Paul, I want to see the stern bridle now, it's next on the list.'

So, this is how this is going to go, thought Paul. Rather than inspect everything on the boat first and then the kit, he would be climbing in and out of the boat all day just so Ian could follow his precious list in the order it was typed. Paul shrugged, passed the phone to Phil and climbed down. Phil gave him a wink and walked to the stern of the boat.

One by one Ian went through the items on his list without comment. Outside of the camera view Paul and Phil made faces at each other, then the phone. They didn't have a clue if they were meeting standards or not.

'The kit now, gentlemen, please.'

Almost all their kit was second hand. They'd agreed that Phil would present and answer questions on some of it, Paul the rest. It seemed to be going well. Phil was able to answer how the items worked, how to use them and what to do if they failed. Paul gave Phil a thumbs-up, then answered his own set of questions.

'Smaller items, next,' said Ian. 'Glucose tablets, there should be four packs.'

'Yes, we have them.' Paul smiled because he had only bought them that morning. At 75p each they were probably the cheapest thing on the boat.

'I need to see them.'

'They're here somewhere, just can't lay my hands on them right this moment.'

'If you haven't got them, then it's a failure. I told you, you need to have everything on the list or you won't be shipping your boat to the starting line.'

Was he really going to fail them over £3 worth of glucose sweets? Where the hell had he put them?

'Wait, wait.' Paul handed the phone to Phil and mouthed at him to keep Ian talking. He ran out to the car. Thank God. There in the side pocket of the driver's door was the bloody bag of sweets. He ran back and put them down on the ground.

'Thank you, let's move on.'

Paul looked at Phil. This was the friendliest tone they had heard out of Ian – maybe they had turned a corner. Ian continued down his list and one by one they presented everything asked of them. When they got to the end of it, they waited for Ian to speak. Paul felt like he and Phil were on one of those talent shows waiting for the judges to announce their decision, a decision that would change their lives. He and Phil stood side by side staring into the phone. All they could see was Ian's profile. He was scanning his list again and again. Come on, say something. It was killing Paul not to blurt out, 'Have we passed?'

Finally, for the first time since the inspection began, Ian looked directly into the camera.

'Congratulations, gentlemen, you've passed. You may now ship your boat.'

'Thank you.'

Paul and Phil held the phone tightly to stop themselves from dancing.

'Well, gentlemen, I can't tell you how surprised I am. I never thought that you'd be able to complete all the work in the timescale you had, so well done.'

'Thank you.'

'Yours was the worst boat I had seen in five years so, again, well done.'

The anger that had driven Paul over the last six weeks was drowned by joy and excitement. Ian carried on chatting, giving them some helpful tips, like making sure to have spare rowing seats and cushions they could swap out to protect their backsides from sores, a back-up plan in case they lost their rudder, and to keep the hatches closed at all times while they were on the ocean. All very useful, but Paul was happy when Ian eventually said: 'Well done, lads, see you in La Gomera in December.' Then he hung up.

Paul and Phil waited to make sure the phone went black.

'Woohoo!'

'We did it!'

They hugged and hopped up and down in the yard like two kids on Christmas morning.

'Quick,' said Phil, grabbing his phone again, 'let's get the post up.'

'Yes, mate, tell everyone we're going.'

Paul was already dialling Nic.

'We did it, love, we passed!'

Chapter 27

31 October 2019

42 days to go

At 10am, Paul pulled up at the fire station where they'd been keeping the boat when they weren't training on the river or using it for fundraising events. The dragon boat racing in August had been a huge success, raising money for the project and the charities, and creating a really fun day for the community. *Didi* was now covered in signatures, almost 3,000 in all.

It was Halloween. His car was loaded with a lot more than sweets, and trick or no treat he wasn't about to give any of them away. Phil rang.

'Sorry, I'm just finishing up at the office. Meme has bagged and tagged all the food. Has she arrived?'

'No, is she not with you?'

'She's enjoying a bit of space. I've been driving her crazy, I'm so excited. I'm sure she'll be along soon.'

'Okay, I'll make a start.'

Paul wasn't normally one to work from a list when packing, but *Didi* was bigger than any suitcase and this was no two-week holiday. She had to carry everything they would need for at least 70 days, maybe 90. There'd be no popping to the shops if they ran out of milk. There's another thing he would miss besides football – a proper cup of tea. Never mind, time to get on. He hoped to be finished by mid-afternoon so he could take a nap before he and Nic had to set off on their seven-and-a-half-hour road trip. The deadline to get the boat to Rannoch Adventure in Burnham-on-Crouch, north-east of London, so she could be shipped to La Gomera, wasn't till Monday, but he was taking no chances. They planned to drive through the night to avoid most of the traffic.

Just as he'd been shown at the inspection, Paul systematically laid everything on the floor beside the boat. Ian's military-style organisation made sense after all. He and Phil had discussed where everything would go, so he started with the heavier items. First up was the life raft. She was a necessary brute but he hoped she'd never have to come out of the forward cabin again. Next in, all the tools and spares, duct tape and torches. He was in the middle of stowing the water bottles they would have to carry for ballast when the phone rang again. A different Phil. Phil Kite, a young man who'd crossed in 42 days, setting a world record for the fastest mixed team in 2018.

'Hi Paul, heard you're ready to ship.'

'Almost. Can't imagine where we're going to put everything.'

'Yeah, but you'll find space. So, how are you feeling?'

'Anxious.'

'What's your biggest fear?'

'The thought of failing.'

'Well, you can put that one to bed, Paul.'

'How d'you mean?'

'Do you have any idea how many people don't make it to the starting line? You've already won.'

It was nice of him to say so, but for Paul it was still all or nothing. He had to cross that finish line.

'I'll be one of your "dot watchers". Good luck.'

'Thanks, mate.'

As Paul stowed the Jetboil, their portable stove, and spare canisters, he thought about how many people would be following their tracks on the internet. For the last three years he'd been one of those watchers; finally he was going to be one of those dots.

Phil arrived and he was indeed bouncing off the walls. 'How's it going? What can I help with?'

'Slow. But should go quicker now with two of us.'

When Meme arrived, she looked upset.

'Everything okay?' said Phil.

'Morgan's having more difficulty walking, I took him to the vet.'

'Oh, what did she say?'

'Says he's got arthritis in his hind legs.'

'God love him, I know the feeling,' said Paul.

'Oh, poor baby,' said Phil. 'Come on, I'll give you a hand with the bags so you can take him home.'

'Thanks. Which ones do you want first, Paul?'

'Let's get the emergency wet rations in first,' he said. 'Might as well stow them at the bottom.'

'Good idea.' Phil handed up over 100 meals that did not require rehydration. Then came the dry packets, more than 500 – enough food for a minimum of two and a half months. To generate sufficient energy to meet the physical demands of the challenge, and to prevent their bodies consuming their own muscles, they needed 60 kcal per kilo of bodyweight per day. That meant eating about 6,000 calories each, the equivalent of 12 Big Macs. With the carbing up Paul had already done, he felt more oven-ready than ocean-ready.

'How are we doing?'

'It's tight, but they're in,' said Paul, securing the last deck hatch.

'I think we are still short of some calories.'

'Pass me that yellow bag, that should bring up the count.'

Phil handed up a collection of breakfast and protein bars.

'Where did these come from?'

'Zoe.'

'What a sweetheart.'

As the hours passed, every corner of space on the boat was stowed and stuffed with items from the never-ending list: matches, lighters, utensils, buckets, roving bilge pump, para-anchor, mooring lines, waterproofs, flags, life jackets, baby wipes, binoculars, as well as spare reading glasses for the pair of them. In addition to the official kit list, they also tucked away their personal gear so they could fly to Tenerife with carry-on only. Among the items for entertainment and crew morale were two Santa hats for Christmas day. The packing seemed endless. One thing Paul had learned about boats – everything cost more than land items and projects took twice as long. His intended afternoon nap was now a joke.

They were still packing when Nic arrived at 10pm. Paul was anxious to get going because they also had to detour to Surrey to pick up the extra set of oars. A new pair cost between £800 and £1,000 but he had found a set he could rent for a fraction of the cost. He wanted to be sure they would bypass London before the early morning rush hour.

Finally, at around 11pm he announced: 'If it's not all there now, we'll just have to sort it later.'

It took the three of them to push *Didi* out of the garage and hook her trailer up.

'Working,' shouted Phil as Paul tested the right indicator, then the left.

'Brakes?' said Paul.

'Yep, all good, skipper. How about your windscreen fluid?'

'Topped up everything this morning.'

Nic slipped into the passenger seat.

Phil tapped the bow of the boat and then stood back. 'See you in La Gomera, *Didi*.'

'See ya.' Paul pulled out and drove towards the motorway.

'So,' Nic asked, 'are you excited?'

He should have been, but he was surprised at how flat he felt. *Didi* was leaving Newcastle on the start of her long voyage and yet he hadn't arranged a send-off. He'd been so focused on the big picture that he had forgotten to celebrate the little milestones along the way.

The roads were quiet but it started to rain. They had only gone about 40 miles when his eyelids felt heavy. He heard a snap and a hiss.

'Drink this,' said Nic, as she thrust an energy drink at him.

He downed it in one go. The caffeine hit his bloodstream almost immediately.

'Thanks,' he said, looking over at Nic. He hadn't noticed the bags around her feet before. They must have contained enough food and drink for a week's self-catering holiday. She flicked through the radio channels and settled on something with an upbeat tempo.

As they passed the exit for Nottingham, Paul felt strange not stopping off to see his mum, but she would hardly welcome a drop-in at 2am. He'd have to make a special trip down to see her before he left. Seventy miles down the road they stopped for fuel. Fully stowed, *Didi* weighed 1,000kg. The car was sucking diesel as fast as Paul was knocking back the sweets and sugary sodas. If he kept eating like this, he'd have to bring even more calories for the trip.

They cleared the traffic hotspots on the outskirts of London as dawn was breaking.

'Fancy a coffee, love?'

'Yeah,' said Nic. 'And the loo.'

As they came out of the garage, Paul cursed.

'Would you look at that muppet. He had all the space in the world but he had to park on top of us.'

Instead of driving out in a straight loop Paul would have to make a three-point turn. Although he'd reversed the trailer down many slips in the past three years, it still felt like a black art. His brain was tired but also addled with caffeine.

'Okay, love, you're going to have to guide me out.'

Nic went to the back of the trailer and started directing.

Paul rolled down the window and shouted: 'Where are you?'

'I'm here.'

'Can you see my wing mirror?'

'No.'

'Well, then I can't see you, Nic.' He got out and showed her where to stand.

After what seemed like a 27-point turn they were back on the motorway. Paul glanced over at Nic, who was tidying the bags at her feet. He felt bad for raising his voice. She'd waited around for him all day, kept him company and fed and watered throughout the night.

'I'm sorry for getting frustrated, love.'

'I know, it's okay.'

Once they collected the oars, they headed for Rannoch. Uncoupling *Didi* from the car and handing her over to the shipping company felt like giving up a child. He wanted to stroke her hull and wish her a safe trip on the cargo boat. He gave himself a nip. People would think he'd lost his marbles.

Nic had booked a boutique bed-and-breakfast nearby and had arranged a 10am check-in instead of the usual 2pm. Paul was tickled with the idea that they would get two sleeps for the price of one. Within minutes, he was snoring. He came to about 4pm when he heard Nic coming in carrying two cuppas.

While they drank their tea, Nic looked through the visitors' guide for a nice restaurant in the area.

'Any preference?' she asked.

'You choose, something close though. Do you want a refill?'

'Please.'

Down the hall, the communal kitchen looked like a diner from the 50s. Paul said hello to a young couple sitting in the corner.

'Well, mate,' the man said, 'looks like a huge journey for you.'

'Wasn't too bad,' said Paul. 'We did it in about eight hours.'

'No, rowing across the Atlantic.'

'Oh, that.' Paul was amazed. Even though Nic had become fed up with how the challenge had taken over his life she'd obviously told these strangers all about the race. At some level she must have been proud of him. It was a nice thought.

Paul was glad she'd chosen a family-run bistro close to the B & B. The checked tablecloths and tealights inside the short red globes gave it a Mediterranean feel. It reminded him of those restaurants they would eat at on holidays. It had been so long since the two of them had been out for a meal together.

'How are you feeling about it all now?' she asked.

'Glad that part's over. Just a month left to get everything else done.'

'There's something I would like you to do for me before you go.'

'What, love?'

Nic fiddled with her serviette. 'Remember when you were in the hospital?'

'Which one?' Paul laughed.

'I'm serious.'

'Sorry.'

'When you had the brain haemorrhage. I thought you were going to die.'

'But I didn't.'

'I know, but I was so scared. And I kept thinking what it would be like without you.'

Paul reached over and laid his hand on hers; it was rare for Nic to talk like this.

'I want you to write me a letter.'

'A letter? What would I say in a letter?'

'About us, about our life together, how we met, what I mean to you, what James means. I want to have something to hold on to if you don't come back.'

'I'm coming back.'

'You don't know that for sure.'

The waiter arrived with their food.

On the drive home the next morning, Nic chatted all the way. It made Paul remember why he fell in love with her all those years ago and just how much he would miss her. Now that the boat was gone, he promised himself he would spend more time with her.

Chapter 28

6 November 2019

36 days to go

Paul sat at the kitchen table with Nic. They'd cleared the dinner dishes and in front of him were forms he had to fill out for TWAC, such as Acknowledgement of Risk, and medical and dental clearances. For his two emergency contacts, he listed Nic and Carl Latimer. The one that gave him pause for thought was the Bereavement Form. He had to make a choice.

> I would / would not like to be informed of any death, serious injury or illness of any of my immediate family members while I am competing in the Talisker Whisky Atlantic Challenge.

In general, he wanted to keep contact from home to a minimum so he could stay focused. But then, if anything happened to Nic, he would need to take care of James.

'What if I say "would not" on the form, but let them know verbally if anything happens to you, I need to be told?

'Okay, but what about your mother?' said Nic.

'I'm hoping she'll be fine.'

'I hope so too, but what if …'

Paul didn't want to think about it, but Nic was probably right. His mother was in her eighties, and still living by herself since his dad had died.

'I'll talk to her at the weekend. Are you sure you don't want to come with me?'

'No, love, it would be nice for her to have you all to herself before you go.'

'You'll miss out on the crisps.'

Nic laughed. It didn't matter what time of day they would go to see her, his mother always had a ham sandwich, a cup of tea, and a packet of crisps at the ready.

On Saturday, Paul turned on to the familiar street of his childhood years. The telegraph pole where he used to play cricket in the summer, and football in the winter, was still there. In those days it was rare for a car to interrupt their game, now there were two in every driveway.

He pulled up to the house. The semi-detached was the same. Little had changed, until the door opened. His mother was no longer the young-looking woman who would call him in for his tea.

'Hello, Paul, how was the drive?'

'Hello, Mother,' he said, giving her a kiss on the cheek.

'Come in, I have the kettle on.'

'Lovely.'

In the lounge, more childhood memories — the owl he'd bought for his gran the first year he earned money because she was a wise old bird too, the horse and jockey statue he'd given his dad because they loved to watch the racing together, and other ornaments that were older than Paul. When he looked closely, he could see where they'd been broken and glued back together.

His mother came in with the tea, then went back for the sandwich, and then, sure enough, the crisps. She sat in the same part of the settee she'd sat in for years.

He took a sip. 'Lovely cuppa, thanks.' He made small talk, but wanted to get it over with. 'Mum, you know when I set off rowing the Atlantic, I'll not be able to come home until it's over.'

'Yes. And I will be able to follow it on Facebook.'

Paul smiled. His mother had become quite the silver surfer. 'I have to tell the organisers what news I want to hear from home … so unless something happens to Nic, then I won't be told.'

'Oh,' she said. 'I suppose if there's nothing you can do about it, you don't need to know.'

Good start, but was she picking up on where he was going with this? He was about to say he wouldn't be able to come back for her funeral when she put her cup down.

'Paul, if I die while you are gone, you can come and see me when you get back.'

'Mum?'

'I'll be above in the cemetery with your dad.'

'I hope not.'

'Don't worry, Paul, you've done enough for us while we've been alive. You've been a good son.'

'Thanks.'

'It took you a little longer than your brothers, but you turned out well.'

Paul munched on the crisps.

For the rest of the morning, he helped out around the house, bringing down the Christmas decorations from the loft, putting the frost cover on the outside tap. Then he drove her to the restaurant to meet with the rest of the family.

Everyone showed up for this farewell lunch. Paul's sons were there: Sean and his baby Noah, Jamie and his young children Katie, Lewis and Archie, and Jamie's partner Natalie and her two children Lewis and Demmi. He was glad that Diane and her husband had come too. The chat was lively. Paul enjoyed dipping in and out of different conversations while his grandchildren made boats out of their serviettes and asked him as many questions about the ocean as the schoolkids did. He tried to remember the last time he had been out with everyone for a family meal. He vowed to visit more often, now that he was retired.

In the car park afterwards, he hugged his two sons goodbye.

'Good luck, Dad, you'll do great,' said Sean.

'We'll be following your tracks,' said Jamie.

'Thanks, lads. I'll come down and see you when I get back.'

His ex-wife came over: 'Mind yourself out there.'

'Thank you, Diane. You take care too.'

Everyone piled in their cars and started driving off.

'Right, Mum, let's get you home. I'm going to take a run up to see Dad and then come back and say cheerio.'

Paul stood at his father's grave in Carlton Cemetery, on the hill above the town where he grew up.

'Look, Dad, there's the streets where I used to do the paper round, and see the bus stop where you and I used to catch the 39 bus to the Raleigh factory.' He chatted away like his father was standing next to him. Even though the man was no longer sick, but dead and buried, and no matter how much Paul wanted to, the one thing he still didn't talk about was the Atlantic Challenge. Even in death, his dad would be disappointed in him if he dishonoured his mother's wishes. His father had been dedicated to her. No matter how tired he would be, having started his day by getting up at four in the morning to walk a mile and a half to catch the 5.05am bus to start his shift at Raleigh, work a full day on his feet, despite his physical ailments, he still helped his wife with jobs around the house when he came home.

Some of his favourites were potato peeling and pot washing. He liked the water to be almost boiling; the man had hands of leather. Paul had the same, something he hoped would be beneficial during the row. But when his dad had become weaker in his final year, he no longer stood at the sink but sat on a stool. Paul remembered the day when he'd said: 'Well, son, I know you should treat all your children the same, but that was not possible with you. I never had to lift a hand to your brothers. Michael just had to be told and he would behave, if I

176

raised my voice to Sean that was enough. But not with you. It wasn't easy being hard on you, but you left me no choice. You were out of control, and that temper of yours brought trouble to our door. I couldn't let you go unchecked.'

'I know, Dad, and I am sorry.'

The hardest part for Paul that day was knowing the conversation was out of character. His father knew he was dying and was putting his house in order. Paul always thought his dad was indestructible. It was something he used to tell James, that the Hopkins men were made of stronger stuff than anyone else. Paul had always believed it to be true, until he'd seen that look of fear on Nic's face the morning after his brain had bled. Paul gave himself a shake. He had to put those thoughts back in the box for now. He leaned forward and kissed the gravestone.

'Miss you, Dad, see you later.'

He pulled his coat collar up around his ears and made his way back to the car. He still had a three-hour drive back to Newcastle. He stopped by the house to give his mother a hug. There was a time she would come to the gate to wave him off, but today she stood in the doorway. Would this be the last time he would see her alive? He locked the image in his memory just in case.

It never dawned on Paul that she might have been thinking the same about him.

Chapter 29

11 November 2019

31 days to go

Phil had spent a lovely evening with Tom, but he couldn't wait any longer. As he got him ready for bed, he said: 'Tom, you know the challenges I do every year?'

'Like the Great North Run?'

'Right, like the run we do together. But you know the other ones I do once a year?'

'Yes, Dad.'

'This year's one is a little bit different. I'm going to be away for almost three months.'

Tom's brow creased; his right arm jerked.

'I'm going to Spain. Remember we went there on holidays as a family?'

'Yes, Dad.'

'I'll be there for about ten days. And I can call you every day.'

'You'll call me.'

'From Spain, yes. Then I'm going to row a boat with Paul. You met him for lunch a few times and he was at the dragon boat racing. We're going to row it 3,000 miles across the Atlantic Ocean.' Phil knew Tom wouldn't be able to grasp the enormity of the challenge, which, in a way, was a blessing. 'You and I will be able to talk, but maybe not every day.'

Phil watched the confusion on his son's face, but carried on.

'It will be different this time. I won't be able to pick up a call all the time, or WhatsApp or do the things we do now, but Alex and Rod will still be here, and your mum, and Meme. What do you think about you and me talking on the phone a couple of times a week? You'd be able to talk to Paul as well.'

Phil knew he was babbling. He stopped. He waited, watched Tom trying to process.

'That would be okay, Dad.'

'There's a good lad.' Phil exhaled with relief.

'How did he take it?' Meme asked Phil when he came home.

'Not bad, I'll go over it with him again. How are you doing with it?'

'Okay. Work will be fine, but what about here, what if we get a buyer for the apartment?'

'I'll get all the paperwork ready, so that you can sign for both of us if needed.'

'I liked that three-bedroom house we saw.'

'Do you think we need that much space? It's only going to be until we retire. Meme?'

'What?'

'Are you having second thoughts about us moving back to the States?'

'Just thought it was cute,' she said.

'It is. I'm looking forward to us decorating somewhere new together.' Phil opened his laptop.

'Aren't you coming to bed?'

'Not yet, just going to finish a couple of quotes.'

'Phil, it's late.'

'I'll just be a few minutes.'

'No, you won't – I can feel you getting all wound up.'

'I'm not.'

'You don't even realise.'

'Meme.'

'Forget it, I'm going to sleep.'

'I'll be in soon. Goodnight.'

Over the next two weeks, each time he was over at Tom's, Phil reminded him he would call every day until the race began. In the meantime, he finished as many last-minute projects at work as possible, trying to leave the business in good shape for Meme.

He also came home earlier from the gym so that he could work off his excess energy in time to spend some relaxing time with her before he left, especially now, since they'd discovered that the vet had misdiagnosed Morgan and he didn't have arthritis. He had a tumour on his hind leg. It was so sad to see him limping in pain.

On 30 November, the night before Phil's flight, he spent the evening with Tom going over the plans again.

'So, you remember I'm leaving tomorrow.'

'Yes, Dad, you're going to Spain.'

'That's right.'

'Will you call me every day like you do now?'

'Of course, please don't worry. And I'll show you around all the boats and introduce you to people.'

'Will there be people there I don't know?'

'You'll know Paul, remember Paul? He's the one who looks older than me.'

Tom laughed. 'He'll be in the boat.'

'Yes. And when we go in the boat, I will call you twice a week on Mondays and Thursdays.' For consistency, Phil had chosen the same days he normally relieved the care staff and put Tom to bed himself.

'Will you call me on my landline? Or on my mobile?'

Phil smiled at how his son was always interested in the finer details, especially when it came to phone calls. 'Whichever you prefer.'

'On Mondays and Thursdays.'

'Yes, Tom. Four o'clock, Mondays and Thursdays.' Phil put his arms around Tom and hid his tears.

'Stay safe, Dad.'

'I will. I love you.'

'I love you loads, Dad.'

Phil turned off the light, not trusting himself to finish with a knock-knock joke.

'Ciao, Tom.'

As he drove away, he felt like he was leaving Tom in the baby ward all over again. This time, it was to the satellite gods he was prepared to sell his soul. He would do whatever it took for a guaranteed phone signal on Mondays and Thursdays.

Chapter 30

1 December 2019

11 days to go

The atmosphere inside the Hopkins' car was as icy as the windscreen Paul had just scraped. His dry-bags were loaded in the boot. One contained personal belongings and the other sweets and chocolates. This was it; they were on the way to the airport. Next stop, the Atlantic Ocean. As Paul drove, Nic looked out the window.

Between last-minute fundraising, training, packing and the farewell parties, the four weeks had flown. Everyone wanted a piece of him, or to tell him what they thought. It had been exhausting. He'd tried to sit down and write the letter to Nic a few times but there were so many other things still on his to-do list before he left. To him, it was a waste of time anyway because he knew he was coming back. But she'd kept banging on about it so much that he'd eventually sat down and written something. The one to James was easier. He'd written how proud he was of him, how much of a pleasure it had been to watch him grow into a young man, how he would miss not being here to see him walk down the aisle, see James' children grow up.

But to Nic? How could he sum up what she meant to him, and the highlights of his life with her? He tore up one page after another. It wasn't the big moments that made up their marriage, it was all the small stuff. Nic never wore her heart on her sleeve, she just got on with it. If he were to list all the little things she did for him, he'd need to write a book. In the end he had scribbled a page or two and put both letters in a drawer. He would burn them both when he came home.

Another waste of time had been the trip to see the sports psychologist. To Paul, his mind was a weird and wonderful place. He was reluctant to let a trained professional start snooping around in there. But since Phil had suggested it might be beneficial in overcoming the mental challenge of the row, he'd gone along with it.

'So, Paul. May I call you Paul?'

'Yes.'

'Let's start with the positives. What are you most looking forward to?'

Paul had relaxed a little, glad they were starting with an easy question. 'I'm looking forward to losing sight of land and rowing in the dark.'

'Really? I imagine that would be what people fear the most.'

'Anyone can piss around in a boat close to shore in the daytime. Where's the challenge in that?'

'How about you tell me where you draw your inspiration from when things get tough?'

'The doubters.'

'Explain.'

'All those bastards who would love to see me fail.'

The shrink made a note. 'What do you mean by that?'

'I imagine their faces, their condescending sneers, their gloating, and it fires me up. I will not give them the satisfaction of being right.'

'That means you're drawing on negative energy.'

'Works for me.'

'It's not a reliable tool.'

Wow, Paul thought, *this guy must be really good. How long am I here, five minutes? And he has already diagnosed me as a nutjob and told me what won't work for me.*

'You need to focus on the positives, that's where you get your best drive.'

'I beg to differ.'

'Positive energy will sustain you more.'

At the best of times, Paul had never enjoyed being told he was wrong. But in this case, even less. It seemed to Paul that he had 55 years more experience of managing his own mental health than the man sitting opposite, no matter how many degrees or accolades hung on his office wall. Paul knew what worked for him. Through countless challenges, both physical and mental, his system had pulled him through and he believed it would again. As far as he was concerned, the conversation was over. Paul had stood up, bade a polite but firm farewell to the confounded psychologist and left.

Then last week, Dave, his former station manager, had taken him out for a beer to have a chat. The two of them had trained for triathlons and run races together so Paul was surprised when he said: 'Right, Hops, I can't let you leave without saying something.'

'What's up?'

'When people say they will do something or die trying, they mean they will do their best and when they can't do it any more, they'll call it. When *you* say you will die trying you actually mean it and in your mind that is an acceptable outcome.'

Paul nodded. It was.

'No challenge is worth dying for, Hops. If it gets to that stage, you have to be brave enough to make the right call.'

'What do you mean?'

'It's not all about you, Paul. You have to think of Nic, your kids, Phil's safety, and of his family. You need to be sure about what you are doing and dying is not an acceptable outcome.'

'Uh-huh.'

He'd heard Dave's concerns, but that was all. For Paul, quitting was simply not an option. If that meant dying as a result, so be it. He thought that was normal. He knew people thought of him as being determined to the point of stubborn, but he was okay with that.

Paul drummed his fingers on the steering wheel while he waited for the traffic lights to change. He only had a few minutes left with Nic. Why could she not be happy for him? He didn't want to admit it, but Paul knew the answer. For the past three and a half years he had been cheating on his wife. Not with a mistress, not with drugs or alcohol but with a 20-foot wooden boat named *Didi*. Last night Nic had made it clear.

'You think more of that damn boat than you do of me.'

'That's not true.'

'No? Well, don't go.'

How could she even ask that? She didn't really mean it. She was probably just sad he was leaving. She knew him well enough to know that he couldn't go back on his word.

But by the time they reached departures, neither the frost on the ground nor the mood in the car had thawed. He unloaded his bags on to the kerb, handed Nic the keys, and drew her into a hug. He could feel her shoulders shake.

'Nic. It's okay, I'll be back, I promise.' He held her, stroked her hair. 'I love you.'

'I love you, too. Be safe,' she said, then turned and got in the car.

Paul watched her drive away, torn. How he wished they'd parted on better terms. If only …

'Hey, skipper.'

Phil and Meme piled out of her car.

'Hi,' he said, relieved by the distraction. 'Well, are we ready?'

'Are we what?'

'Stand together,' said Meme, holding up her phone.

Bags by their sides, the two men posed for a photo outside Newcastle Airport, about to set off on the adventure of a lifetime.

Chapter 31

2 December 2019

10 days to go

It seemed fitting that the final leg of their journey to the starting line was by sea. On yesterday's 40-minute ferry crossing from Tenerife to La Gomera, Paul and Phil had stood out on deck to enjoy the sunshine and scenery while many of the other rowers had gone inside to try the local brew. As the island came into focus, they could see the whitewashed houses of San Sebastian stretching up into the hills and a harbour filled with sailboats and motor yachts.

'Look, look, there they are,' said Phil, pointing.

In the car park next to the marina, 35 rowboats sat on their trailers, waiting.

'Wow,' said Paul, 'we're really here.'

They disembarked and walked through the narrow Spanish streets. Local kids kicked a football while a couple of tourists posed next to the statue of Christopher Columbus, who'd made his final stop here in 1492 before his voyage of discovery to the Americas. For a moment, the atmosphere made Paul feel like he was arriving for a week's escape from the English winter, but he knew their time here would be far from a holiday.

The hotel was modest. Compared to what they would be living in for the next couple of months, the room he and Phil were sharing was five-star, but more importantly, it was close to the boat park. This morning would start with the first pre-departure briefing. The inspection they'd passed in August gave them permission to ship the boat here, now they had to undergo a pre-race inspection before they would be allowed to put her in the water. Paul was off his food. After all the years of preparation, it came down to these next ten days.

He and Phil arrived early. As soon as the gates opened, they walked down the line of bright and shiny boats.

'There she is!' Paul grinned and jogged the last few paces. Sandwiched between two new, expensive vessels, *Didi* sat proudly on her trailer, the only wooden boat and the poorest vessel in the fleet.

'Hey, girl, how was your trip?' Paul ran his hand along her gunwale.

'She's looking good,' said Phil. 'Can't wait to get her in the water.'

But they would have to.

At 9am sharp, Carsten welcomed the teams to the briefing tent and played a video of highlights from last year's race. Thirty-five teams, 103 rowers from 18 countries fidgeted in their chairs like greyhounds ready to explode through their cages. As it faded to black, Carsten turned to the room and said: 'Now it's your turn.'

The hare had been released. Paul was so energised he felt he could swim across, never mind the easy task of rowing.

'Let me introduce the rest of the staff of Atlantic Campaigns.'

Paul only had eyes for one – Ian.

Carsten passed the mic to his safety officer.

'Congratulations on getting this far,' said Ian, 'but no one is ready for the race yet.'

Shoulders dropped. Faces fell. *Here we go*, thought Paul. It wouldn't be the condition of the ocean or the many miles to row that could impede them getting to Antigua, in Paul's mind, it was this man. He was convinced Ian would find something wrong and eliminate *Didi* before the race began. Although, he knew if Ian hadn't pulled them up on the inspection in July, making them work all hours during those six weeks, they wouldn't even be sitting in this tent at all. Even though he knew Ian was doing his job and trying to keep all the teams safe out there on the ocean, his foot still jiggled with the desire to kick him from here to Tuesday.

'The final inspections will start in three days. You need to pass those before you can launch. Since there are 35 boats this year, I will be conducting some and Fraser will do the rest.'

Paul nudged Phil. 'You can bet he'll be coming to inspect us himself.'

Phil nodded.

'When you are sure you are ready, book a time slot with Nikki.'

After the meeting, rowers drifted off towards their boats. Gone was the excitement, back were the nerves. Sandwiched between teams Oarsome Foursome – who were now only three having lost a team member due to seasickness during training – and Row Off the Wall, whose skipper, Sarah, at 64, was hoping to become the oldest female to row the Atlantic, *Didi* waited. Paul and Phil still had work to do.

It was slow going the first day. People kept coming over to talk, asking about the signatures and if they too could sign what would become, unbeknownst to everyone at that time, the last wooden boat ever to attempt the Talisker Whisky Atlantic Challenge. But over the next 48 hours, in between briefings, media requirements and getting checked out by the doctor, they managed to get through most of their list.

'Okay, skipper, do you think we're ready?' said Phil.

'Yeah, better to get it over with.'

'Shall I book us in for Thursday?'

'Yes, mate, see if you can get an early time slot, before it gets too hot.'

Chapter 32

5 December 2019

7 days to go

Paul didn't sleep on Wednesday night. His mind was on full alert, trying to remember where this or that bit of kit was stored. He must have dozed off at some point because when the alarm went off, he jumped.

They got to the boat park just as it opened and began to unload all their gear from the deck compartments. By 9.45am they had laid most things out on the tarp, including the spare solar panel that had been housed beneath their mattresses. For the first time since the boat had arrived in La Gomera, Paul could access the lockers beneath their beds. He opened the first one.

'Phil, quick, hand me the bucket and a sponge.'

'What's up?'

'There's water under here.' Paul started to soak it up. 'Whoa, my hand is tingling. That's not water, that's battery acid.'

'Shit, are you okay?'

'Never mind my hand, we've only got ten minutes.' Paul opened the battery compartment and found that one of their two brand-new wet-cell batteries was laying on its side. 'Must have got knocked over during transport.'

'We had them tied down,' said Phil.

'I know. Bloody rope.' If only they could have afforded the extra £100 for two AGM batteries that stored the electrolyte

189

in a 'dry' state. Those were supposed to be maintenance free. 'Pass me one of the spare straps.'

After Paul secured the battery, he nipped over to the toilets to wash the acid off his hand. He was back at 9.59am and stood next to Phil. The door to the tent flapped open.

'Nope, it's not him,' said Paul. 'Fraser, and someone else.'

'Another team must have the same time slot as us,' said Phil. 'But I don't see anyone else with their kit out?'

The two of them looked up and down the line. 'Yeah, look, far end. The American team, I think.'

'Lucky them.'

'Okay, lads, are you ready?'

Paul spun around. 'You're doing our inspection?'

'Yes,' said Fraser. 'Any problem with that?'

'No, no. We're ready,' Paul indicated all the kit on the tarpaulin.

'Thanks,' said Fraser, 'but first let's start with the towing eye.'

'What? That's not on the list for today. Ian inspected that back in the UK.'

'Yes,' said Fraser, 'but I have to physically inspect everything Ian saw on the video.'

Great, thought Paul, *we're getting inspected before the inspection.* How many more hurdles would they have to overcome?

Fraser worked his way through his sheet. What had seemed like a long list back in the UK felt even longer here. Paul watched Fraser's pen. Each tick was another milestone. He finished the first page and started on the second. But it didn't make Paul feel any more secure. Phil motioned to him to chill.

'That's all looks fine, now on to the pre-race inspection.'

Halfway there, thought Paul. Tick, tick, tick. This inspection was going faster, until: 'I don't see a spare bulb for the navigation light.'

'It's here, it's here somewhere,' said Paul.

'Yes,' said Phil, 'I saw it earlier.'

Paul tried to think. Where the hell was that bulb? But it didn't matter, the first X went on the sheet. At least they had gotten down to the small items; Paul felt good about that. They were almost finished when Fraser asked to see the toolkit. Paul relaxed. Not only did he have everything on the list, he'd put in a few extra tools.

'Looks good,' said Fraser, 'but you are missing a couple of drill bits.' And another X went on the sheet.

'Okay, just those two items,' said Fraser.

'We'll get it sorted, thanks.'

When Fraser left, Phil suggested they head off for a cup of tea.

'Why not,' said Paul, 'we deserve a break. Let's get the food on board first. Don't want the chocolate melting.'

They found a mini-mart in town that looked tiny from the outside but extended back a long way inside and sold everything from flyswatters to tinned sardines. Here they purchased the drill bits. They even found bulbs, but Paul couldn't bring himself to spend more money. He was determined to find the one he knew he already had.

'Here's to us,' said Paul, when they sat down at a café.

Phil clinked his teacup with Paul's. 'To Atlantic Dream Challenge.'

'To getting the final tick.'

On the walk back to the boat they passed two other teams unloading their gear for inspection. One lad was handing the toolkit down to his team-mate.

'Plastic storage box,' Paul said to Phil.

'What?'

'The bulb. It's in the box on the top of the toolkit.'

Sure enough, when they got back to *Didi*, Paul opened the box and there it was. 'Where's Fraser?'

'He's down the far end.'

'Keep an eye on him, let's grab him on the way past.'

Paul climbed on to the boat and Phil began handing up the 300 Eco For Life water bottles which Paul stowed below the deck for ballast. As the sun beat down, they continued to reload the rest of the kit.

'I think he's finished.'

Paul watched Fraser making his way towards the tent. People kept stopping him to ask questions. *Come on*, thought Paul, *leave the man alone. We need him.*

'Fraser, Fraser.'

At last, Fraser started walking towards *Didi*.

'Here you go, mate,' said Phil, holding out the drill bits.

'And here's the bulb,' said Paul. 'Can you tick them off your list?'

'Congratulations, gentlemen. I'm pleased to say you can now put the boat in the water.'

Paul and Phil couldn't stop grinning. After *Didi* was fully stowed, they got ready to celebrate. Over dinner, Paul treated himself to a second beer and Phil updated their social media accounts, letting all their supporters know that they were officially in the race. Finally.

Firefighter Paul Hopkins on his last day at work. *Photo by kind permission of Tyne and Wear Fire and Rescue Service*

Phil Pugh in the Great North Run pushing Tom's all-terrain wheelchair

Tom Pugh. *Photo by Phil Pugh*

Paul and his wife Nic. London circa 2001

Meme and Phil, Lake Tahoe circa 2003.

Phil and his son, Alex, on Santa Monica Pier, California, after bicycling Route 66 from Chicago

Atlantic Dream Challenge Team Photo Phil Pugh (L) and Paul Hopkins (R)
Photo by kind permission of Atlantic Campaigns

Paul and Phil training together on the water for the first time.

First inspection at Byker Fire Station. *Photo by Phil Pugh*

Paul and Phil's first view of the boat park in La Gomera, Canary Islands. *Didi* is the only wooden boat in the 2019 race. *Photo reproduced by kind permission of Atlantic Campaigns*

Carsten Olsen signs the boat. *Photo by kind permission of Atlantic Campaigns*

The Starting Line. *Photo by kind permission of Atlantic Campaigns*

3,000 miles to go. *Photo by kind permission of Atlantic Campaigns*

On deck showing foot steering and entry to cabin. *Photo by Phil Pugh reproduced by kind permission of Atlantic Campaigns*

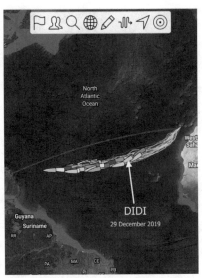

'Dot Watching' *Didi* on 29 December 2019. *Photo by kind permission of Atlantic Campaigns*

Bird on the bow. *Photo by Phil Pugh reproduced by kind permission of Atlantic Campaigns*

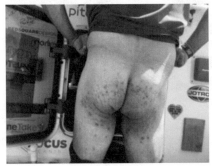

Salt Sores caused by being constantly wet

Flares Up. Moment of Triumph. *Photo by Niamh McAnally*

Certified Race Time 70 Days, 9 hours, 11 minutes. *Photo by Niamh McAnally*

Ian Couch, Safety Officer applauding Paul and Phil's arrival.
Photo by Niamh McAnally

Paul Hopkins Before and After. *Photo by kind permission of Atlantic Campaigns*

Phil Pugh Before and After. *Photo by kind permission of Atlantic Campaigns*

Didi Before. *Photo by Phil Pugh*

Didi After. *Photo by Niamh McAnally*

Nelson's Dockyard, Antigua. L to R Gary Krieger (author's husband) Phil Pugh, Niamh McAnally (author) and Paul Hopkins, taken before dinner onboard Gary and Niamh's sailboat home, *Freed Spirit*. Three hours later the idea for this book was born.

Chapter 33

6 December 2019

6 days to go

Paul and Phil had developed a bit of a swagger as they walked through the boat park the following morning. They were now part of the more relaxed group who'd passed the inspection and felt sorry for those who still had to go through the ordeal. Inside the tent, all 35 teams waited for the daily briefing.

Since it would take them a few days to get their sea legs, they were advised to bring some bottled water to help ease the transition from fresh water to the desalinated kind produced by the water maker.

'… and if you have any spare containers, you can fill them here at the marina for free,' Carsten was saying.

They had bought a few bottles of water at the market but they also had two five-litre jugs they could fill at the tap.

'You might also bring some takeaway food from the local restaurants.'

Ah, pizza. Paul's stomach started doing backflips in delight, even though it was only nine in the morning. He knew just the place where he was going to buy a large pepperoni with black olives. And he would also pick up some sandwiches. It would be a long time before he would have bread again. He was still thinking about food when Ian took the stage.

'I'm disappointed to say we've had more failures than passes. This is the time for fine-tuning, not for us to identify major issues. You've only got a couple of days. Those of you who need to schedule a second inspection, make sure you are ready.'

Ian was followed by the doctor who would be sailing across in one of the two sailboats. The doc planned on checking each team's medical kit and reminded everyone that, if anybody caught an infection during the race, it was important not to delay in starting a course of treatment. A couple more speakers and then the briefing was over. The teams began filing out.

'Paul.' Ian stopped them at the door.

'Yes, mate,' said Paul.

'Just wanted to say congratulations on your inspection. You've come a long way since the first time we saw you. Honestly, I thought you wouldn't make it, so well done.'

'Thanks, Ian, that means a lot.' Paul hesitated. 'If you don't mind me saying, I wish you'd take a look at what you call an advisory meeting. I know your job is to make sure we're safe, but if we'd known it was actually an inspection, we would've been better prepared.'

'Fair comment,' said Ian. 'I'll have a think about that. But, trust me, once you get out there, you'll be glad about all the preparation you've had to do. The things that will mean the most to you will be the worst things you've had to overcome.'

'You've rowed it twice,' said Phil. 'What made you go back out again?'

'There's nothing like it. Your first day or two you'll be carried through by your adrenaline and expectation. Then the seasickness comes. Those 20-metre waves won't be rolling underneath you; they'll pick you up and toss you down the front of them. But you'll settle in and by day seven you'll be an ocean-going nomad.'

Paul started to hear Ian, the man, not the drill sergeant, and realised how passionate he was about the race and his job ensuring everyone's safety.

'Your life will be on the boat and nothing will prepare you for what you'll experience out there. I promise you one thing, when we meet again in Antigua, you'll agree that it is life-changing.'

'Thanks, mate.' Paul reached out and shook Ian's hand. He'd never gone from hating someone to warming to them so quickly.

As he and Phil left the tent, Paul's phone rang.

'I'll catch up with you later, Phil. It's Nic.' Paul walked towards the water. While he felt bad about how he and Nic had parted at the airport, he was glad they'd managed to talk on the phone every night since, and the atmosphere between them had been warmer.

'Hi, Nic, how are you? You'll never guess what—'

'What do you call this?'

'Call what?'

'The letter.'

What was she talking about?

'The one you left for me, it's rubbish.'

'You opened it? What the—'

'It's rubbish.'

He could feel his face flush. 'You asked me to write you something in case I died. Last I checked in the mirror this morning I was very much alive.'

'It was the one thing I asked for.'

'We haven't even left La Gomera.'

He knew she wanted him to say sorry, but in Paul's mind that was not her letter to open until he was dead. And she had the cheek to complain about it? If only he'd left it with someone else who would have kept it safe until he returned.

'Nic, I told you, I'm coming back. Nic?'

He was talking to himself. He put the phone in his pocket. He would call her later when she was calmer. Meanwhile, he had a battery to sort. It would be a struggle to get a new one shipped in time, not to mention the burden on the credit card. The other option was to obtain some deionised water from the local garage. It was worth a try. The walk would do him good.

Once they topped up the levels, Paul connected the battery to the solar panel. As soon as he switched it on, the monitor read 43 per cent. Not good. During the sunny afternoon, it rose to 70 per cent. Better. By the end of the day, it was fully charged.

'That was a close one,' said Phil.

'Yes,' said Paul, 'glad we didn't have to come up with more money for a new one.'

Chapter 34

10 December 2019

2 days to go

The population of San Sebastian on La Gomera had almost doubled in size since the race officials, the rowers and their families had arrived. Tonight, the bars and restaurants were pregnant with the boisterous teams, each one anxious to get on the water. Only two more sleeps before the race.

Paul and Phil enjoyed the energy, but seeing the other teams with all their families made them miss their own even more. They walked through the town, each of them on the phone to their wives. Nic had stopped talking about the letter but was still a little cool.

'I love you, Nic, I promise I'm coming back.'

'I hope so.'

'We're still hoping we can get Phil's contact with the travel agent to sponsor you all to come out to Antigua when we get there.'

'I'm not counting on it.'

'It's a long shot, I know, but if it doesn't happen then you and I should go on a holiday when I get back. Just the two of us. Your choice where.'

'Okay, that would be nice.'

'Maybe sometime in March, that will give me time to get back and rest up before we go.

'It would be nice to go somewhere warm then.'

Phil was walking over. He looked upset.

'I love you, Nic, I'll talk to you tomorrow.'

'Love you too.'

He disconnected and heard Phil say: 'I wish I was with you. I know.' And Meme was saying something. 'I love you. I will be praying. And … tell him to come to me when I am out on the ocean.' Then Phil hung up.

'What's the matter? Everything okay with Meme?'

'No. It's Morgan. He's got sicker and sicker since we left. The tumour metastasised. He's in so much pain, they're going to have to put him down tomorrow.'

'Oh no, I'm sorry, mate.'

'The vet is coming to the apartment, and they'll do it at home. All the employees are coming to be with Meme, and to say goodbye.'

'How awful. Are you sure you still want to go out to eat?'

'Yeah, somewhere close.'

They slipped into one of the quieter restaurants and sat at the bar by themselves.

'What do you think all these families do that they can afford to fly out here just to wave their teams off?' said Paul, trying to take Phil's mind off Morgan.

'Who knows?' said Phil. 'But even if we had the money and every one of our lot could get the time off, I still think it would be better to have them at the finish line than here.'

'Absolutely. Anyways, let's go through our daily task list in case we've missed anything.'

'I was thinking,' said Phil. 'There's no rule saying we have to stick to the two hours on, two hours off rota.'

'No, it's just a suggestion. Makes sense for the solo rowers, though. But I can't see myself getting enough sleep in two hours.'

'What if we rowed together for 18 hours out of 24, taking turns with 15-minute breaks on alternate hours and then we could both sleep for six? The autohelm should keep us on course.'

'It's worth a shot.'

The barman put a cerveza in front of Paul and handed Phil a mug of tea.

'Gracias.'

'Cheers,' said Paul. 'Right, what else?'

'Phil pulled the sheet out of his pocket. Social media updates — I've talked with Ellie from my networking group and she is going to liaise with Meme on the blogs and Facebook posts. And of course, I have my calls to Tom on Mondays and Thursdays.'

'Have you the calls to the schools on there?'

'Yep.'

'Hey,' the tall blond from the Row for Veterans team called out. 'What are you guys doing over there? Come join us.'

'Hey Lars, be right over,' said Paul. 'I think we've covered everything for now, don't you, Phil? I'm starving.'

'Yeah, let's eat.'

Paul took a seat next to the Danish rower. 'Fancy meeting you here.' Paul had followed Lars' and Mads' progress all through the 2018 race and wasn't surprised they won the pairs category. 'Still can't believe you are going to do it all again, but I'm glad we're going to be in the same race after all.'

'It was such an amazing experience, I decided to go again,' he said. 'This year I am rowing to raise awareness for Danish veterans who suffer from PTSD.'

'Good on you. Should be quicker this time with four of you.'

'Yes. How are you doing, Paul, are you ready?'

'Boat's in the water, can't wait to go.'

'I mean, can you cope?'

What an odd question, Paul thought. 'Yes, I can cope.'

'What I mean is, are you prepared for all the thinking you will do out there?'

'Lars, you know I don't do all that "thinking" stuff.'

'I know, and neither did I. But once you are out there, your mind wanders. You'll think things you've never thought of, solve problems you didn't know you had and if you let it, your mind will take you places you never wanted it to go.'

'Don't worry, Lars, I'll be fine.' Paul knew how to keep the box at the back of his mind closed. 'But thanks for the heads up. Are you going to eat that bread roll?'

PART 2

Chapter 35

12 December 2019

Race day – 3,000 nautical miles to go

The room was quiet. The curtains were still drawn when Phil woke, although it appeared that Paul had already gone. He stayed in bed a moment longer, thinking about Meme and how upset she was yesterday. He couldn't believe Morgan was dead. The apartment would seem so empty without him. And the office. For the past eight years he'd been their greeter and mascot. Clients and employees adored him. Everyone would miss him, but for Meme he was more than just a dog. Morgan was her baby. Even though he was getting older, they had both assumed he would be her constant companion while Phil was gone. Why had the vet not found the sarcoma eating away at his bone sooner?

He wished he could have been there to hold her as they'd put Morgan down. If this were any other trip, he would have flown home to be there for her, but she was so understanding, knowing he couldn't back out now. He had to get in that boat with Paul and row it to Antigua. The thought made him tremble. All his previous challenges seemed like a Sunday stroll in comparison. He and Paul had encountered so many setbacks on the journey to the starting line that he'd rarely allowed himself to believe they would get this far. But here they were, about to dive into the unknown, all 3,000 nautical miles of it, the equivalent of 5,550km on land.

He padded to the bathroom, thinking of all the last-minute calls he wanted to make. The shower was hot, full pressure. He stood an extra minute, letting it cascade over him, soaking up the last drops of fresh water. This would be his final shower for two months or more. The idea seemed preposterous.

He joined Paul in the dining room. They exchanged a look, both afraid to utter a word. In the days and months to come it would just be the two of them, alone on an ocean, weeks from civilisation.

After breakfast, they gathered the last of their items. Phil checked the satellite phone and back-up were functioning and fully charged. Every piece of kit was vital, but these were the lifelines to loved ones back home. Phil could feel the clock pushing him from behind; it was time to make a move.

'I have to drop by the post office on the way,' said Paul.

'Right. Meet you on the promenade.'

Phil merged with the rest of the rowers walking to the race tent for the final briefing. Some teams were silent, others laughed, some sang. No matter their country of origin – America, Australia, Austria, Belgium, Denmark, Germany, Norway, South Africa, Switzerland or the UK – they all had the same destination in common: Antigua. Phil felt the energy in the pit of his stomach and took a moment to think about the last 65 years of his life and everyone he was leaving behind, just so he could spend the next few months pushing himself to his limits. How would Tom cope with his absence? Had he told Rod and Alex how proud he was of them, had he said a proper goodbye? He kept thinking about Meme and how badly he felt about leaving her to cope with everything – the business, the apartment – without him, especially now she was without her darling Morgan.

'Good morning, everyone,' Carsten greeted the group. 'This is it, guys. After all your training, this is it.'

Phil looked around the tent at all the other rowers, who in turn were looking around the tent at everyone else. Most appeared to be wearing a small round plaster behind their right ears – a scopolamine patch to prevent seasickness. Even Paul, who had slipped into the seat beside him, had one on. Phil wondered if he had made the right choice opting for anti-seasickness pills instead. Since they were using both strategies, hopefully one of them would stay well enough to pull the other one through.

'Before you leave,' Carsten continued, 'Thomas is going to take one last look at weather with you.'

Phil watched the expert talk about systems and intensity, expected wind and seas. It was difficult to understand what he was saying, as he spent most of his presentation looking at the screen, but it seemed like they were in for some rough weather. Phil could only hope Paul was taking it in, although part of him knew it didn't matter. Gauging the weather was like playing Russian roulette anyway. The bottom line was summed up by the final farewell from Carsten: 'Good luck, everyone, looks like the start of this year's row is going to be fast and furious.'

What did that mean? They didn't need luck. They were prepared, they were ready. Deep down, he believed their protection would come from their precious boat and the belief that he and Paul had in each other.

'But don't forget,' said Carsten, 'we are here, we have your backs. You *will* do this, you *will* succeed.'

It all seemed a little *kumbaya* to Phil, but then if Carsten had reminded them of the horrors ahead – the storms, the pain, the dark moments – he supposed half of the rowers probably wouldn't want to leave the tent, never mind the dock.

But everyone stood up, shook hands, and hugged people who only ten days ago had been strangers. Now they were friends and fellow adventurers, about to take on the biggest challenge of their lives. They filed out of the tent into the bright sunshine and walked down the ramp to where the boats were all lined up against the dock wall. Their fourth-hand wooden boat stood out in the fancy fleet. *Didi* was covered in over 3,000 signatures; even Ian and Carsten and some of the TWAC staff had stopped by during the week to add theirs.

Phil and Paul hopped aboard and busied themselves with last-minute nothing. They knew they were only marking time, waiting for their departure slot. The team on the boat next to them was discussing waypoints, which made Phil feel anxious to check his phone, but he knew there was no need. He'd already programmed the 15 different points of longitude and latitude they'd need to steer towards to keep them on course to Antigua. He checked the tracker, which the organisers had secured to the bulkhead by the cabin hatch before *Didi* had been put in the water. The independent GPS device, about the size of a smartphone, would transmit their 'dot' to the TWAC website and show their tracks and stats as they progressed across the Atlantic. Tampering with the tracker would disqualify them from the race. Not that they would want to. In the event of an emergency, it would show their last known position.

On the other side, their neighbours were discussing supplies – in particular, shampoo. Phil smiled. That was one piece of kit neither he nor Paul would need. Rowing the ocean might be a turning point in their lives but it was hardly going to cure baldness. Still, it made him wonder if they had enough marine soap to keep their bodies clean.

Phil told himself to relax. They'd packed everything they'd need in a calm and logical manner. This was just last-minute nerves, the kind that inveigled your mind after cramming for an exam and waiting for the test papers to be handed out. But still, was there anything else he could or should do before they set off?

He'd read about seeking Poseidon's blessing before embarking on a long and dangerous sea voyage but neither he nor Paul had followed through on any ceremony. He remembered the St Christopher medal a couple had given them at one of the fundraisers. Perhaps the patron saint and protector of travellers could liaise with the god of the sea to keep them safe. Phil pulled the medal out of his pocket, kissed it, and attached it to the bow of the boat. There. May it protect *Didi*, Paul and himself.

'Hi, Atlantic Dream Challenge.'

Nikki Holter stood on the floating dock.

'Hi,' said Paul, 'how nice of you to stop by.'

'Well, Paul, how could I not? Of all the people who signed up for the 2017 race, you are the last man standing. Everyone else has either dropped out or made it across.'

'It seems so long ago now,' said Paul.

'Congratulations to you both. It's been a struggle but you made it. Are your families here?'

'No,' said Phil, 'but we're hopeful they might be able to meet us in Antigua.'

'Even better,' said Nikki, turning to Phil. 'You make sure you get this man across.'

'Yes, ma'am.'

'I'll be watching out for you.'

Phil looked at the big grin on Paul's face and felt proud that, not only was he doing this for Tom, he was also the man who would help Paul complete his dream.

At 10am the cannon fired; the crowd cheered as the first team rowed off the dock. Phil and Paul waved. The challenge had begun. At 10.05 another boom, and the second team left San Sebastian harbour. The departures continued, five minutes apart, as team after team pushed off the dock. The sight was overwhelming. Phil wished Meme was here to see them off, but he knew she would be watching the livestream back in England.

When it was their turn, Phil and Paul stopped fiddling, gave each other a slap on the back and strapped themselves into the footplates. Deep breath. They manoeuvred *Didi* to the starting line.

'Ladies and gentlemen, let's hear it for Paul and Phil of team Atlantic Dream Challenge.'

The cannon fired. They dipped their oars and pulled hard. The world was watching: Meme, Tom, Rod, Alex, Debbie, all Phil's employees at Adept, Paul's family, the kids at Hadrian Primary and Excelsior Academy, the firefighters at Byker – everyone who had supported them would be following their departure on the internet. The next time they would feel anything other than water around their boat would be at the dock in Antigua.

They navigated their way out of the harbour by foot steering and pulling on the oars, making sure to stay clear of the main shipping channel. As they approached the first turn, Phil called: 'Left oar only.'

Three more strokes on the left, and bang. They had run into the large yellow marker.

'Oops,' said Phil, 'the other left.'

Chapter 36

12 December 2019

2,999.5 miles to go

Paul turned his head and looked at Phil. 'So much for that auspicious start.'

'Do you think anyone noticed?'

'You mean apart from everyone on the dock and the thousands back home watching on the internet? No, no one at all.'

They both laughed. As they straightened the boat out, Paul thought about all the people on the dock who had waved their loved ones off. Even though he had told himself it didn't matter, he still wished Nic and James had been there for one last hug so he could tell them how much he loved them, that he couldn't wait to see them in a few months. But now those emotions had to be stored in the box; they had to focus on the next task, which was to get clear of the Canaries. Past teams had got caught up in low-pressure weather systems that circulate between the islands. Because those teams had required outside assistance, they'd been disqualified from the race when they'd still been within sight of land.

'So, Phil, before we make any more turns, just wanted to check how many more left arms do you have?'

Phil's chuckle was drowned out by the sound of the cannon and another boat leaving the dock. Paul was unperturbed about boats passing them at this stage. They weren't in a race against them. Their race was against the Atlantic and if they got to the other side, they'd be winners.

When they cleared the headland, they felt the true effects of the sea conditions. *Didi* started to pitch and roll. Already it churned much more than they had experienced in the North Sea. Now that they were in open waters, someone had to climb into the cabin and open the rear hatch to attach the linkage to the autohelm, so that it would guide the rudder for them. But as soon as Paul opened the cabin hatch, his stomach heaved. He turned back to Phil.

'Any chance you could fit the linkage for me?'

'Sorry, I think I'm going to be sick.'

No sooner had Phil said it, Paul himself vomited, right beside his rowing position.

'Sorry, mate.'

'Are you okay? Here, have a drink.'

'Thanks.'

Paul swilled his mouth. A wave washed over and cleared the mess away, making him feel a little less embarrassed, but he still needed to attach the autohelm. He climbed into the cabin but the feeling was back. This time he managed to get the hatch at the stern open just in time to throw up overboard.

Come on Paul, get a grip. He attached the linkage and backed his way out of the cabin.

'Well done, Paul. Are you feeling okay?'

'Not the best, mate, how are you?'

'Not good, not good at all.'

They could hear the autohelm adjusting the rudder, keeping *Didi* on course. At least *she* was feeling okay. The boat continued to roll and slide about. As much as they had mastered rowing in unison on the river, and the North Sea, it was impossible to stop their oars from clashing here. When they pulled, one oar would dig deep into the wave on one side but only catch the surface on the other. They tried alternating, one rowing for five minutes, then the other. The wind became stronger in the afternoon, whipping up waves on top of the swell.

In the second rowing position, Paul could only see Phil's back, but he could tell his energy was waning.

'Do you want to try some pizza, Phil?'

'Not really, but I suppose we should eat something.'

Phil retrieved two sandwiches from the cabin, and handed one to Paul. With both sets of oars stowed, the sea tossed them about even more, up and down and side to side.

'Thank goodness we brought these,' said Paul. 'There's no way we could set up the Jetboil in this.'

Phil had only taken a couple of bites when he grabbed the railing.

'Are you okay, mate?'

'No, I'm going to be—'

And he was. Luckily, over the side.

'Sorry, Paul, I'm going to have to lie down.'

'No worries. Try and rest.'

Phil climbed into the cabin and locked the hatch shut, a necessary evil to keep it watertight and, in the event of capsize, to keep them buoyant. But Paul could imagine how dank it would be in there when Phil was feeling so poorly. He wasn't the best himself. Three minutes later, the sandwich catapulted out of his stomach too. At least he was in the fresh air. He kept rowing. He wasn't getting very far but the forward momentum helped reduce the four-way bronco ride to just up and down. He looked at his watch. If an hour on the stationary bike had felt long, an hour at sea felt like forever. Only 20 minutes had passed since he last checked the time. Wait. He stowed the oars.

'Phil, Phil.'

'What?'

He hated to rouse him, but ... 'It's ten past four.'

'Oh God, thanks mate.'

Phil dialled Tom and Paul got back on the oars. Poor Phil, he was doing his best to cheer up for Tom's sake but Paul could tell he still felt awful. The other thing Paul noticed was that having a private phone call on this journey was going to be impossible.

The afternoon became evening, and the clouds turned from grey to charcoal. So much for Paul's romantic notions of the two of them toasting their first sunset at sea. The sun had sunk beneath the horizon behind him and he hadn't even noticed. Within 30 minutes the sky was dark. He kept rowing, trying to keep his stomach from retching. He wasn't sure how late it was when the Automatic Identification System (AIS) beeped, alerting them that there were other marine vessels within a five to seven-mile range. It was too dark to see. Since so many rowboats would be in close proximity that first day, he expected there would be a lot of alerts, so he wasn't too concerned until: '*Mein Schiff, Mein Schiff*, this is Oarsome Foursome on channel 16, over.'

Paul remembered the three ladies who'd been next to them in the boat park. They'd left shortly before them.

'Oarsome Foursome, this is *Mein Schiff*, switch channel 13, over.'

Paul dialled the hand-held VHF to 13 and listened in.

'*Mein Schiff*, this is Oarsome Foursome. We are in a small rowboat off your starboard bow, we are not under power, repeat, we are not under power, over.'

'State your vessel again, over.'

'Rowboat, over.'

'We are a cruise liner.'

A cruise ship? Shit. Guess they didn't get the memo about 35 rowboats leaving port today. A cruise ship could plough right over them and not even feel the bump. He heard Oarsome Foursome's skipper reply: '*Mein Schiff*, we are not under power and cannot manoeuvre out of your way, over.'

'Roger, Oarsome Foursome, *Mein Schiff* over and out.'

Paul tried to get a visual fix on the cruise ship but the seas were at least five metres. As *Didi* rode up them, he could see some lights off to the right but he couldn't be sure if that was the ship or the lights from Tenerife. On the next rise, he saw her; she was large. *Didi* fell into the next trough, then rode up again. Paul tried to work out how close they would pass. Their AIS was not sophisticated enough to give specifics as to the vessel's size or if they were on a collision course. All he could do was continue to monitor his position relevant to the ship. She was close enough that he could see her clearly now, the string of lights down her middle. By the time she came level with *Didi*, she looked to be about a mile away. In terms of distance at sea, and their being in a 20-foot wooden boat, that was like driving a mini next to an articulated truck on the motorway on a windy day. Five minutes turned into ten and the lights became a little smaller. The closest point of contact had passed and Paul relaxed a little.

He checked on Phil. It was hard to tell if he was asleep, with his body rolling back and forth with the swell, but he didn't look like he was ready to row any time soon.

Right, thought Paul, *time to get back on the oars*. But that was easy to say. The seas continued to grow and the wind was blowing 26 knots, a strong force 6. *Didi* was tossed about so much that Paul was knocked clean off his seat, even though his feet were still strapped to the footplate. He felt a sharp pain at the back of his calf. His leg was wet, not surprising in these conditions. He flipped on his head torch, another gift from Zoe. It wasn't salt, it was blood. Not too bad, though, he would sort it later. He got back on the seat, got thrown off again. If he couldn't row, how would they ever get free of the islands? As he looked over the stern, he could see the lights of Tenerife seemed further away than before. Good. The wind and waves were coming from behind, pushing them forward. But the full moon had risen, backlighting a monster cloud that towered skyward. This was no ordinary weather pattern. They were being chased down by a storm.

Paul grabbed the railings, put one foot on each side of the boat, stood up straight and balanced. As he shifted his weight, he felt the boat catch a wave and slide down the backside of it. Wow, was that a fluke? He waited. *Didi* rode up the next wave and on the crest, he shifted his weight and sure enough he skimmed down into the trough. *Didi* rode up the next one, he rode it down. Well, would you look at that. The conditions were too rough to row, but he could surf. He looked over his shoulder. The storm kept coming but he still had some time. It took every muscle in his legs and abs to maintain his balance, but as he focused, he felt his body tune to the motion of the boat. Up she climbed, down he surfed. He thought of nothing other than riding the sea and outrunning the tempest. His quads were on fire, his glutes trembled. The sky lit up; it wasn't the moon. The wind was so loud he never heard the thunder. Okay, Paul, time to go in and let *Didi* and the autohelm keep them on course.

He squeezed in feet first, trying not to disturb Phil too much. Easier done when the boat had been sitting in the harbour. Phil groaned and rolled.

'Sorry, mate.'

Phil seemed to be asleep. Paul tried to do the same but with the constant motion his stomach was at his feet one minute and in his throat the next. He lay there for what seemed like hours, but sleep eluded him. He gave up and hauled himself out through the hatch again. If he'd missed the sunset, maybe he could watch their first sunrise.

Chapter 37

13 December 2019

2,968 miles to go

Paul sat on deck; the wind whipped at his ears. The seas were just as rough but seemed a little less frightening in the early light. As for sunrise, the sky was one big grey mess. He scanned the horizon. No other boats. They'd lost sight of La Gomera but could still see El Hierro, as expected.

Phil climbed out of the cabin and tried to stand up, but he threw up and quickly retreated like a groundhog. Although he knew Phil loved a good joke, Paul thought it might be too soon to mention that his face looked like the mystical colours of Ireland – 40 shades of green.

'See if you can keep some water down.'

Paul knew they were going to learn a lot about each other on this trip and his first lesson about Phil was that he did not function well with dehydration and seasickness. Some previous rowers who could not get their bodies attuned to the conditions had fallen at this first hurdle and had needed to be rescued. Paul had not come this far to let it happen to either of them. Despite not feeling great himself, he got on the oars and tried to keep the boat moving, but having had no sleep, and not digested any food, every stroke cost him precious energy for little reward.

Phil seemed to be sleeping again, somehow, so he tried to take a nap himself. He lay there heaving instead. He'd sooner get back in the air. He turned on the satellite phone and spoke with Ian. The good news was they weren't the only seasick crew; the bad news was the winds from the north were likely to back to the north-west and work against them. *So much for the middle route*, thought Paul.

After another invisible sunset, the light faded, the wind whistled and again the clouds rose up. Decision made. He didn't have enough energy to fight another storm. It was time to deploy the para-anchor. Although he was tethered to the boat, Paul held tight to the handrail, inched his way to the forward locker and opened the hatch.

The life raft and anchor were on top. Thank you, Ian, for that advice. He confirmed one end was secured to the bow, then threw it over the leeward side. As the line paid out, the red and yellow parachute filled with water then disappeared. *Didi* knew she had been collared and swung around, the anchor pulling her bow into the oncoming waves. It was the safest position for the boat, but as Paul was about to learn, not the most comfortable ride.

He joined Phil in the cabin. *Didi* struggled so much in the oncoming waves that his face rolled into Phil's feet one minute, the hull the next. With much heaving and groaning, he turned around, put his head next to the hatch and braced himself shoulder to shoulder with Phil. The howling wind and water rushing past the hull at uneven rates made it feel as though the boat was spinning. Every time the line snapped taut, he felt his neck jerk. Even Phil couldn't sleep through this.

'I suppose this is what they meant,' said Phil.

'Fast and furious?'

'Yeah. Welcome to the 2019 Talisker Whisky Atlantic Challenge.'

'We could use a bottle of that right about now,' said Paul. 'Too bad you don't drink.'

'Actually, it's a good thing I don't drink. That's not something you want to see.'

The boat continued to twist and surf, zigzag and spin. Inside the cabin the two men's stomachs roiled.

'Hey, Paul?'

'Yeah?'

'I think your laundry is almost done.'

If Paul hadn't felt so rotten, he might have chuckled. Seasick, dehydrated and now a night of hell inside a washing machine; he wondered if it could get any worse.

Beep, beep, beep …

'What's that?' said Phil.

'No idea mate, but doesn't sound good, does it?' Paul checked the monitor. The battery on the port side read 100 per cent. Great. The battery on the starboard side? Thirty per cent. Shit. Why was that? Oh God, that was the battery they'd topped up. Was it leaking again?

'Let's turn everything off that we can do without,' said Phil.

Paul disconnected two of the biggest draws on power while the boat was under way – the autohelm and the GPS. The beeping stopped. 'Well, that's something, I suppose.'

'Shall we wait till morning to get under the mattress to check it out?'

'Fine by me,' said Paul, 'we need some sleep.'

But sleep remained a far-away dream. The boat continued to be tossed about by the confused seas and the noise inside the cabin was deafening. Paul thought about all the ways you could torture someone. This form of hell would have to be top of the list for any interrogator. He would have told them anything if it would mean getting off this horrific roller coaster. And this was only the second night.

He needed a wee. He felt around for the sports bottle. To keep them from falling overboard they planned to stay in the cabin and urinate into a bottle. He lay on his side with his back to Phil, lined up his manhood and started the sweet release. But on the next wave, *Didi* pitched him on to his back, cutting off the flow. Okay, he was going to have to time this.

217

Penis in one hand, bottle in the other, he rolled on to his side and was almost ready to start again when the ocean tossed him backwards. Third time lucky, here we go. This time he anticipated and started to pee before he made it on to his side, but the waves hit at a different angle. Not only did he miss, but the contents of the bottle splashed back on his hand. Where did the bloody cap go?

'Phil?'

'Yeah?'

'Hate to ask, but could you help me out?'

He always knew they'd have to perform bodily functions in close proximity but he hadn't thought he would need Phil to help him in the process.

Phil sat up. 'What do you want me to hold?'

'Not that.'

'How about I roll on my side and support you from behind?'

'Excuse me?'

To keep Paul from rolling, Phil curled into the foetal position, pushed his feet against the hull on his side, and lined his back up against Paul's. 'Does that work?'

'Ahhh.'

'I'll take that as a yes.'

When Paul was finished, he capped the bottle and grinned at the absurdity.

'Pleased to make your acquaintance, Mr Pugh.'

'Likewise, Mr Hopkins.'

Chapter 38

14 December 2019

2,952 miles to go

Paul was relieved to see it getting light outside. The night of horrors was coming to an end. *Didi* was still bow to the waves, but the sea state seemed to have improved, and the jerking motion had subsided a bit. Maybe today would be better, and tonight they would sleep. But first they had to sort out the starboard battery. Phil rallied enough to help Paul lift the mattress to gain access. It was still upright, hadn't leaked, but now showed less than 28 per cent full. They couldn't afford to let it run down to zero, so they disconnected it for now. Thankfully, the second battery could work independently but they would have to ration power and the biggest draw was the autohelm and the water maker. They needed sun.

'Glad we got that extra water,' said Paul. 'We need to keep hydrated. Feel like eating?'

'Maybe. I'll try and make some Bovril.'

Paul put the mattress back while Phil set the Jetboil into the gimbal and somehow managed to boil some water without scalding himself. He made two cups. Paul took a mouthful and spat it out.

'Yack, that tastes like shit.'

'Yeah,' said Phil, taking a sip. 'Sure doesn't taste like Bovril.'

'Is that the water from the marina?'

'Yes.'

Paul put his cup down, annoyed at himself for not tasting the 'free' water before they'd left. Frustrated, he stood up to bring in the para-anchor.

'Let me help,' said Phil.

The two of them pulled against the drag but Paul could tell Phil had no strength.

'I'm so sorry.'

'It's okay.'

Paul heaved and pulled until he got it on board. He bagged it but left it on deck. 'Do you feel well enough to row for a bit?'

'I'll give it a go,' said Phil.

If they were going to make any progress, they needed to row together. Phil got into position; Paul took up the oars behind him. But once again the foot steering was no match for the power of the sea. The current pushed against the rudder, Paul's foot snapped the wrong way and the boat turned off.

'Let's switch to hand steering.'

Between them, they disconnected the footplate and fastened the ropes to a couple of clamps on the side of the boat. Once they set the steering in line with the GPS heading, they tried again. But the wind and swell continued to beat them up. So much work for so little progress.

'Sorry, skip, I've got to lie down again.'

Paul stayed on deck and kept rowing. When he stopped to adjust their course by pulling on the hand steering, the rope went slack. He looked over the side and saw the line had snapped close to his position. He checked his harness was secure, reached over and tied the two ends of the line together and then continued on, fighting for every stroke. But no matter how hard he tried, he was making no progress against the wind. By dusk there was no point in burning energy; the boat wasn't going forward.

Once again, he deployed the para-anchor and squeezed into the cabin next to Phil. They were in for another night from hell.

Paul wasn't sure if he could fall asleep. He was dehydrated because he couldn't stand the taste of the water, exhausted from effort and lack of food, and feeling like he had lived like this for weeks already. He thought it couldn't get any worse until he heard an almighty bang, loud enough to stir Phil.

'What was that?'

The crash was so loud it sounded like their wooden boat had splintered. Before either of them recovered from the noise, there was an even louder bang.

'Shit,' said Paul, 'sounds like she's breaking up.'

'How long have we got?'

Paul twisted around to look out. They were still afloat.

'I'm going to check.'

He struggled into his harness, opened the hatch and clipped himself to the deck. The wind was icy.

'Bollocks.'

'What is it?' Phil called out.

'Hand steering is gone and the footplate broke loose.'

'What?'

'Footplate,' Paul shouted, but he doubted Phil could hear him over the wind. The hand steering line had snapped again but it was too far away and too dangerous for Paul to reach.

'Cheap polyester piece of shit,' he yelled at the wind. The wind spat back and the footplate smashed against the hull again. He grabbed it and tied it down. The rest he'd have to sort out in the morning. He climbed back into the warmth and sealed the hatch.

'Everything okay?'

'Not really, mate, hand steering line's gone and the foot steering doesn't work.'

'What are we going to do?'

'Same as we always do. We'll find a solution.'

Chapter 39

15 December 2019

2,964 miles to go

Phil stared at the ceiling 12 inches above his head. If he didn't know better, he'd think he was in a coffin and he'd been buried alive. How many days had he been drifting in and out of semi-consciousness? He remembered coming to during the storm, knowing Paul was out there by himself in the eye of it. He'd never felt so ill or guilty. He'd wanted to pull his weight, but hadn't been able to raise his head off the mattress. If Paul hadn't reminded him, he would have missed his call with Tom completely, something he could never have forgiven himself for. He vaguely remembered the conversation with his son, trying to tell him they were doing fine. Was that the first night? And then the dreams – Morgan running towards him but then turning into a ball and rolling away, Meme pulling something out of the back of a rabbit that was carrying a drum, the giant toothbrush his mother was using to clear her clothes of soot.

He remembered being on deck at some point trying to help Paul row, but his body had rebelled, and he'd kept vomiting till he was empty. His temples had throbbed until he'd lain back down and passed out. Then there was the crash and the freezing wind when Paul opened the hatch.

As he pieced the last three days together, his brain fog started to lift. This morning felt a little calmer. He rolled on to his tummy, propped himself up on his elbows and looked out.

Paul was rowing. But, he remembered, they were still in trouble. Before he went out there, he needed to think things through.

He mentally listed the problems they faced.

Because of the storms, he knew the rudder had been thrown about and the autohelm had taken a battering trying to make adjustments to their course. It couldn't keep up. After all the work he had done calibrating it before they left, setting the movement of the piston to guide the rudder, it was disappointing. The foot steering couldn't function in these seas. And they were severely down on power. They still had at least 60 days to go. Could they survive another beating? What else might break? They knew their kit wasn't top quality but it was the best they could afford with the funds they'd had. Phil's mind kept weighing the odds, balancing probabilities of success versus failure.

He checked the gauges and miles to go. Backwards? They'd actually gone backwards during the storm. Or was that sideways? Either way, they were now 12 miles further from Antigua than they'd been before. Phil did the maths. This meant they were less than 70 nautical miles from land. What options did they have? They could turn back, repair *Didi* and maybe rejoin the race, even though they would be at least a week behind. Or, if that didn't work, they could try again next year. The more Phil mulled it over, the more he understood his worst fear: what if they found themselves in real trouble 2,000 miles out? There'd be nowhere to hide, nowhere to run. They'd be at the mercy of the sea and would have to wait to be rescued, which could take anywhere from days to a week or more. Or worse, the unimaginable. What if by the time a support boat arrived all they found was *Didi* drifting by herself …

It wasn't like Phil to focus on all the negatives, but this was no afternoon row. He schooled his mind back to pondering solutions. First, he had a question for Paul. He crawled out and welcomed the fresh air.

'How are you feeling?' Paul asked.

223

'A little better, I think. You?'

'Not too bad.'

'Can we talk?'

'Sure.' Paul kept rowing.

'Sorry I've been so useless over the past few days.'

'It's okay, mate. It's been a baptism of fire and dehydration is a killer. Hopefully the seas will settle a bit, now that the storms have blown through.'

'Let's hope,' said Phil. 'About the boat, I just wanted to review where we're at. We've lost one battery. We've barely enough power for the water maker. The water we have from the marina tap tastes like a sewer. The autohelm is useless, even if we did have enough juice to power it. The sea is too powerful for the foot steering. We've lost the line for the hand steering.'

'Yes, mate, that about sums it up. But I've come up with a solution.'

'What's that?'

'I can dismantle the foot steering and use the Kevlar rope to rig a new line for the hand steering. That stuff's bomb-proof.'

'So let me get this straight ... we're going to cross the Atlantic with only a compass and two bits of rope?'

'Don't forget, we still have our four packets of glucose sweets.'

'Funny.' Phil didn't laugh. 'There's another solution I'd like you to consider. And before you say anything, I want you to know I'm fine with whatever you decide. We're only a couple of days from land.' He could see Paul's jaw tighten, but he needed to ask. 'Do you think we should turn back and try again another time?'

Chapter 40

15 December 2019

2,963 miles to go

As Phil had been talking, Paul felt himself tensing up. He could sense Phil's question, and in a way, wished he'd just spit it out. Finally, there it was. Phil wanted to know if Paul thought they should turn back. Despite all the months training together, and the days and nights they had just endured, it seemed Phil hadn't quite grasped that Paul was hardwired to never quit. He must not have told Phil the story of his 2013 triathlon.

Three weeks after Paul had crashed his bicycle into the lorry, and against all medical advice, he was getting out of his wetsuit having completed the swimming portion of the triathlon. See? No problem. Six hours and 40 minutes after that, he had cycled 112 miles, his fastest time yet. Next, the run. Just as he switched shoes, his left calf cramped. A volunteer offered to help, raised Paul's leg and pushed back on his toes. Paul cried out. His entire hamstring constricted. Excruciating pain. He tried to stand but his right leg also cramped. He collapsed on the ground and thrashed about like a break-dancer. After 20 agonising minutes, Paul finally got to his feet.

One of the medics approached. 'The race is over for you.'

'No.'

'Sorry, sir, we can't let you out on the course. You've lost too much fluid, it's not safe.'

Paul was handed a glass of electrolytes and told to sip.

'Someone will bring you back to the starting line where you can collect your gear.'

'Okay, doc.'

As soon as their backs were turned, Paul ducked out of the tent. Seven hours left before he would be disqualified and only 26 miles to go. Game on.

For the first mile, he was spurred on by seeing Dave on the road ahead and managed to jog. He took on food and water at every station but as the miles ticked slowly by and the heat became more oppressive, he forgot. He knew he was struggling when a bloke with two prosthetic blades instead of legs ran past him.

Paul didn't want to admit he had pushed himself too hard on the bike. Keep going, Paul, don't let anything beat you. He felt like a boxer who had instinctively got back on his feet after a knockout but who did not know what he was doing.

Never give up. His dad never gave up, neither would he.

His feet felt like lead weights. He saw the 17-mile mark, shuffled forward. Only nine to go. Was he out of time? In his haste to escape the transition tent, he had forgotten his watch.

'Are you okay?' said a voice beside him.

Paul was confused by the German accent. Until he remembered. *Okay. That's right. The triathlon is in Germany. I'm in Germany.*

'No, mate, I'm in trouble.'

'Come with me, do what I say.'

Four hundred yards on, they reached the next station.

'Wash your face with this sponge.'

Paul did what he was told. The cool water was a glorious treat.

'Here, drink this. Slowly.'

Paul took a gulp. The cup was smacked from his hand.

'Slow. Or I will knock it away again.'

Paul sipped.

'Better. Now take some banana with you. Let's go.'

Like a five-year-old child, Paul followed his instructions. The man kept pace with Paul's shuffle. They didn't talk. Paul nibbled the banana and sipped from a bottle. At the next station, he ate and drank some more.

'Now, we try to jog.'

Every time he renourished, Paul gained a little more strength. The man never left his side.

'Who are you?'

'No one. I saw you struggling when my friend and I passed you. I had to come back and help.'

'Thank you. Do I have enough time?'

'Yes, but I have to go now to help my friend. Keep close.' The German ran off.

Paul pushed on, his spirit lifted by the sight of his new friend ahead. He was going to finish. He was not going to let himself or anyone else down. As the route entered the forest the light faded. The track started to twist and turn and then the Germans were gone. Paul's mood slipped. The cramps returned and fear of failure haunted him once more.

It's over this time, he thought, *there's no one to save me.* He shuffled around the next bend. A couple of teenagers walked along carrying a pizza and a large bottle of Coke. They spoke no English, Paul no German. He tried miming eating but they didn't understand, so he just took their food from them. Pizza in his mouth, Coke to wash it down, life was good again. But then both legs cramped and he fell over. His calves burned and his quads knotted into strands of steel. Even though he'd stolen their food, the kids took pity and helped him to his feet.

But Paul was sure he had run out of time. He had failed. He trundled out of the forest and then the stadium came into view, but before the finish line there was still another mile to go around the village of Roth. Should he do the full course? Pride propelled him towards town and the final timing mat. He saw a figure running towards him. Who was that? Dave? No, can't be. Dave must have finished hours ago.

'Come on, Hoppy, you have eight minutes to do the last half a mile.'

How could that be?

'I'll pace you; I'll get you home, mate.'

Adrenaline flooded Paul's limbs. They were getting closer. I'm going to finish, Dad.

Paul's calf locked up and brought him to a stop.

Two race officials shouted: 'Hurry up, you'll run out of time.'

'Leave him alone,' yelled Dave.

Paul tried to breathe the pain away.

'Come on, slow and steady.'

They set off again. The lights from the stadium got brighter, he could hear the noise of the crowd. They entered the chute, the walls lined three-deep with people clapping, cheering, egging him on. Then, as the end of the tunnel opened up into the stadium, he heard the announcer call 'PAUL HOPKINS'. A giant roar. He saw his image magnified on the jumbo screen. He waved at himself. All around the railings, hands were raised in high-fives as he passed. He could see his fire service buddies, Carl and Mickey, waiting. Paul ran across the finish line and collapsed into their arms.

So, no. The answer to Phil's question was no. Despite what the storm had done to both of them, despite the cuts, the bruises, the lack of sleep, the nausea, despite how it had pummelled *Didi*, despite the broken steering, the failing battery, and despite still being close to the Canary Islands, quitting was not an option. But maybe, just as the German and Dave had helped in his time of need, and had got him across the finish line, maybe it was Paul's turn to spur his team-mate on. As Paul pulled on the oars, he looked at Phil and said: 'This boat is going to Antigua.'

'Okay, skipper, I just needed to hear you say it.'

Chapter 41

17 December 2019

2,889 miles to go

Paul rowed on. And on. As day six dawned, life as he knew it was settling into a routine. A life on the oars, interspersed with some questionable meals, some dodgy sleep and having a bowel movement in a bucket just a few feet away from Phil. This was his new life.

They'd been forced to abandon their schedule of rowing for 18 hours and sleeping for six. They'd lost ground during the storms and had been pushed south, leaving them further from Antigua than they had been two days ago. Plus, *Didi* was heavy. If they didn't row, she didn't go. They'd agreed on a new plan. Since Paul was stronger on the oars, he would row from 8am till 2pm and 4pm till 10pm (with breaks for lunch and dinner) and midnight till 5am, a total of 15 hours out of 24. Phil would row the other nine. In addition to Phil's shifts, he would operate the water maker, cook all their meals, relieve Paul while he ate, keep up on all communications and social media reports, and monitor their course and mileage. Paul was happy with this new system. He'd been prepared to row solo if Nic had agreed, so even if Phil never picked up an oar, he was Paul's ticket into the race; anything else he did on board was an absolute bonus.

Paul had expected the race to be tough. He'd even been invigorated about facing storms at sea, willing to take on Mother Nature. But so far, every battle had been a one-sided fight. If the rest of the crossing was going to be this hard Paul would have to summon every ounce of physical strength, access every source of inspiration.

Perhaps now the weather would settle into the traditional pattern they'd expected to take advantage of at this time of year – trade winds blowing from behind them. Otherwise, what was the point in missing Christmas at home with the family? Come on, god of wind or whoever you are – how about you start smiling on us like you did Columbus? We're not greedy. We've no plans to discover a new continent, just to find a small island called Antigua.

A small dark-plumaged bird with a white belly glided along the trough of the wave parallel to *Didi*, then landed on the bow. Where had it come from? Paul watched it peck at the wood as though it could eat one of the signatures. No, you don't, bird. That person paid for their ride across and we are going to get them there. Paul thought of every last person who had come to their fundraising events and dropped money in the bucket and signed their name in support. Despite these rough conditions, Paul owed it to them to finish.

As he rowed, Phil's question kept playing over in his head: should they turn back? At their first meeting, Phil had called him 'skipper', and had said there could only be one. And he was right, especially with two alpha males on board. Only one person could make final decisions. But Paul understood how hard that must be for Phil. He was a natural leader, a business owner who was used to being the decision-maker. One of the things Paul admired about Phil was his logical approach to problem-solving, his ability to assess their circumstances, to predict what the sea might do to them and what precautions they should take to protect *Didi* and themselves. No doubt Phil had given it all careful consideration before he'd opened up the idea of turning back. And what had Paul done? Shot him down. The only factor he'd considered was his own fear of returning home an embarrassed failure.

For the past four years, Paul had been laser focused. He paused now and thought about what people had been trying to tell him. Dave had said death was not an acceptable outcome, Carl had said family was more important, and the sports psychologist had questioned his motives. At the last minute Nic had asked him not to go. But all Paul had heard was *wah-wah, wah-wah, wah-wah*. He had committed to this race and nothing, not even death, was going to stop him. But now he began to ask himself if it was worth dying for after all. He'd spent years putting himself in danger, risking his life to save others. If he'd got killed firefighting, then there was a point to it. But this? Was it really worth that risk? It wouldn't matter to him, he'd be dead, but what about those he would leave behind? Nic didn't ask for this; his kids would want their dad alive. Maybe it was time to start thinking things through, to stop with his knee-jerk reactions, to tackle his bloody-mindedness.

Had he even told Phil what a great job he was doing, how much he appreciated his efforts? No. Just another mistake to add to the already long list. Paul had promised Meme he would bring her husband home alive; it was time to start assessing risks with a more critical mindset and stop making decisions based on his own stubbornness. There. See? He could be rational.

The bird flew off. It must have realised Sharpie ink had zero nutritional value. But the bird had reminded Paul of his own hunger. He'd kept little down in the last three days, and still couldn't stomach the water from the marina. The desalinated water didn't taste much better. His muscles cramped and his inner critic mocked him. He'd saved €30 by filling their jugs from that tap. Today, he would gladly remortgage his house for a sip of fresh water that didn't taste like it had been filtered through a condom at the bottom of a swamp. But if he was going to survive out here, he knew he'd have to eat and drink.

As if he'd read Paul's mind, Phil popped his head out of the cabin.

'Morning, skipper, hungry?'

'Morning, mate. Starving.' Paul didn't bother to ask Phil how he'd slept. The cabin hatch should've had a sign reading: *Sleep deprivation guaranteed for all who enter here.*

'What d'you fancy? Spaghetti bolognese?'

'God, no.'

'Okay, what about chicken tikka? You like that one.'

'Ugh.' Paul could imagine masala coming out both ends. If only their budget had allowed for better food. They'd bought many of their meals at a discount – the leftovers from last year's race. Of course, those were the ones the other teams hadn't liked.

'Here's one. How about porridge with blueberries?'

'What?' It was as if Phil had called all six of his numbers in the lottery. There was an *actual* breakfast? 'Yes, please.'

Previous rowers had told Paul about all the wonderful things he would experience at sea: the wildlife, the magnificent sunrises and searing sunsets, the night sky, the feeling of being an infinitesimal part of the grander galaxy. They'd said the effects would be life-changing. Many of them had gone on to change careers, move house, start a family. *All very fascinating*, thought Paul, but right now the only thing he cared about was how fast Phil could boil the water and rehydrate his breakfast.

He watched the steam rise, watched Phil pour the half-litre into his own meal, then tear the top off the small silver packet of porridge. As the water soaked the granules, Paul could smell the magic starting to happen. He counted his strokes. Fifty more pulls and his gourmet feast would be ready.

Phil started to eat his first and talked about their overnight speed, miles to go, and the weather forecast. Carl had confirmed the winds were settling for the next few days and their course looked good. The more Phil talked, the slower he ate. Paul wished he would hurry up. He counted 220 more strokes before Phil finally put his packet down.

'Ready, skip?'

'Yes.'

'Shall we swap?'

Paul got off the oars and displaced Phil from his perch faster than any Formula One pit stop. He picked up the packet and scooped the first spoonful. Unlike the packet meals he'd tried before, it didn't look like mush. He could smell the earthiness of the oats and, oh my, his taste buds somersaulted on the first bite.

He squelched a blueberry between his molars. Its sweet juice squirted on his tongue. He ate slowly, allowed the flavours to melt in his mouth, savoured every morsel. He felt like the kid from that old TV ad for Ready Brek, walking to school on a winter's morn cocooned in an orange glow. How could porridge bring so much cosy joy?

'How is it?'

'Good, thanks mate.' Paul couldn't share his mental ramblings lest Phil thought he had gone quite mad.

Whether it was the first time he had stomached a full meal, or sheer exhaustion, as soon as he climbed into the cabin, Paul fell asleep. He had no idea how long he had been down when he heard: 'Paul, Paul.'

Bloody hell, he thought, *could the man not just manage a couple of hours on the oars without waking me?*

'What?'

'A ship.'

A ship? Shit. Why had AIS not alerted them? Despite *Didi* pitching in the waves, Paul scrambled into his clothes and climbed out. If he was about to meet his maker, he wasn't going to be half-naked.

'Look, there.'

'Where?'

'There.'

'Oh, for God's sake, you could have saved me a fright if you'd told me it was a sailboat.'

'Sorry. Do you think it's the Talisker safety sailboat?'

233

The VHF squawked: '*Dream It, Do It, Dream It, Do It*, this is *Billy Milly, Billy Milly*, over.'

'*Billy Milly, Dream It, Do It*, comeback.'

''Allo. It's you.

This was not the safety vessel, but a sailboat heading to the Caribbean for winter. Paul and Phil had met the French crew, two men and a woman, in La Gomera before they'd set off. The sailors had been amazed to see little rowboats leaving the dock and had hoped to meet at least one of them under way.

Paul heard them switch from sail to motor so they could come close enough to dispense with the radio. She wasn't the prettiest sailboat, had seen some seas, but compared to *Didi*, she was a superyacht. As they came alongside, the captain called out: 'I make photo of you.'

Phil grabbed their camera too. For the next few minutes both boats snapped away, capturing images of each other's grinning faces. What a boost to meet other humans out here in the middle of nowhere.

'Can we give you something? Water, food?'

Oh, the thought of fresh water.

'Sorry, mate, we're not allowed to accept outside help.'

'No?'

'Race rules. If we do, we'll be disqualified.'

But temptation scratched at the back of Paul's throat. He'd just eaten his best meal, and could imagine the cold liquid sliding down like ice cream. Paul felt like Eve in the garden of Eden and the French boat was offering them an apple. Unless there was a satellite passing or a drone hovering, who would know? He couldn't make eye contact with Phil, in case he was wavering too. If Phil said yes, they might both have jumped overboard, swum to the sailboat and guzzled.

'Thanks, but no thanks.'

God, that hurt to say. What was wrong with him? He'd just passed on fresh water that would probably taste like clean mountain dew, a babbling brook, a filtered stream of loveliness.

As painful as it was, he and Phil both knew it was the right decision. *Well done us*, he thought.

'Wait, wait,' said the Frenchman. 'We must have something we can give you.'

One of the crew waved a fishing rod. It was a nice thought, but even if they were permitted to take it, they had no way of cooking fish. They watched the Frenchman attach something to the line and cast it in the direction of *Didi*. Paul could hear the line pay out as the package flew through the air and landed on their deck. Phil untied it and the Frenchman reeled in the line.

'Something of us,' the captain shouted.

Inside the parcel were three individually wrapped Ferrero Rocher chocolates, part of the French crew's limited treats for their transatlantic voyage. Their generosity brought tears to Paul's eyes. As he shouted their gratitude across the gap, he knew the French crew could never grasp how much the encounter had lifted Paul's and Phil's spirits. They already had chocolates on board, but the sight of these faces, and the sound of other human voices in the middle of the ocean, was as valuable as any treat. They were on such a high already that they agreed to save them for Christmas.

When the two vessels parted ways, they watched the sailboat ride the waves all the way until it became a dot on the horizon. Then it disappeared from view. But the joy from such a chance meeting where five strangers had connected in the middle of the vast ocean would be something Paul and Phil would cling to in the weeks to come.

Chapter 42

18 December 2019

2,848 miles to go

Phil had heard Paul struggling in the cabin for the past hour; he was trying to get to the battery. Everything that was stored on the cabin floor under the mattress, including the spare solar panel, had to be moved before Paul could access it. Phil knew it was an exhausting job in the tight space while the boat was in calm water, but near impossible in five-metre seas.

Then he thought, *but hey, here I am rowing away in those five-metre seas as though it's normal, when only a few days ago I was dying.* He was looking forward to his next phone call with Tom tomorrow. He'd be ready with a few jokes.

When Paul came out, he was soaked in sweat.

'Any luck?'

'I've topped it up. Again. Just need to get some air.'

'You're supposed to be sleeping.'

'Can't,' said Paul, scratching at the stubble now growing on his neck and chin. 'Have to put everything back before I can stretch out. Is yours itchy?'

'Not too bad. You remind me of my mum.'

'Are you calling me a girl?'

'No, but she was just like you.'

'A bearded lady, was she?'

'No, numpty. Determined.'

'How so?'

'She ran away from home at 15.'

'Why?'

'She didn't want to get stuck in Wales married to a miner, so she got on a train to London and never looked back.'

'Wow, that was young, even back then.' Paul sat in the corner near the hatch.

This is nice, Phil thought. Here they were, just chatting away like on the river. Ian was right, only a week into it and they were now nomads of the sea. 'Yeah, 1933. My dad was broken-hearted. Even though he was only 15 himself, he knew he had lost his sweetheart.'

'I assume he followed her?'

'Not at first. He played football, won several caps playing internationally for Wales.'

'Really? He must have been very good.'

'Yeah. Then he got picked up by Tottenham and moved to London.'

'Tottenham, wow. I'd love to have met him. So, he found her?'

'Yeah. By that stage she was 21 and the youngest matron in the UK, but then World War II happened. Eight years she waited.'

'Wow.'

'It was looking less likely they'd have kids, but she never gave up. And surprise, surprise, I came along in 1954.'

'They must have been thrilled.'

'You know, it wasn't until Tom was born that I began to appreciate everything they went through. Especially when they nearly lost me at birth.'

'Why? What happened?'

'When she was delivering, the cord got wrapped around my throat and I couldn't breathe.'

'That must have been very scary for them.'

'I wonder what they would have thought of all this.'

'Yeah, I often wonder what my dad would think if he could see me now.'

'Do you think he ever knew?'

'Maybe. Sometimes, when we thought he was asleep in the hospital bed, we'd be chatting about it. He told my mother once, "Our Paul is going to row the Atlantic Ocean."'

'What did she say?'

'Told him he was mistaken, that we'd been talking about a friend of mine. He didn't even think I should be off running triathlons instead of staying home with Nic, although secretly, I think he was proud.'

'Funny the perspectives different generations have on life.'

'Yes,' said Paul. 'He was an amazing man, though. Never wanted anyone to know he was in pain, kept it all to himself.'

'My father was the same but didn't have the health issues your dad had to endure.'

'Did you miss having brothers or sisters?'

'Yes and no. That's a hard one to answer,' said Phil, 'because I didn't know any different. There were about seven or eight kids my age on the avenue, but I also enjoyed playing by myself, making up fantasy worlds. I had a really happy childhood. They didn't spoil me, although my dad did shower me with gifts at Christmas and my mum would scold him for that.'

Paul laughed. 'Your mum ruled the roost?'

'Oh yeah. She was only five foot two, but she was a powerhouse, a nuclear reactor. They were sweet together, though. He would always carry her handbag, open doors for her, walk on the outside of the footpath to protect her. It's something I still do myself today. Although that seems to annoy some women.'

'I know, like somehow the chivalry our parents believed in is now seen as chauvinism.'

'It's so ingrained in me, though,' said Phil. 'My father always taught me to stand up for myself, you know. Like when I was tortured at school about my last name, and bullied for being a fat kid, he would take me aside and show me some boxing moves. Mind you, he always had a slipper ready for when I was naughty. Spanking was just the norm back then.'

'Yeah, same in my house. It was an open-handed smack when I was young. It didn't work though. I was a difficult child with a terrible temper. By the time I was a teenager and got in trouble with the police, I had graduated to the belt.' Paul wiped away the sea-spray that had landed on the back of his neck. 'Could you imagine what would happen if you hit your kid nowadays?'

'Times have changed; you'd probably be arrested.'

'I know my dad didn't want to do it, but I pushed and pushed until I left him with no option. I'm grateful for his "tough love". If he had taken the easy way out and let me run wild, who knows where I would have ended up.'

'I remember this one time I really got it,' Phil laughed. 'It was a Saturday night; they were going out and I was supposed to be doing my homework. I loved science, so I decided to run an experiment on one of the fireworks Dad had bought for Guy Fawkes.'

'Uh-oh.'

'Have you ever seen those Catherine wheels?'

'You're talking to a firefighter, mate.'

'Right. Well, I wanted to see if I could light the starting paper but snuff it out before it reached the spinning part.'

'Let me guess ...'

'I was just about to pinch it out when a spark jumped across on to the wheel and the whole thing started spinning flames.'

'What did you do?'

'Ran to the kitchen to get water. By the time I got back to the sitting room the top of the sideboard was on fire. I'll never forget the sizzling smell after I threw the bucket on it.'

'You were lucky.'

'I didn't really think so when my parents came home.'

'How old were you?'

'Ten,' said Phil.

'Wow, there's no way my dad would have trusted me by myself at that age.'

Just then the boat pitched to starboard as it slid down the back of a large wave.

'Watch out,' said Phil, grabbing tight on the oars.

Paul ducked into the cabin before the next, even bigger wave broke. Phil, however, got a thorough soaking.

'You okay, Phil?'

'Yeah. That water is still cold, let me tell you.' As he shook himself like a dog, he couldn't help thinking it was too bad that amount of H_2O hadn't been around when he was ten. It might have saved his parents' furniture and maybe, just maybe, he might have avoided the spanking his father had bestowed upon his then chubby arse.

Chapter 43

19 December 2019

2,803 miles to go

To relieve the monotony of a seemingly endless voyage, Paul had mentally broken the trip into three sections of 1,000 miles each. Each one was punctuated by specific dates or events to look forward to, like Christmas and New Year in this first section. Tuesday's encounter with *Billy Milly* had been an unexpected bonus.

Today, he was looking forward to the phone call they'd arranged with Hadrian Primary School on their final day of term before the Christmas holidays. Phil was just finishing up with Ian first.

'So, what's new with the fleet?' Paul asked.

'Almost everyone has been sick but a lot of the four-person teams are further west and missed the worst of the storms.'

'I bet Lars and his gang are out there.'

'Probably. He says most have recovered, although *Mad Giraffe* is still having a tough time.'

'Must be tough being sick and solo. At least we have each other,' said Paul.

'I don't know what I would have done without you back there.'

'You too, I'd still be trying to pee in the bottle.'

'Maybe we'll keep that to ourselves for now,' Phil laughed. 'Signal's good, are you ready?'

'Absolutely.'

Phil sat close so that Paul could continue rowing.

'It's ringing.'

Paul could see Phil was just as excited to speak with the kids as he was.

'Hello,' one of the teachers answered. 'Can you hear me?'

'Yes, yes. We hear you.'

'The whole school is in the assembly hall and we have you on speaker.'

'Hello, boys and girls,' Phil shouted down the phone, 'can you hear us? It's Paul and Phil calling from the middle of the Atlantic Ocean.'

There followed a massive spike in static.

'We might have lost them,' said Phil.

'Wait, I don't think so.' It had taken Paul a moment to process that what they were hearing was the sound of 300 children cheering all at once.

'They want to know how you're feeling,' the teacher said.

Phil looked at Paul before answering. 'We're doing great.' They'd agreed not to tell them they were having major problems. 'We were a little seasick, but feeling better now.'

'The children have a surprise for you. Can Paul hear too?'

'Yes, he can. He's on the oars but I'm sitting right beside him.'

For a moment they heard nothing more. 'Did we lose them?'

Then, 'Jingle bells, jingle bells, jingle all the way.' Paul stopped rowing. From thousands of miles away, 300 little voices were singing Christmas carols to the two men at sea. As Paul listened to every word of 'Jingle Bells', then 'Silent Night', he thought of all the times he'd sung carols at midnight mass with his mum and dad; of Nic, and how she loved to put up the decorations; of James opening his presents; of the Christmas spent sitting around his dad's bed, waiting for him to die. A tear rolled. He looked at Phil and saw he was weepy too. In the middle of a challenge that demanded all their strength and determination, the two of them sat huddled together over the satphone, pulling every ounce of joy from every melody, crying like a pair of softies.

'Happy Christmas,' the children yelled when they were done.

'Happy Christmas, boys and girls. Thank you so much. Enjoy your holidays.'

Phil pressed the red button and then they were gone. The sound of the wind filled the void. Paul could see Phil wasn't ready to talk either. He picked up the oars and rowed, every stroke helping him process all the emotions the children's voices had stirred.

Chapter 44

23 December 2019

2,643 miles to go

Monday. And it was a busy one. Phil laughed when he thought about all those questions they'd been asked like: *What will you do on the boat all day?*

Won't you get bored or sick of each other?

If they only knew. Between checking weather, navigation, calls to TWAC, making meals, making water, maintenance on the boat, creating posts and dictating them to their social media team, there was little time for anything else. Often, one of them was sleeping while the other person rowed. But they did carve out an hour for an after-dinner discussion each evening.

They'd usually pick their topic in the mornings to give them a chance to think about it during the day.

After he finished cleaning the salt off the solar panels, Phil called Meme.

'Hi, Phil, how are you doing?'

'Lovely to hear you. All good. Made 45 miles yesterday.'

'Well done. You've had almost 200 likes on your last post.'

'Great, any more donations for Tiny Lives?'

'Some. By the way, Ian mentioned you in his report.'

'Really, can you read it to us?' He came out on deck. 'Paul, have a listen, Ian gave us a mention.'

Paul shouted a greeting to Meme and then she read: 'When Paul and Phil had their initial advisory inspection, it did not go well. When they arrived in La Gomera, it was a transformation. This pair have grasped the challenge and are making every day count. They call in daily and it is always a pleasure. When they step off in Antigua, they will have achieved something very special.'

'Nice,' said Paul.

'Very cool. How's everything else with you, Meme?' said Phil, going back inside.

'Good, work's fine. I've been spending more time with Chris at his house.'

'I'm sure the apartment must feel empty at the moment.'

'Yeah. And they're not coming to inspect the cladding until March.'

'Oh, so we can't sell before then.'

'No.'

'Oh well, s'pose on the bright side, it means you don't have to move before I get back.'

'Don't worry about it for now. Anyway, isn't it almost time for you to call Tom?'

'Yes, how do you think he's doing with me away?'

'So far, so good. I'll see him on Christmas Day, will let you know.'

'Thanks. I miss you. I'll call you tomorrow.'

'It's okay, you don't have to call every day. I'm fine.'

'I know, I want to.'

After they disconnected, Phil put the phone on charge for a few minutes. He was so lucky to have Meme. She understood him, knew he loved her as his wife, but also recognised that his bond with Tom was different, his love for his son limitless.

He was anxious to hear Tom's voice.

'Hiya, my bestest pal. How are you?'

'Hi, Dad. I'm fine. I want to introduce you to Em.'

Phil greeted Emily as he did with whichever member of staff Tom introduced at the beginning of the call.

'What are you doing, Dad?'

'Still rowing across the Atlantic.'

'Right now?'

'Paul is actually rowing right now, I'm taking a break to call you.'

'What are you doing after this?'

'Making the dinner for myself and Paul.'

'What will you eat?'

'Oh, I don't know, maybe chicken tonight.'

'Chicken?'

'Chicken.'

'What did you make yesterday?'

'Might have been chicken too.'

Tom laughed. 'Chicken,' he repeated, then on to the next question. 'Have you spoken to my brothers?'

'Yes, I talked to them yesterday.'

'What did you see today?'

'We saw three birds circling the boat.'

'Have you spoken with Mum?'

'Yes, I've talked with your mum.'

'What are you doing tomorrow?'

'Tomorrow we are going to row some more.'

'Okay.'

'How about you, Tom, what have you been up to? Do you have a joke for me today?'

'What do you call a cow with no legs?'

'I don't know Tom, what?'

'Ground beef.'

'Good one. I've got one for you. What do you call a bee that can't make up its mind?'

'I don't know.'

'A maybe.'

Tom's laugh infused Phil's heart with love. 'I enjoyed chatting with you today, Tom.'

'Me too.'

'I'm looking forward to talking to you again. When will that be, Tom?'

'Thursday.'

'Yes.' Phil didn't mention he'd call on Wednesday for Christmas too; he didn't want to confuse him. 'What time on Thursday?'

'Four o'clock.'

'Right. Thursday at four. I love you.'

'I love you too, Dad.'

Phil disconnected and sat for a moment. To anyone listening, their chats might sound superficial and Tom's focus scattered, but for Phil their conversations were as deep as the ocean under him. He loved to hear Tom's voice, the words he chose, his jokes, the way he laughed. Everything about Tom's personality brought him joy. Despite how full Phil's days were, without Tom his life would be empty. Tom was the reason he kept living, kept striving to be everything he could be for him. Tom's grandma, Debbie's mother, once said to them: 'God gave you Tom because He knew you would be the very best parents to take care of him.'

Simple but profound. And Phil had taken those words to heart. In caring for his disabled child, he'd come to understand that meaning in life could only come through connection with others. Tom brought joy and laughter to those he met. His innocent approach to life helped those jaded by it, gave the disillusioned a reason to be grateful.

His disabilities forced him to request help from those with no physical worries. And in receiving and accepting their help, Tom gave them the gift of caring and a sense of contribution and connection. It taught Phil to cherish Tom's role in society, have patience with his limitations, but above all to give him love and more love.

It made Phil's guilt for what he had done years ago even more unbearable.

On an ordinary Saturday afternoon, Phil had been assisting six-year-old Tom with his physiotherapy, encouraging him to walk to prevent his legs from becoming permanently crossed, a potential side effect of cerebral palsy. He was used to the back-breaking hours he spent supporting Tom under his arms and walking him. On this day, his son was struggling, and Phil, who so desperately wanted the best for him, lost his temper. He shouted at Tom and smacked his legs. Tom didn't cry, but Phil saw the look on his face. It was as if he'd said: I am doing my best, Dad, why did you do that to me? Phil was so ashamed he never told anyone, not even Debbie.

Even now, lying in the cabin, the burden of guilt he'd carried for so many years overwhelmed him and the tears fell. Why had he lashed out at his beautiful son while his real frustration had been with God? Tom was an innocent being, born into a compromised body over which he had little control. No matter how many adversities Phil had to face in his own life, nothing compared to the hardship Tom dealt with every day. Not only did Tom cope with his physical challenges, he did so without blame. Instead, he carried himself through life by bringing joy and laughter to those he met, which made Phil feel even more guilty for hitting him. He could never forgive himself. He'd crossed the line that day from light to dark, down into the horrors with the worst of humanity. In his mind, his action was as abhorrent as any atrocity inflicted by the worst tyrants the world has ever seen. He'd broken his vow to love and cherish his son and had spent every day since trying to make it up to God and Tom. But it would never be enough. Phil's only consolation was knowing that on the day he would meet his maker, he would seek forgiveness.

He wiped his tears with the heel of his hand. He had to pull himself together, get out on deck and make their evening meal.

'How was Tom?' Paul asked.

'Good. He was in good form.'

'Any new jokes tonight?'

'Em …' Phil couldn't remember, then made one up. 'Yeah. What do you call a funny mountain?'

'Don't know.'

'Hilarious.'

Paul chuckled. 'He's hilarious alright.'

After their meal and evening discussion, this time about animal cruelty, Paul retired to the cabin and Phil got back on the oars. The sun was down but the last light of Monday and Phil's guilt lingered on. And as if that shame wasn't enough company, the bird landed on the bow, and glared at him. Another mistake from his past had come to haunt him.

As an only child, Phil mostly played by himself. For his twelfth birthday, he'd been given an air rifle. In the garden, he shot at targets. One day, though, he wandered into the nearby woods. Springtime buds appeared on many trees, and birdsong filled the forest. In front of him, a blackbird sat on a low branch, its head cocked. Without thinking, Phil aimed and fired. The bird fell from the tree and hit the ground with a thump. Phil had stood there, transfixed. What had he done? He started crying before his feet moved toward the bird. It was lying on its side, one eye looking at Phil, the other against the dirt. Blood oozed from the hole the pellet had created. Phil thought he would be sick. How could he have harmed such an innocent thing? As disgusted as he was, he couldn't leave it in pain. He shot it again, but the bird wouldn't die. Twice more he had to aim his rifle. Finally, the bird stopped moving. Phil ran home and never picked up a gun again.

As the sky turned dark, and Phil rowed on, he kept asking himself why his two most shameful moments plagued him tonight. What was the message? What was he supposed to learn?

He thought about Tom and all the challenges he'd undertaken in his honour, about how much it made his son smile. But did it? Or was that just when he did events with Tom, like the Great North Run? Consistency was a comfort blanket in Tom's life. How did Tom really feel when his routine was interrupted by his father's absence? On previous trips, Phil had been gone for a couple of weeks, but never months. Was this challenge of facing the mighty Atlantic an act of bravery or, having deserted Tom and the family, simply selfish?

If he was honest with himself, yes it was selfish, but not in the way people thought. Every challenge, not just the last five, every gym workout, every run, swim, bike ride, had been a way to push himself into pain. It was the closest thing he could do to punishing himself on Earth while he waited for judgement day.

As he rowed, and looked out over the water, Phil saw a room with a padlocked door, with bars across it. He's afraid to open that door because he knows behind it, locked inside a box, is the bottle filled with his love for Tom. It's a love so deep, so wide, that, even though he knows he will never hurt another innocent being, if anyone, be they man, woman or child, were to try to harm Tom, he would unleash that love and kill to protect his son.

Another image floated before him – he is a warrior, the apocalypse is here, he picks up his son, cradles him and carries him beyond this world, into eternity together.

And then, he heard the wind whisper: *Perhaps it's the love that's selfish.*

Phil stopped rowing, rocked himself with the swell. Was that it? Had his guilt, his bargain with God, and his drive to protect his grown son – seeing him three or four times a week, calling him twice a day, substituting for his carers, which denied him the opportunity for more social interaction – caused Tom to be emotionally dependent on his father? Was he still treating his son as a boy and not encouraging him to be the man he was destined to become?

Was this the Atlantic's lesson?

Chapter 45

24 December 2019

2,600 miles to go

It seemed like a short three hours since Paul left the oars at 5am. Could it be he'd actually slept? Through the hatch he could see blue sky. Maybe they were in for easier weather at last. He checked the phone. There were several texts in Spanish. As the only words of the language he knew were *cerveza, por favor* and *gracias,* none of which seemed in evidence here, he had no idea what the texts meant, though he did spot a few words that were the same in English, like *radio.* Maybe Phil would have a better chance of translating. Meanwhile, he checked the mileage, their longitude and latitude, and was about to go on deck when he noticed the VHF was on channel 15. It must have got knocked off 16 when they'd been crashing about during the storms. He set it back to the emergency hailing channel and climbed out. What a glorious morning it was. Not a cloud in the sky, the sea seemed settled and it actually felt warm for a change. Phil too seemed in better spirits than yesterday.

'Hi, how was your shift?'

'Wonderful, skip. I'm thinking it's a great day for a swim under the boat.'

Paul nodded. The water looked clear and enticing. *Didi* had been sitting still in the harbour in La Gomera for a week and they'd been another 12 days at sea. Even though she had antifouling paint applied to her hull beneath the water line, it was still possible for molluscs and algae to cling to her bottom and slow them down. If the paint didn't slough off and take the growth with it, they would need to scrape it clean by hand. It would be no bother to Phil; he was an excellent swimmer. Paul had become more competent through competing in triathlons, but there was something about jumping off an almost perfectly good boat in the middle of the Atlantic that gave him pause for thought.

He wondered about the creatures of the deep. There was at least one mile of ocean underneath them and no rescue boats on the horizon.

'This may be the calmest day we get,' said Phil.

'Let's hope there are more like this, but you're right, we need to check.'

'I wonder if anyone has ever worked out a formula to calculate the negative effect,' Phil said.

'How do you mean?'

'Like if half an inch of algal growth equals X decrease in speed which equals Y number of extra strokes we'd need to row to get across.'

Too complicated for Paul's brain before breakfast. While he ate his food, he tried to push the scene from *Jaws* from his thoughts. He wished he had never seen that moment when the shark's open mouth lurched out of the screen and scared him senseless. He felt that Great White could have swallowed his 11-year-old body whole. If he'd been a parent back then, he would never have allowed his kids to watch it. How many people were afraid to swim in the sea because of one damn film?

'Would you like me to go first, skipper?'

'Sure.'

Paul cleared the breakfast bowls while Phil gathered the gear.

'Don't forget the most important piece.'

'Not a chance,' said Phil, waving the small purple plastic box. He disconnected his short tether and attached one end of the long floating swim line to his harness and the other to the D-ring on the deck. That would keep him attached to the boat while he was in the water. Paul unfurled and secured the rope ladder over the side.

'All set?'

Phil pulled the goggles over his eyes and stood there a moment.

'Ready.'

Splash. Paul watched the spread of white bubbles. It seemed like forever before Phil's head broke the surface.

'That's not warm,' he said, gasping to catch his breath.

Lovely, thought Paul, *deep ocean, sharks, and cold water. What could be better?*

'Okay, here goes.' Phil adjusted his goggles and swam under the boat. Paul had to count to 11 before Phil re-emerged and dropped the scraper over the gunwale.

'It's spotless.'

'Really? That's great.'

'And now for the best part.' Phil reached up.

'Here you go mate.' Paul opened the purple box and handed him the marine soap.

Phil scrubbed his head, face, armpits and all the other bits, delighted with how the soap could foam in salt water.

'Not the warmest bath I've ever had, but that feels so much better than baby wipes.' He passed back the soap. 'Now for the fun and games.'

Paul moved to the opposite side to balance the boat while Phil began the tricky task of trying to climb up the rope ladder. It swayed from side to side as the waves hit the hull. Phil grasped the gunwale near the oar gate. 'Damn. It's curling under the boat, can't get leverage.'

'Try kicking backwards.'

'I am, skip, I am. The webbing is cutting into my feet.'

253

Paul transferred his weight further away so Phil could swing his legs out. In one giant move Phil landed on deck like a flopping fish. He rolled on to his back.

'Well done, mate.'

'Thanks. I'm amazed at how clean the bottom is, not a thing on her.'

'Same can't be said for you. You look like a Smurf.'

The front of Phil's legs and belly were bright blue.

Phil laughed. 'Looks like the ablative paint is ablating.'

'Want to get in and wash again?'

'I'll pass, thanks. Your turn.'

Paul knew he didn't need to go in. Phil had checked the hull and *Didi* was clean. Cleaning himself would be nice, even if the effect would be temporary; however, he wanted to be able to say he swam in the Atlantic over 5,000 feet out of his depth.

He harnessed up and jumped over. *Whoa.* Phil had not been joking, the cold water made his skin tingle. But once he surfaced and settled his breathing, he took a moment to languish. He stretched his arms and legs out and floated like a starfish, his body rising and falling with the swells. He thought of his mother and his birth; he was on his way out into the world, testing the waters, but still attached by the umbilical cord. And his first view of the world was blue: the sky, the ocean, the bottom of the boat. *How cool is this?* He rolled and began to scrub his body, clearing away all the crud and sins of his youth. He called out to his father: 'Look, Dad, I'm taking a bath in the middle of the ocean on Christmas Eve.'

Would his father be proud?

'Don't mean to rush you, skip, but you might want to get in now.'

'What? What?'

'I saw something in the water.'

Paul had no idea how fast or ungainly he was scrambling back up the ladder, but he was on board before Phil had finished his sentence.

'What is it?'

'Not sure. Looked like a fin.'

'Where?'

'A little way off port.'

Paul unclipped himself from the swim line, reconnected his tether to the boat and peered in the direction Phil was pointing. 'Oh, I see it.'

'Dun-dun, dun-dun.' Phil hummed that scary theme.

'Stop,' said Paul. 'Oh God, there's more. Should we get in the cabin?'

'Wait, look. Oh my God,' said Phil. 'Dolphins.'

'Wow.'

Paul watched the pod switch direction and swim towards them. There must have been 20, no, 30 of them. Like synchronised swimmers, their dorsal fins broke the surface one after the other as though they were one continuous wave moving through the water. They kept coming, now only ten metres away.

When the leaders reached the boat they split, some crossing in front of the bow, some the stern. Two of them passed underneath. Shafts of sunlight penetrated the clear water and bounced off their backs. As they emerged on the far side and came up for air, drops of water cascaded down their sleek-looking skin like a waterfall of diamonds.

Mesmerised, Paul and Phil had lost all vocabulary other than *wow*.

Further off, a dozen or so seemed to be playing leap-frog, coming halfway out of the water as though trying to get a better look at *Didi*. And then, like something out of a movie, one of them jumped clean out of the water and somersaulted, revealing a spotted belly. He hit the water on his back, sending a fountain of spray into the air.

'Oh my God, did you see that?'

'Wow.'

Two more leaps, each one more spectacular than the last. Then, as if the leader had set off a sonar command, they all regrouped, and headed back in the direction they'd been travelling.

Both men sat, the oars still stowed, and watched these beautiful creatures fly through the water. Within a minute, they had sped out of sight. The ocean was empty once again.

'That was something,' said Phil.

'Amazing,' said Paul, his mouth still open. 'What a way to celebrate Christmas Eve. I can't wait to … Oh, no.'

'What?'

'We forgot to get the camera.'

Their proposed dinner conversation – ideas to improve transport strategies for the UK – was completely abandoned. All they wanted to do was talk about the dolphins. It had been a glorious day on the water, the sky was blue, with only the occasional white puffy cloud. Nothing like an English Christmas Eve at all.

'What an amazing experience,' said Phil.

'Fabulous to see them in the wild like that,' said Paul.

'There were so many. Can't believe we didn't get a photo for the post.'

'Yeah, but I was thinking, maybe it was better. If we'd been messing about with a camera we might have missed them jumping. This way we got to be present and see it all.'

'You're right.'

'You know what they say about Facebook and Instagram – half the people spend their day documenting their lives instead of living them,' said Paul.

'True enough. You can't say we're not living ours.' Phil took the Jetboil out of the gimbal and packed it away. 'Look at this sky, Paul. Why don't you take a break? I have a feeling tonight might be our first real sunset.'

'Why not?'

The pair of them turned and sat facing the bow. The sun was still a circle of light but deepening in colour with every passing minute. As it started to sink, yellow became gold, then gold turned to orange. The ocean blue transitioned into the indigo of the sky, making it hard to tell where one ended and the other began. A flying fish leaped out of the water as if to watch the wonder too. And when the sun kissed the edge of the world, it spilled red rubies on the tops of the waves. In its final farewell, right before it disappeared, it flung an emerald flash into their eyes. Surrounded by a 360° panorama of colour, of pinks and tangerines, aqua blues and violet, unlike anything they'd ever seen from land, it felt as if they, and their little wooden boat, had rowed right inside the sunset.

Chapter 46

25 December 2019

2,552 miles to go

At 7.45am on their thirteenth day at sea, Paul woke with one thing on his mind — Nic. She would struggle today. Christmas, her favourite day of the year. Even though they'd talked almost every night while he was in La Gomera, she'd still been upset with him.

He'd written her a new letter to tell her how sad he was about the coldness that had come between them and how deeply he loved her. This time the words flowed, filling page after page — how he adored her smile, the way she made him feel, what a wonderful mother she was, and how he would make it all up to her when he came home. He couldn't wait to call her and hear the joy in her voice after she opened the Christmas card and the —

'Fuck me.'

He felt a familiar, sharp pain in his right foot. He pulled it out of the sleeping bag to take a look. If Rudolph had gone on strike, Paul could have guided Santa's sleigh with his severely swollen big red toe. Just what he needed — gout on the high seas. The thought of having to cram his foot into his shoe filled him with dread, and he'd have no luck borrowing a larger one from Phil, as they were both the same size. Rowing barefoot was not an option; the footplate and strap would shred his skin. Nothing for it but to loosen the laces, remove the insole and offer his foot up to the trainer. The boat rolled and his foot crashed into the hull.

'Bastard.'

The pain was unbearable. *Come on, Paul, man up and put on your damn shoe.* He lined his foot up again, red skin against the black trainer, pushed his toes in and stopped to breathe. Nearly there; he just needed to slip a finger into the heel to horn his foot in the rest of the way. The boat continued to pitch. *Oh, come on ocean, give me a break.* Had the gout been on his left foot he would not have had to battle the reduced flexibility of a replaced knee. He manoeuvred on to his side and torqued himself into position to reach the heel. In what seemed like a game of solo Twister he made one final almighty attempt and shoved his ankle in. His scream reached Phil out on deck.

'You okay in there?'

'Yes. Just got banged up a bit.'

There was no point in telling Phil – what could he do about it anyway? Paul tied his lace as loosely as possible and climbed out of the cabin. Phil vacated the oars; Paul took the seat. He slid his feet under the straps and waited for Phil to tighten them.

'How's that?'

'That's good.'

But that was the left foot. Paul waited for the pain he knew was coming. It shot from a five to a nine. So did his panting.

'Thanks, mate, I'm in.'

Bending at the knees, he reached forward and placed the oars in the water behind him, the first part of the stroke. The pain eased a fraction, but he knew what was coming. When he pushed through his legs and pulled, the pain shot right back up to a nine. He would have loved to call it a ten but that would leave him nowhere to go.

Phil continued the handover: 'What's our long and lat, skip?'

'Sorry, mate, I forgot to check.'

'No bother. I'll get it.'

As the minutes wore on, the only thing that subsided for Paul was his positivity. As if this wasn't going to be a long, tough day already. But he couldn't share it, didn't want to bring Phil down. He wanted him to get his calls made, to enjoy time with his family.

Paul had to distract himself. He focused on his first thoughts upon waking – calling Nic. Was that only 20 minutes ago? During these past two weeks, he'd had plenty of time to think, to realise how he'd completely missed the point. For four years Nic had put her life on hold to support his dream, everything they did had been about getting him to the starting line. Regardless of whether he wanted to write the letter, or if it was ever even read, it had been important to Nic so it should have been important to him too. He hoped the second letter would make amends for his failings.

After Phil made some of his calls, they switched. Paul dialled her number.

'Hello.'

'Hi, Nic, it's me. How are you? Happy Christmas. How's the weather? Did you like the card? Did you like the letter?' Paul was so excited he hardly took a breath.

'What card? What letter?'

'What do you mean what letter? I put it in the Christmas card. I posted it the morning the race started.' He was in full panic mode. 'I was nearly late for the briefing. I sent one to you and one to James.'

'A letter arrived for James. Nothing for me.'

Paul could hear her voice break. Her voice never broke.

'It's Christmas and I have nothing from you.'

'I posted them together, Nic, you must have it. Why would I send one to James and nothing to you? Please Nic, you've got to believe me.'

'No card, no letter, no present, no nothing.'

'You told me not to buy you anything. You saw how busy I was, how hard I was working to get everything done in time, you told me not to bother.'

Paul tried to rein his frustration in. Why did women do that? Tell you one thing but mean another. How was he supposed to know she really wanted him to buy her a gift? But the emotion in her voice told him he had made a mistake. A big one. Never before had he wanted to forget about the boat. But now all he wanted was to be at home, face to face with Nic to make amends. But he couldn't. He was stuck in the middle of the Atlantic, his foot was screaming and his chest was tight. She was in a bad place and he had put her there. Bottom of his list of priorities. How could he have been so selfish?

Then, just when he thought he couldn't feel any worse, she said: 'I can't cope. I can't cope with this any more.'

'Nic, I'm sorry—'

'I've had enough, Paul. It's over for me. Please don't ring again.'

The phone went dead.

Phil saw Paul slump over.

'You okay, skipper?'

Nothing.

'Paul?'

As much as Phil hadn't wanted to listen it was impossible not to overhear Paul's side of the conversation. 'Everything okay?'

Paul emerged from the cabin. 'Why don't you take a break, make the rest of your calls.'

'Are you sure?' said Phil. 'I can wait.'

'No, it's fine, I could use a spell on the oars. Phone's on charge for you.'

Whatever Paul was dealing with, Phil knew he wasn't ready to talk.

'Okay, thanks.'

Phil checked the time; Tom should be at his mother's now. He moved to the cabin and dialled. Rod answered.

'Hey, Dad, how are you?'

'Hi, Rod, you're at your mum's too? How lovely.'

'Yeah, we're all here, let me put you on speaker.'

'Hi, Dad, hi, Phil, hello, Merry Christmas,' everyone shouted at once. Phil could make out Meme's and Debbie's voices, as well as Rod's partner, and Alex and his partner. His entire inner circle were all there together – without him.

'Happy Christmas, everyone.'

'Glad to hear you didn't get arrested,' Meme said.

'What?'

'Apparently, another boat tried to hail you and you didn't answer.'

'Oh, yeah. The VHF got a knock and we weren't monitoring channel 16 for a while.'

'Well, from what I understand they thought you were an illegal migrant vessel because you were moving so slowly. They called it in to a friend in the navy. Apparently, they were about to send a fast boat out to board you.'

'What? That's crazy.'

'Supposedly several texts came into your TWAC account. Ian had to convince the coastguard that you were rowing.'

'Well, I think if we were human trafficking, we'd pick a boat with an engine. Too funny though. Wait till I tell Paul.'

'Did you find the cards?'

'Cards?'

'Check in the bag with the wet rations?'

'Okay, thanks. Is Tom there?'

'He's here, Dad,' Rod answered, 'he can hear you.'

Between the wind noise and the slight static, Phil couldn't quite make out the conversation going on in the background.

Rod said: 'Tom, do you want to tell Dad a joke?'

When he didn't hear Tom speak, Phil said: 'I've got one for you, Tom. Why did Beethoven get rid of his chickens? …

Because all they said was "Bach, Bach, Bach."' And there it was, Phil finally heard Tom laugh.

'Hang on, Dad, he does want to tell you one.'

'Dad?'

'Hiya, my bestest pal.'

'Where do tough chickens come from?'

'I don't know, Tom, where do tough chickens come from?'

'Hard-boiled eggs.'

Phil was relieved to hear Tom engage with him at last. He'd been nervous about today. How would his family feel about his absence, especially Tom? It was his first time being away from him on Christmas Day, and oh, how he missed him. But he was surprised that hearing them all enjoying themselves together brought him more joy than sadness.

The laughter that reached Paul on deck could not penetrate his despair. The pain in his foot had been swallowed by the gaping hole in his heart. What was he going to do? How was he going to get through the next few hours, days, weeks? Loneliness swamped him. Questions picked at his brain like a woodpecker destroying a tree. Was his marriage over? How would he survive without Nic? Where would he live? What about James? Would they have to sell the house so that they could both afford somewhere? Or maybe it would be better to let her keep it. He'd have to find some cheap bachelor pad because he'd spent his retirement package clearing the mortgage, paying off debts, financing the return shipping for *Didi*, and buying Nic a car – the yellow Citroën DS3 she'd always wanted. The lump sum was gone.

He hadn't worried about it because they still had her wages and his monthly pension. But now? Hell of an age to have to start over. His life was on a board of snakes and ladders and as much as he had climbed and as far as he had reached, he had just slid down the biggest snake of all. Right back to the beginning. A part-time job wouldn't do it, he would have to start full time from scratch, presuming he could find an employer who would hire a 55-year-old.

He could hear Phil wrapping up his call, promising his family that they'd all be together next Christmas. Phil came out and related the story about the coastguard.

'We need to be more careful,' said Paul. 'Make sure you check all the switches and radio frequency when you're in there, especially when you get thrown about.'

'Sure. By the way, the battery is down to 30 per cent again. It's not holding a charge even with all that sun yesterday.'

'For fuck's sake. Sorry.'

'Everything okay, skip?'

For the morale of the boat, Paul knew he should probably talk to him, explain that he thought his marriage had just died. But then if he did, if he said it out loud, it would be true.

'It's fine, mate, Nic's just a bit lonely on Christmas.'

'Sorry, Paul, hopefully she'll feel better in a few days.'

'Maybe.'

After lunch, Paul spoke to his mum, but making small talk was so unbearable that he chose to text the rest of his family instead. As Phil called his friends, Paul shouted 'Happy Christmas' to whomever. He posed for the photos Phil would email for the Facebook post wearing a Santa hat and a fake smile. In between his shifts, he tried to relieve the pain in his foot by propping it up or immersing it in a bucket of seawater, anything to relieve the swelling. If living inside the washing machine of the cabin during the storm had been the longest night of his life, rowing with gout and a broken heart was the longest day. He replayed Nic's words over and over. No volume of music in his earbuds could drown them out. She was done.

What if she moved on? He remembered the pain of seeing his two eldest boys living under another man's roof when Diane had remarried. God, he couldn't think about that. Life without Nic was one thing, but seeing her with someone else? And then that bastard would move into his house, sleep in his bed?

He couldn't go on like this. With 50 or maybe 60 days left to row, these thoughts would destroy his mind before the ocean would break his body.

'She said they're in here,' said Phil.

'Sorry?' Paul was so wound up in his thoughts he'd almost forgotten Phil was on the boat.

'Time to celebrate,' said Phil, who was opening one of the lockers where they'd stashed the wet rations.

'We can't eat those.'

'No,' said Phil, still rummaging. 'Here they are.' He pulled out a plastic bag of cards.

'Where did those come from?'

'Meme said she packed them as a surprise. Let's have a read.'

Paul set the oars in the gate and took the first one. On the cover were two stick figures, a little boat and a smiling sun wearing a Santa hat.

'Oh my.'

Phil passed him another. This one had a boat with a mast, complete with Christmas tree branches filled with ornaments instead of sails.

'How about some chocolate?'

'Totally forgot, thanks, mate.'

And so, this was their Christmas celebration, the two of them nibbling the Ferrero Rocher they'd saved since their happy encounter with the sailboat *Billy Milly* and reading all the handmade Christmas cards the children of Hadrian Primary School had drawn for them.

Chapter 47

26 December 2019

2,513 miles to go

On Boxing Day, as soon as Paul woke up, the tennis match of pain began again. When he got his mind off his foot, the ache in his chest took over. He thought he had envisioned every highlight and every hardship he would face at sea. What if they capsized or one of them fell overboard, could they deploy the life raft in time? All the big stuff, the kind of events that would cost him his life, never thinking the biggest cost would be to his heart. He couldn't believe how one phone call had turned him inside out. He tossed off the sleeping bag and started getting dressed.

Nic, his beautiful Nic.

He thought about the first time he saw her. He'd just broken up with his live-in girlfriend. Having been married and divorced twice already, he'd been reluctant to make another commitment until he was sure. He still believed there was a woman out there that he wanted to grow old with, and who wanted to grow old with him.

He'd know her when he saw her, but for now he was sworn off women and there was nothing better to take his mind off his life than going on a good old-fashioned stag weekend for his mate, Tony. They'd driven up from Nottingham for the Newcastle races, and were staying in the seaside town of Whitley Bay.

After a heavy session on Friday night, and miserable losses on the horses, they headed out for a Saturday night on the town. The weather was good, the pubs lively, and the whole place had a friendly atmosphere. Paul spied a beautiful woman walking past him on her way to the bar. He wasn't sure what attracted him, whether it was her pretty face, her dark hair, or that she was singing along with the music. Maybe it was that she just seemed so happy.

'You look like you are having a good time.' *God, what kind of a line was that?*

'Yeah, I love 80s music. You're not from here, are you?'

'Visiting.'

The barman put two girly drinks in front of her. Paul was pleased she wasn't on a date.

'You're here with a friend?'

She pointed at a girl on the dance floor who was gyrating next to a man who should probably already have been at home sleeping it off.

'I'm going to drop this round down to my mates,' said Paul. 'Okay if I come over after that?'

'Yeah, we're over there.'

Paul carried the three pints back to the lads. 'I'll be back,' he said.

'Thought you were staying away from the ladies?'

'I am.'

He had intended to. But Paul knew he had to talk to this woman who seemed to have such a zest for life. And he'd better be quick before her friend finished propping up the legless bloke.

'So, I'm Paul, by the way.'

'Nicola, but my friends call me Nic.'

'Nic, lovely name.'

As soon as they started chatting, Paul realised how easy it was, nothing awkward, no fumbling for great lines, just an everyday conversation about what brought him to Newcastle and how she had grown up here. They danced, chatted, danced some more. It felt natural. When the pub closed, the lads drifted off, but he didn't want the night to end. Her friend's date announced that the bar at his hotel was still open. Knowing he had to drive the minibus back to Nottingham tomorrow, or rather later today, Paul had already stopped drinking earlier and had been on water for the last hour or two. This seemed to both surprise and please Nic. He tagged along, happy to be able to continue talking with her.

'So, were you ever married?' he asked.

'Yes, you?'

'Twice.'

'Me too,' said Nic.

'Really?'

'I was too young the first time, I thought the second time would work, but no.'

'Me too,' said Paul, fascinated.

'There was something missing,' she said. 'I want to feel special.'

'I know exactly what you mean.'

'And I want a partner to feel the same way.'

It was late. Reluctantly he put her and her friend in a taxi and made his way back to his digs, but not before they'd exchanged phone numbers. He needed sleep, but lay awake thinking about her.

How mad was it that the minute he was not looking for anyone he might have found the one?

In the past, he would have agonised over when he should contact a woman after that first meeting – too soon, the woman would think he was desperate, leave it too long and she'd think he didn't care. Balls to the dating rules. With Nic, he didn't want to play any games. After breakfast, when the lads were loading the bus, he snuck away to text her.

Good morning, I really enjoyed meeting you last night. Would love to see you again.

Apparently, she wasn't caught up in the rules either because within seconds she replied: *Me too, safe home. Ring me later. Would be lovely to chat some more.*

'Hey, Hoppy, are we going home this century?'

'Would you look at him, all dopey.'

'So much for his woman-free streak.'

'Are you going to call her?'

Paul couldn't wait to drop off the lads and the minibus so he could get home and phone her, but he wasn't about to tell them a thing.

He talked with Nic every night that week. For hours. They would pick up the conversation where they'd left it. She invited him to come back and visit the following weekend. As far as his mates were concerned, he was going walking by himself in the Lake District, a quiet time to sort himself out, and it was highly unlikely he would get a phone signal up there.

He felt like a teenager again, couldn't wait till Friday, and spent most of the week thinking about a girl. When he got to Newcastle, he and Nic fell into a rhythm as though they'd been lifelong lovers. Having grown up in the landlocked town of Nottingham, his only trips to the seaside had been on the annual family holiday. It made walking the coast with Nic even more special. He would take her hand and stroll along in the marine breeze. When they'd stop or sit on a bench, he found himself looking out into the North Sea and wondering what was out there past the horizon. All too soon it would be Sunday night and he would once again long for Friday.

The first weekend she came down to Nottingham, she wasn't bothered by having to bring her own cup, plate and bowl to his bachelor pad, and that endeared her to him even more. He vowed he would have it sorted by her next visit. That thought caught him sideways. Her next visit. He was so sure there would be one, and he wanted there to be one, and one after that. Would he spoil it if he came on too strong? Why were matters of the heart so difficult?

One Saturday night, when they were lying in bed together in the afterglow, she looked at him and whispered: 'I love you.'

Paul was surprised, shocked, thrilled, scared, excited, happy and couldn't help responding in kind: 'I love you too.'

He lay inside that bubble of joy, convinced they'd found the piece that had been missing for both of them in previous relationships.

Once the words had been spoken it was only a matter of weeks before it was time to meet the parents. Nic warned him to enjoy her mum's cooking no matter what and to be understanding with her dad, who suffered from Alzheimer's. Just like his own dad, hers loved to talk about horse racing and football, so Paul was off to a good start with him. Nic would sit on the arm of her dad's chair just to be near him, and always made sure he had whatever he needed.

While the weekdays seemed long and the weekends too short, Paul hardly noticed the months stacking up. They'd been dating five months when she gave him a surprise.

'I'm pregnant.'

'Really? That is amazing.'

'Yeah, shows you what doctors know.'

Paul thought about his sons, Sean and Jamie, who were already 16 and 14. How would they feel about a younger sibling? And Diane, how would she feel if he left Nottingham? But Paul knew Nic was the woman he had longed for and now she was carrying his child. He had to be with her. And so, the whirlwind continued. Within the year, he moved to Newcastle and started a new job.

Nic was the shoulder every one of her friends leaned on when times were tough. Paul loved her caring heart. But it broke his to see her hurting when her father's mind continued to deteriorate and her mother made the decision to put him in a care home. Even though James was two at the time, Nic still found time to visit him every day. Watching her mourn her dad slipping away was painful. All he could do was be there for her.

Christmas, Paul learned, was a special time for Nic and her family. During her childhood, no matter how tight things were for her parents, she would come downstairs on Christmas morning and delight in the sofa full of presents for her and her brother and sister. The first year they were together, Paul was surprised to see the tree go up the first weekend in December and down on the 27th. Such different traditions compared to the 12 days of Christmas his family celebrated, but he was happy to adopt hers. She lavished gifts on James and loved to watch him open them one by one. Paul received more presents from her than he could ever remember as a child. He would unwrap a gift from Nic and instantly cherish something he hadn't even known he always wanted. She wouldn't open a single one of hers until everyone else had opened theirs. She didn't need him to give her anything flash or expensive but she liked it when it appeared he had put some thought into it. The wrapping paper had to be just right, the card had to have nice words and he had to write some of his own. They were small things but he knew they all added up to the joy he could give her.

So why couldn't he have remembered that sooner? Paul chastised himself as he tied his laces. Why couldn't he have bought a little something, wrapped it in pretty paper, hid it in the house and called her on Christmas to tell her where to find it? Instead, he had kicked her in the teeth from a thousand miles away. Nic was a strong woman. To have heard her voice breaking had been a shock; to know he had been the cause, devastating. He had taken her love for granted. What a fool.

He longed to be with her, to show her how much he loved her. But he couldn't fix it from here. He had to push through. He had to row this boat across that finish line, then fly home to England and try to win her back.

271

Then came a thought from the abyss. She'd be alone for at least another two months; would she even *want* to wait for him? Would she ask him to let her go so she could have that partner who made her feel special, a marriage where the man would at least sometimes put her needs above his own? But Paul wanted to be that man, he could be that man — if only she would give him a chance to prove it.

He still had a few minutes before his shift. He needed to talk to someone, someone who would be pleased to hear his voice, someone happy who could give him a boost and ease his despair.

Zoe. Who better? He dialled; it rang. Great. It continued to ring. *Come on, Zoe, please pick up.*

'Hi, this is Zoe, leave a message.' Paul didn't want to talk to a bloody machine.

Dave. Dave Linsley from the fire station, he was a good mate and had followed the challenge every step of the way. He would cheer Paul up. Again, the phone rang and rang. Another machine. No, no, no. Paul needed human contact. He needed warmth and joy to get him through the day, the next hour, the next few minutes.

Carl? Carl had already done so much for them in the first ten days, he hated to bother him during his family time on Christmas, but … Once more Paul heard a phone ringing, only this time: 'Hi, mate, how are you? It's great to hear from you.'

Paul heard the genuine joy in Carl's voice and let it course through his veins like a drug.

'Katrina, Poppy, come here,' Carl called out. 'It's Hops, he's on the phone.'

'Hi, Hoppy,' said Katrina's bubbly voice in the background. 'We are so proud of you.'

'Thank you.'

'Just keep doing what you're doing and you'll make it.'

'Thank you so much.'

Then young Poppy: 'You are amazing, we love you.'

Paul soaked up the happy, embraced their pride in him, cherished their love. 'I just wanted to say "Happy Christmas" to you all.'

'Okay, mate, be safe.'

'I will Carl, thank you for everything.'

Paul pressed the red button. He allowed the tears to flow freely. Life would be very difficult without Nic, but with the help of friends, somehow, he would get through it. And dealing with gout would take his mind off it for now. He opened the hatch and clipped himself to the jacklines. Phil was at the oars, his jacket soaked through.

'Rough one?'

'Yeah, had two waves break on top of me.'

Paul grasped the rail on starboard to allow Phil to get off the oars and move back on the port side. He settled on to the padded seat, which squelched.

'How are the blisters?'

'Not bad,' said Phil, holding up his hands. 'Two of them burst, sting like shit but they should start to harden soon. They're doing better without the gloves, though. Hungry?'

Paul didn't feel like eating but he knew he needed the calories. 'Sure. Do you want to change first?'

'Into what?' Phil laughed as he pulled off his jacket and what had been his last dry shirt and tied them both to the flagpole. He grabbed his towel and grimaced. 'Nothing like a little free spa exfoliation with a salty towel.'

Paul appreciated Phil's attempt to lift his mood. 'Sorry I've been in the dumps.'

'No problem. Christmas is a tough time to be away from home.'

'It's more than that.'

'Want to talk?'

Paul didn't really want to, but bottling it up wouldn't help the atmosphere on the boat either. 'I've screwed up with Nic,' he said, and then, with every pull on the oars, the rest of the story came tumbling out.

Phil listened. Didn't advise, didn't contradict, just listened.

The phone rang, startling both of them out of the conversation.

Ian said: 'Hey, lads, how are you? You're making good progress.'

'Thanks,' said Phil, 'we're hoping to make our next waypoint tomorrow.'

'Sounds right, should still have a north-east wind today.'

'How's the pack?'

'Spreading out.'

'Don't tell me,' Phil said, winking at Paul, 'we're not in the lead.'

'You could say that.'

Phil laughed.

'How's the wildlife?' said Ian. 'Seen anything cool yet?'

'Yeah, we had an amazing visit by a pod of dolphins on Christmas Eve.'

'That's great, they're so cool to see in the wild, aren't they? Told you guys you'd have some spectacular sightings once you're miles from land.'

'Speaking of which, we keep seeing a small dark bird, kind of has a square tail. Can't believe it flew all the way out here.'

'Does it have shortish legs and a light colour on the underbelly?'

'Yeah, exactly.'

'It's probably a storm petrel. They live at sea. Only come back to land to breed.'

'Wow.'

'You're not superstitious, are you?'

'No, not really. Why?'

'Some say they got their name because they seemed to be harbingers of bad weather, but looking at the forecast I'd say you're going to be okay for a while.'

'Good to know.'

'Okay, lads,' said Ian, 'keep up the good work, and be safe.'

'Will do, thanks, Ian.'

After he made breakfast, and they both ate, Phil went to lie down and Paul was once again alone with his thoughts. He knew he had to get control of his thinking. He remembered the mantra he and Phil had adopted for life on the boat. Focus on the solution, not the problem. What was the solution to his problems with Nic?

She'd asked him not to call her again. Right. He would give her time, respect her wishes. But surely, if there was any hope of building bridges, he'd need to make contact? How about a text? Just a short one. As soon as he got off the oars, he punched out a few words.

Hi love, hope you are okay. I am so sorry, Love Paul.

He put the phone down and tried to sleep but every ten minutes he checked it in case he had missed a ping. Did they have a signal? Was it fully charged? When he ran out of excuses, he let the truth in — she didn't want to text back.

His next shift felt pointless, despite the calmer weather. Every stroke in the direction of Antigua pulled him further away from her. Yet each one took on a rhythmic effect, calming his mind until he was able to see the lesson. He'd always felt the day would come when someone would break his heart. He deserved it. He'd crashed through other people's lives like a human hurricane, leaving catastrophic damage in his wake. As he continued to row, he thought of each person and how he might have hurt them. Wives, children, family, friends. Time to make amends.

Looking at the sky, he begged forgiveness from each one. As he did, another pound of weight seemed to lift from his shoulders, the fog began to dissipate. On land it would have taken Paul days, even weeks, to change his emotional state but life on the ocean had the capacity to both compress and expand time and within several hours, he had brought his mind under control and the pain in his chest was beginning to diminish.

The next day he sent another text, and although he was hopeful for a reply, he felt a little less needy in the waiting. Little milestones. That's all he could reach for right now.

Chapter 48

28 December 2019

2,428 miles to go

'Are you sure there's no other option?' Paul asked.

Phil had just got off the phone and was emptying the first aid kit. 'Fraser says we have to manage these pressure sores now or they'll get infected by the bacteria in the salt water.'

'But with that?' said Paul, eyeing the evil plastic bottle in Phil's hand.

'He said surgical spirits would be better, but since we've run out, hand sanitiser is the next best thing.'

'Pardon me for mentioning it,' said Paul, 'but I believe the objective of hand sanitiser is to apply it to your hands, I don't remember hearing anything about smearing it on your *balls.*'

In the last three days they'd been rowing across the waves rather than running down them. Their clothes and skin were constantly wet. Pulling on an angle had caused severe chafing and salt sores. Their scrotums were now red raw.

'It's got to be done,' said Phil.

'Okay, mate, you first.'

Phil got into the cabin, but then popped his head back out.

'Maybe if you watch the waves, I could open the back hatch so we can get a bit of airflow.'

'Sure, mate.'

Paul thought he had seen everything there was to see on this trip, until he found himself looking at Phil, on all fours, his bare backside pointed straight at him. That was one more back hatch open than he'd ever wanted to see. And as for Phil's, it looked like both cheeks had lost the fight against measles.

'Okay, here goes,' said Phil.

The scream that pierced Paul's ears would have rivalled that of any woman in the throes of labour. Paul was tempted to call him a sissy but he knew it was his turn next.

'You okay, mate?'

Nothing.

'Phil?'

'Can't breathe.'

'Sorry, mate.' Trying not to laugh, Paul focused on the waves. Now was not the time for one to roll into the cabin. The next one broke under them and *Didi* rolled up one side and down the other.

'Ow. Ow. Ow.'

Paul could only imagine the pain Phil was feeling as his balls slapped the inside of his thighs like a pendulum.

'Sorry, mate.'

When Phil recovered enough to put his shorts back on, he closed the stern hatch, came out and handed Paul the bottle.

'Your turn.'

'Maybe mine aren't as bad as yours.'

'Get in there, skipper.'

Paul climbed in and lay down for a bit. Two days had passed since he'd sent the text to Nic. No response. Perhaps it was time to leave her alone. Or maybe he could try something else – text his son. Anything to delay his tender region coming into contact with Dante's Inferno.

Hi James, how are you? Is Mum okay? She didn't respond to my text.

Done. He wasn't going to check the phone, but within half a minute it pinged.

Hi Dad, I'm fine, will tell Mum you asked about her.

With that little titbit from home, Paul braved up and put on the gel.

'Very quiet in there, skipper.'

'All good,' said Paul. Blood still dripped from where he'd bitten his tongue.

The topic for dinner conversation that evening was the need to change the way Britain farmed commercially, to encourage families to grow their own food, which kept Paul's brain engaged for an hour. Between the emotional drainage and physical tiredness, he managed to sleep on his 10pm to midnight break. The 12am to 5am shift was always the toughest but with the help of the compilation album James had given him last Father's Day, he focused on the music and the thousand or more times he dipped the oars in the ocean. The last track ran out ten minutes before the light in the cabin came on and Phil relieved him on deck.

Another day. Routine brought comfort.

After breakfast, Paul was nodding off in the cabin when the phone pinged. He ignored it. Probably not for him. But what if it was? He picked it up, just in case, and recognised the last three numbers.

Hi, is everything okay? James said you tried to text me.

Another ping.

You can ring me if you need to.

Was he reading this right? Maybe sleep deprivation had confused his brain. Tired or not, now he was wide awake. The signal was strong. He dialled, it rang, she answered.

'Hi Paul, are you okay?'

'Yes. I am now, love.'

'Oh?'

'I've been so worried about you, Nic. You were so upset at Christmas and you never answered my texts.'

'I never received any texts from you. James told me that you sent a text, but there's nothing on my phone.'

279

First, she never got the Christmas card with the second letter, and now she was saying no texts either? How could that be?

'If it's easier, you can always phone me,' said Nic.

'You said not to—'

'I know. I was so low at Christmas I couldn't cope, but I am okay now.'

In that moment, the truth bored into Paul's brain like a pneumatic drill. He'd been crazy to think he could move on without her, or even tolerate the idea of another man taking his place. She was *his* love.

'Can I phone you once a week?'

'Yes, you can phone any time.'

'Thank you,' said Paul, breathing easier for the first time in days. 'Can't wait to see you. Phil is still working on trying to get that travel agency to fly you and James and his lot out to meet us.'

'It's a nice idea but how can I make plans for time off if I don't even know when you'll be there?'

'I know. Well, let's see how it goes. I love you.'

'Love you, too. Mind yourself.'

After he disconnected Paul settled down to sleep. So much for the plan of not wanting to have contact from home. He needed it, needed to hear her voice. It would help him get across the miles. He slept and dreamed of dolphins.

When he awoke, he was sweating. He lay there a moment, reflecting on the emotional journey of the last few days and the relief he now felt, but what had happened to his texts? Out of curiosity he picked up the phone. There it was. Since he hadn't planned on calling often, he'd never bothered to programme her contact info but had dialled from memory. Two days of needless pain caused by sleep deprivation, an anxious heart, and his dyslexia — he had inverted two digits in the middle of her number.

Chapter 49

30 December 2019

2,340 miles to go

Phil had been rowing in the dark for an hour when he sensed it approach.

'Incoming.'

It didn't matter that Paul was asleep; they both needed to hang on tight for what mariners referred to as a rogue wave. High winds and strong currents would cause several sizable waves to merge into a monster one. Even a larger vessel could drown beneath its weight.

It often came from the south, having travelled hundreds of miles uninhibited. Phil could usually tell the wave's intent moments before it broke. When it arrived, there were three possibilities: it would either break underneath them and the boat would twist and turn as though pulled tight by an elastic band before being pushed up the 15-metre wall of water and then being released with a twang to plummet down off the top; or it would break overhead and crash on the opposite side, leaving them no option but to surf the tunnel until they were spat out the end.

This wave was the third kind, the one they feared the most, the one they'd nicknamed the Torpedo. It would come fast and hard with a deafening crack. He pulled the oars in and yelled:

'Brace.'

The wave slammed into the side of *Didi* with such force that it knocked Phil completely off the seat. His world slowed into separate beats. He bounced hip-first on a locker cover, his elbow crashed into the gunwale and the butt of the oar jammed into his shoulder. He reached for the railing, but he knew this cartwheel would continue until he was pitched overboard.

But. Everything. Slowed. Down.

Then, as if someone had pushed the play button on a recording, his nightly prayers began. He heard the voice in his head saying: God bless Meme, Debbie, Tom, Rod, Alex, all my family, my friends, my employees. God bless *Didi*, Paul, the race. God bless all those who are suffering and may the leaders of the world bring peace and light to all.

Next, the darkness came. A wall of water cascaded down on top of him. The weight pushed down on his head and it felt like his chest had collapsed. He couldn't breathe. Couldn't open his eyes. But he saw something move, something bounding along the water, parallel to the boat. *Morgan?* Come here, buddy, come here. Morgan ran along in slow motion, carefree like a young puppy playing in puddles. Each splash sparkled like bioluminescence on a moonless night. A quick jerk on Phil's harness snapped everything back to normal speed; he had reached the end of the tether. Morgan floated away.

He gasped for air, tried to push himself up out of the water, tried to stand, but he couldn't see his feet. *Didi* was full to the gunwales, as though she was swimming just below the surface. Then he felt her tip and roll almost to that point of no return. Drill, drill, remember the drill. Okay. If *Didi* goes over, let her settle, then push away from underneath. But what if the waves pushed him against her? Under, he could swim under the waves until she righted herself and he would climb back on.

But that wasn't *Didi*'s plan. No. She was the boat that never capsized. Instead, she groaned and gurgled. Before Phil's eyes she began to drain the water, slowly at first, over the gunwales, gallons at a time. Then, she pushed it through the black spring-loaded flaps that Roger Haines had installed on her sides. And when she had forced it all back into the sea where it belonged, she once again rode up and crested the waves. Phil stood, astonished, in only the shallow pools that remained.

He heard a knock on the hatch. He knew Paul wouldn't open the airtight cabin until he knocked back, telling him they were safe from capsize. When he did, Paul opened it a couple of inches.

'You okay, mate?'

Phil tried a deep breath; his lungs felt intact. 'Peachy. Just another couple of bruises for the collection. You?'

'Yeah, thanks for the warning. I managed to pivot sideways and brace just in time.'

'At least, on the next call with the kids from Excelsior, we can tell them we really do know what a 15-metre wall of water can do.'

'Do you need me to take over?'

'No, I'll be fine, thanks. Try and get some more sleep.'

'Okay, but holler if you need me.'

'Will do.'

Phil closed the hatch and turned towards the bow. The waves had settled back to their normal Atlantic swell but the wind still whipped his ears. He sat awhile, thinking of all the near misses in his life. He wasn't afraid of dying; he knew his soul, his energy, would continue on in another realm. It was a belief that he and Meme shared. They'd often talked about how she would come back to help him transition should she pass before him, and vice versa.

But what about the rest of his family, about everyone who loved him, about Tom, how would they cope without him? Phil couldn't die now. He was still only 65. Even though many of his peers were starting to slow down, he was on a mission to give back to all those who had supported Tom from birth, through his childhood, and into his adult life. Raising money for Tiny Lives was fundamental to that.

With each passing year though, it was getting harder. He knew he was starting to exploit the generosity of the same group of friends and colleagues. Whenever they'd see him enter a room, especially during the run-up to his annual birthday challenges in June, and the Great North Run in October, they knew he'd be collecting. To capture their interest, and squeeze out that extra penny in the name of charity, Phil felt compelled to make each challenge more daring than the last. This one was definitely the toughest, and demanded as much mental strength as physical. But Tom would be so proud of him. Knowing his son's personality, Phil felt it would be just the kind of adventure Tom would want to do. There were days when Phil would allow himself to fantasise about what Tom's life would be like if he weren't disabled. Wouldn't it be something to have the four Pugh men row an ocean together?

The boat lurched; the wind had not let up. It was too soon for another Torpedo but Phil steeled himself anyway. No, he could not die out here.

Moonlight shone across the bow and the medal of St Christopher, the protector of travellers, caught his eye. After 19 days exposed to the sea, it was no longer shiny but covered in salt. Much like himself. He and Paul were now true ocean voyagers but they needed to reach land eventually.

He paused.

Maybe he needed to pray to the gods of the sea as much as the god of the heavens. He stood in the footwell, held fast to the bulkhead and beseeched the help of Poseidon and Neptune.

'We don't want to fight you; we know this is your world and we are just passing through. You don't have to make it easy, just bless us with fair winds and following seas.'

He waited. Nothing changed.

'Please.'

He prayed again, harder, just like he had when Tom lay in that incubator. He looked again at the St Christopher medal.

'Help our efforts to get to Antigua.'

He listened. The howl of the wind eased. He felt a presence, but it wasn't God, nor was it Poseidon or Neptune. It was the voice of ...

Didi?

He ran his hand along the painted wood, crusty and wet, and felt an impulse from her. Others would think he was daft, but he could almost hear her chuckle. She had a personality of her own and while he and Paul might be visitors on the water, this was where she was completely at home. She was enjoying playing in the waves and dancing in storms. She bathed in the sunshine and showered in the rain. She offered up every plank of wood, every joint, every ounce of glue that held her together in support of them.

A sense of calm came over Phil. He had no need to worry; *Didi* would take care of them. She was heavier than any other vessel in the fleet, she had carried three other teams across. She knew what she was doing, all she asked was that they trust her. And to prove it, she was carrying them forward, riding the waves without him rowing. Phil brought his fingers to his lips and touched *Didi* with a kiss. She wasn't just their borrowed home; she was their protector. They were not a team of two, they were a trio.

Didi: Dream It, Do It. Paul and he had dreamed it; she was doing it.

Chapter 50

31 December 2019

2,262 miles to go

Just before midnight, in the final few minutes of 2019, Paul came on deck to relieve Phil. The moon was still sleeping, and for the first time on the crossing, it was a cloudless night.

'Wow, look at that sky,' said Paul.

'Isn't it wonderful?' said Phil. 'This is what we've been waiting for.'

The wind was mild and the water slapped. Miles from civilisation and light pollution, the night was black. Stars pierced the canopy that extended from the horizon to infinity. Some gathered in constellations, others formed clusters in galaxies far away. Planets reflected the sun: Venus, Jupiter and even Mars vied for attention. Saturn spun her rings. There was a softness to the stardust and yet an expanse so vast it eluded human comprehension.

A miracle of creation. Paul, Phil and *Didi* floated beneath the awe.

'Oh,' they both said, as two shooting stars streaked down the sky. And then another.

'It's like God's up there shaking glitter in his personal snow globe,' said Phil.

'Better than any fireworks on land.'

'Absolutely. Look, there's Cassiopeia, see, the one that looks like a W. And there's the Plough.'

Paul followed Phil's finger all the way up till they found the North Star.

Phil turned around, looking lower on the horizon, 'Ah, there it is. Orion. The Hunter. See his shield and club?'

Paul peered but couldn't make out the shape. 'I'll take your word for it.'

'This is amazing, and here we are. Happy New Year, skipper.'

'Happy New Year. What a party.'

'Absolutely. I'd sooner be right here, right now, out in the middle of this with you than stuck indoors with a bunch of drunks.'

'Meant to be, mate.'

'Welcome to 2020. It's off to a great start.'

As Phil got ready for bed, Paul settled himself on the rowing seat, the VHF hand-held radio and jelly sweets tucked by his side. He was about to put on his jawbone headphones when the light in the cabin went out, throwing the deck back into darkness. As his eyes adjusted to the black, the stardust burned brighter. His music could wait.

Somewhere up there was the star formally known as CS-427-D, now called Gentleman Jim. His mother had chosen the name. Paul's father, Jim, had been a gentleman indeed, and tonight, on the third anniversary of his death, Paul wanted to finish the year and start the new one remembering the man who made him who he was.

If there was one reason Paul had decided to take on his toughest challenge yet, to row the Atlantic, it was to see if he had what it took, to be as great a man as his dad, to persevere without complaint and to be the son that would make his dad proud.

His dad had never climbed Mount Everest or run a marathon. His greatest aspiration had been to own his own home and raise his three children to be good, kind, successful human beings. He had a determination some might call stubborn; Paul liked to call it focused. And just like Paul, his father never did anything by halves. Even when he contracted dementia, he had to get the worst strain of the disease.

When Paul had gone to visit him in the hospital, he didn't recognise the man dressed in trackie bottoms and a tee-shirt that seemed three sizes too big. His hair was a mess and his face unshaven. This could not be his father. Even when his dad gardened, he would dress properly. His eyes, which used to contain his warmth and personality, were now empty. Paul struggled to make conversation and keep the tears down. He knew his father would be uncomfortable if he were to make a show of himself in public, but all Paul wanted to do was hang his head in his hands and cry.

Why? Hadn't his dad suffered enough in his life? There were so many bad people in the world; why was this not happening to them instead? It wasn't fair. This horrible disease was going to rob him and the family of everything.

A damp patch appeared on his father's tracksuit; it got bigger and bigger.

'Oh, Dad, why didn't you say something?'

'Sorry son, I didn't want to be a bother.'

After Paul helped clean him up and settled him back in bed, he had to get away. It was as if part of his own soul was dying in that hospital too. He had no memory of walking back to his car but when he got there, he sat in the driver's seat and cried.

When his father was discharged into his mother's care, he and his brothers took turns to stay overnight with their dad. Over the weeks, Paul had become accustomed to the narrow and uncomfortable camp bed but he remembered one night in particular when it was impossible to sleep. In the bed beside him, his dad was snoring. Then it went quiet. *Good*, thought Paul, maybe now he could nod off himself. But wait, was he breathing? Was this the moment his father's pain and struggle would come to an end? He listened. Yes, it was over.

His dad had stopped breathing. Wait, no, he was back. Paul continued to lie there, listening intently. His father's breathing stopped again, this time for longer. As much as he wished for his dad to be pain-free, he would prefer if he didn't pass during Paul's watch, for fear the family wouldn't believe he'd died of natural causes.

Paul started to count the seconds between breaths. He counted 25 seconds, 30, no breath, 40 seconds, still no breath. He sat up and leaned in, his face inches from his father's. No sound. It was now more than one minute since he had heard his father breathe. His hero, his mentor, his dad was gone.

'What's up, son, can't you sleep?'

Paul nearly soiled himself.

'Sorry, Dad, I thought you were dead.'

'Not yet, son, still life in the old man. Go to sleep.'

Paul remembered that night with a chuckle. The doctors had told them his father would die by Christmas, they'd just forgotten to tell the old man which one. But three years ago, tonight, he'd finally left Earth and became Gentleman Jim.

Paul paused the oars a moment and lay back. The more he gazed at the stars, the more he felt like a dot − a single human in a massive ocean on a small planet spinning around the sun. Who was he to think he had a plan, that he was in charge of his destiny? Did he believe in an almighty God, a single being that controlled the universe? He wasn't sure, but he recognised the power of the ocean surrounding him, the fragility of Earth, and that the human race was fucking it up. What if someone from one of those other planets landed on Earth, how would we ever explain ourselves? That on one continent we have people starving to death because they don't have enough food, but on another, people eat themselves into an early grave. That as a society we spend more money buying weapons to kill people than on food or medicine to save them. Or that our civilisation marks progress by cutting down rain forests, deflating the lungs of the planet on which we live. *Yes, Mr Alien*, Paul thought, *we have raped and pillaged our home. Perhaps we are not as clever a species as we would like to think.*

Paul shook his head as though his ears were waterlogged. Where had all these thoughts come from? Was this what Lars had been talking about, the effect of living in the wilderness? Paul was not a thinker, he lived in the moment. But tonight, only 20 days into the row, here he was contemplating the universe like Stephen Hawking.

Chapter 51

8 January 2020

1,918 miles to go

Already a week into the new year, the days were adding up. Routines had fallen into place, but they stopped to notice even the tiniest sighting in the natural world. It never mattered who was on deck, as soon as either of them saw it, they would call out: 'The bird is back. Twenty feet off starboard,' or, 'On the bow.'

They liked to think it was the same one each time, although they knew it probably wasn't. They'd also decided it was female since they had no room for a third alpha male. She was contact, not human, but at least another life form out there with them. They would look at her with admiration. How could this small, brown-feathered creature, no bigger than a blackbird, fly this far out into the ocean? At least they had a boat.

Other times they would look at the water, studying how the waves took on different hues depending on the sky. Clouds came and went, bringing shapes they would ponder. Sometimes they would both see the same image, other times they had to explain. Sharing these moments gave them a lift, a distraction to keep their minds off the open salt sores that covered their bodies, the pain that cramped their muscles, and the number of miles left to row.

The other highlights of their days were mealtimes and after-dinner conversations.

This particular morning Paul was on the oars as usual while Phil made breakfast. Phil had become adept at the delicate art of filling the food packet with boiling water before a wave could knock him sideways. No matter how moderate the seas were between meals, as soon as Phil tried to boil water, Poseidon would have one of his coughing fits.

'Almost ready, skip. Do you want to eat first or shall I?'

'You made it; you eat first.'

Paul smiled at the exchange; the ritual never changed.

'So, what should we discuss tonight?'

At that moment the sun broke through a cloud and Paul caught part of his reflection in the cabin hatch. 'Maybe the state of my beard.'

'Yeah, you should be concerned about that straggly scrap.' Phil snapped a photo and showed it to Paul.

Paul looked at it in surprise. 'Whoa. Where did all that grey come from?'

Phil laughed. 'When's the last time you grew a beard?'

'My dad used to say there are only two types of men that grow beards – ugly ones and lazy ones.'

'Well, I'll have you know—' The satphone pinged. Phil reached into the cabin to grab it. A headline sent by one of his friends. They'd expressed their desire to keep clear of most news from back home. They'd deliberately banned all conversation about Brexit. The idea of living at sea, free from political pundits for a couple of months, had been very appealing. But it seemed Phil's friend had thought this message was important. He read aloud: 'Prince Harry is stepping down from his royal duties.'

'Oh, wow,' said Paul, 'such a shame.'

'What? We should shoot the lot of them.'

'You can't be serious.'

'I am.'

Paul continued to row. They'd faced so much together – storms, equipment failure, physical pain – and throughout it all

Phil had been as calm and steady as a tortoise crossing a road. But it seemed the subject of the monarchy had riled him up. 'Looks like we've found our after-dinner conversation.'

Paul liked to think he had an opinion on most things and was unafraid to share them. So far, he and Phil shared a similar philosophy on almost every subject, from immigration laws to battery farming and from gender equality to prison reform. Everyone said they would have arguments and tension but since rowing off the dock, they'd never spoken a cross word or raised their voices. Well, except for a couple of times when Paul got hangry because he wasn't eating enough to offset 15 hours a day on the oars, but Phil started to anticipate it and got up earlier to cook meals with a higher caloric value for him.

Tonight was one of the few times they were going into the dinner discussion knowing they had opposing views, but no matter what, Paul did not want them to fall out over it.

'So,' Paul said that evening, as he put his spoon into his packet of mush, formerly known as beef stew, 'you're not a fan of the royal family, then?'

'They're a bunch of overprivileged fools.' Phil pulled on the oars with a lot of gusto. 'They're a symbol of an elitist class based on a culture that should be removed. Their wealth should be spread evenly to every citizen.'

'Hold on, Phil, the royal family does a lot for our country.'

'Complete waste of taxpayers' money.'

'I agree there are a lot of hangers-on, but I don't think they should all be shot.'

'Okay, not actually shot, as in shot dead, but definitely done away with. My hard-earned money could be spent on something better.'

'I think the money the royals bring in,' he said, 'outweighs the amount spent on maintaining them.'

'Why should we have to pay to maintain or renovate their houses? I have to pay for my own.'

'Fair comment, mate, but I don't see a large crowd of tourists outside your apartment when you appear on your balcony.'

'But how often do they see them? The tourists come to see the buildings.'

'So shouldn't we maintain the buildings then?'

'There's too bloody many royals. Who cares about the Queen's second cousin twice removed?'

'Well, you have me there. I would agree with a smaller royal family. The Queen and her children and grandchildren would be enough for me,' said Paul, with his mouth half full.

'What would you do if I said you had to stop eating right now?'

'I'd tell you to shut your gob.'

'Yeah? Well, you know you'd have to stop if the Queen had finished her meal.'

'You have a point,' said Paul, shovelling the last two spoonfuls in. 'It would be good to see William and Kate make the royals more accessible.'

'They don't represent me.'

'What would you replace them with? Are you saying we should have a Donald?'

'God no, I don't want that either but there has to be something better. We should have a say without being dictated to. We should have a referendum to see what people want. We need to disassemble the class structure.'

As had happened during many of their evening conversations, they'd started on one subject and ended up on another.

'It's a great idea, Phil, but how do you get that concept through when the politicians and lobbyists have their own self-interest at heart?'

'We need a party that stands for social change. Time for universal equality.'

'And how would you see that working?'

'If we stopped spending money on guns and missiles and armies worldwide, we'd have a chance to end poverty.'

'You're not wrong there.'

Paul noticed that Phil's rant was running out of steam, and so was his energy.

'Ready for me to take over again, mate?'

'Sure, skipper.'

As Paul got back on the oars, he thought about how simple it seemed out here on the ocean. He and Phil had started on opposite sides of a debate but somehow found common ground and come together to agree on something. From eradicating the environmental threat to the planet to creating a more caring culture in which all citizens had the same opportunities, they had the answers, they knew what needed to be done. But if they were to voice their opinions back on land, people would probably laugh at them as though they were two contestants in a beauty contest looking for world peace.

Chapter 52

14 January 2020

1,642 miles to go

Phil disconnected the satphone and came on deck to give Paul the update.

'That was Ian.'

'How'd we do?'

'Says we did 48 miles yesterday.'

'Great, we've been flying along this week. Didn't someone say when we're halfway we'll be closer to the space station than land on either side of the Atlantic?'

'Yeah. Amazing.'

'What did he say about the weather?'

'Mix of wind today, from 15 knots down to eight and then picking up this evening.'

'Not too bad,' said Paul.

'Except, Ian says we're being pushed too far south.'

'Oh. That means——'

'Yep, we're going to have to cut across these waves and head north.'

'Right.' Paul eased the left oar and pulled hard on the right. As soon as the boat began the turn a wave broke over the gunwale and swirled around the deck. Paul slid right, but pulled himself back to the centre of the seat. 'What else did he say?'

Phil watched Paul struggle on the new course, and wondered if he should tell him the rest. '*Fortitude* arrived in yesterday.'

'Wow, good for them.'

'Yep, and the Aussies are due in tomorrow.'

'Hard to believe they've already finished and we're just halfway.'

'Don't forget there's four of them.'

'Yeah, and a much lighter boat. Wonder how they'd do facing another 30 to 40 days out here.' Paul pulled hard across the waves. 'Can't believe they've already slept in a dry bed though.'

'And walked upright for more than five steps.'

'Eaten a steak.'

'Dried their bums,' said Phil, thinking of the state of his own. The salt sores were becoming more painful every day. He pulled the Jetboil out of the locker and set about making breakfast. Thinking of the lads who'd finished and were on their way home reminded Phil about how much he missed Meme. He enjoyed thinking about when they could sell the business, retire, and spend more time in the US. He filled the pot with water, then sifted through a few packets of food until he found one with over 900 calories for Paul.

'Beef stroganoff today, skipper?'

'Thanks, mate. What're you having?'

'Might try the sweet and sour chicken.'

As Phil tore open the packets, he was thinking about Meme's recent texts. Mostly updates on the business. She'd won a major contract with the NHS. He had to admit she was doing a terrific job managing everything in his absence. And she was trying to chase things up on the apartment issues.

'Water's boiling,' said Paul.

'Oops, sorry.' Phil turned it off. They couldn't afford to waste a drop in steam. In the last few days, the second battery wasn't charging to 100 per cent. It had taken over two hours for the water maker to produce only one litre yesterday. 'Shall I eat first?'

'Of course.'

Phil twirled the spoon around and around the packet.

'Everything okay?' Paul asked.

'Yeah, no bother. Just thinking about the apartment.'

'Any sign of a buyer?'

'No. We're still waiting for the cladding to be certified. We've had the fire service out a few times over the years but it still hasn't been sorted. Hey, maybe it was your station?'

'Don't think so. The only time I was out to your building was for a burst pipe.'

'One of the joys of apartment living. We're lucky on the top floor though. There was a bad flood a few years ago, two floors below us—'

Paul stopped rowing. 'A Chinese lady?'

'Yeah,' said Phil, putting his spoon down.

'Around dinner time?'

'Yeah. Why?'

'I knew it,' said Paul.

'Wait, was that you in the stairwell?'

'Yes, mate, that was me and Billy.'

'I gave you the number for the property manager?'

'Yeah, mate, that was us.'

Phil roared laughing.

'What's so funny?'

'Bet you never thought that three years later you'd be asking me to help you pee in a bottle.'

'No,' said Paul, 'but then I never thought I would have to deal with having your bare arse shoved in my face either.'

Chapter 53

22 January 2020

1,266 miles to go

'Hello, Paul.'

'Vicki?'

Although it had been over 20 years since he and his second wife had divorced, Paul wasn't surprised to see Vicki, sitting there while he rowed. She was perched at the foot of the cabin hatch eating a packet of food, just like Phil would do. Only yesterday Paul had been telling Phil how he'd met Vicki, and almost all the women in his life, in a pub. It had been on a Friday. He and his mates were having their usual few in the local. Busy night, the bar was three-deep. Paul noticed this pretty, well-dressed woman. She and her friend were struggling to get served. He walked up behind them and grabbed the barman's attention.

'Yeah, Paul, another pint?'

'Not me, these ladies are ahead of me.'

When their gin and tonics arrived, she thanked Paul.

'You're welcome.' It was her air of quiet confidence that attracted him.

'See, there are still some gentlemen left in the world,' he said.

Her friend bit back. 'Just because you helped us get served doesn't make you a gentleman. Men don't know how to treat a woman. A real gentleman would invite a lady to dinner or a movie.'

'What a great idea,' said Paul.

'Are you asking me out?'

'No, not you. But if your friend here would give me her phone number ...' Vicki turned to Paul and smiled.

Their first date led to a second and a third. Paul could see a future with her. She was engaging, light-hearted and had the right amount of self-reliance. She was also into football, so his mates loved her too, even though she followed Derby County and they were avid Nottingham Forest fans. She loved his kids and his whole family adored her.

Tonight, she looked as pretty as she did back then, her stylish haircut, her eyes so blue. She'd kept her slim figure all these years.

'How are you, Paul, how is your mum?'

'She's okay. She misses Dad.'

'I miss them both.'

'I'm so sorry, Vicki.'

'I know.'

'You deserved someone better.'

Vicki looked out over the water. 'Maybe. But I loved you.'

Paul felt a pain in his chest, like he was hurting her all over again. She turned back to him.

'Would you have told me?'

Paul could see it still — the moment his car keys hit the kitchen floor. 'I don't know,' he said.

She seemed to consider this. He wanted to reach out and touch her hand. She was a good woman, kind, loyal. 'I wish I could take away the hurt.'

'You're not a bad person, I just ...' He watched her lick the spoon. 'I couldn't try a third time, Paul.'

He hung his head. Paul had had it all: a wonderful wife who'd forgiven him, twice, a lovely home that she kept clean and tidy, enough money for two trips a year, weekends away with the lads if he wanted. So why on God's blue ocean had he pushed it?

'I am so sorry.'

Vicki said nothing, continued eating. Then, as if the thought had just occurred to her, she asked: 'Are you hungry?'

'Starving.'

She held out the packet. He reached over to take it, but it wasn't there. The cabin door opened and Vicki disappeared.

'You okay, skipper?'

'Yeah, mate, why?'

'Thought I heard you talking to someone out here.'

'Vicki, she was just here.'

'Huh?'

'She made me dinner and now I can't find it.'

Phil watched Paul searching the deck of the rowboat.

'I can't find it.'

'Come on, Paul, let me take over the oars for a while.'

'No, still got another hour.'

'You need sleep, skip.'

'I …' Paul stopped, looked at Phil. 'Ah, no …'

'Yep.'

'Shit.'

'It's okay,' said Phil. 'Well, at least now we know they weren't lying about hallucinations.'

'Yeah. But I didn't think it would happen to me.'

'It's okay.'

'It was so real. Wow.' Paul stared at the water for a moment, rattled his head. 'Anyway.' He picked up the oars. 'Wind?'

'Eighteen knots.'

'Feels like 30.'

'North-north-east.'

'Damn.'

'Why don't we both row a while? Grab back some north latitude?'

'Sure.'

Phil settled into the second rowing position. They had rarely rowed at the same time since they'd left La Gomera.

With the new wave direction, it took a few minutes to sort out their stroke.

'So, what was she like?'

'Looked as pretty as the day I met her.'

'She was a blonde, right?'

'Oh God.'

'What?'

'Stupid, stupid. I should've realised her hair wasn't blowing.'

'Might've been a clue, but … How come she's still on your mind?'

'Dunno. S'pose, since yesterday, I just started thinking how she deserved to be treated better.'

'What'd ya do?'

'Blew eight years.'

'Oh. Right. How did she find out? Hang on. Left oar, left oar.'

'What?' Paul's brain had been so foggy he hadn't seen this one coming. 'Shit.'

He pulled on the left to see if they could take the wave on the bow but not soon enough. *Didi* dug into the belly of it, knocking them both off their seats. When the water spilled over the side Paul shook himself and got back up. 'You okay, mate? Phil?'

'Yep. It could have been worse. You?'

'Yeah. God, that water is still cold though.'

'Nothing like an Atlantic salt shower to brighten your day.'

'Well, we didn't hallucinate that. Must be brewing down south.'

'Hope the sun breaks through soon,' said Phil. 'I have some laundry to hang out.'

'What? You don't want to use the dryer?'

'Nah, I'm old-fashioned. Ready?'

'Yeah.'

'So, what happened with Vicki?'

'She wanted to move my car.'

'Oh no, you left something in it?'

'No. She dropped my keys and the little plastic photo frame cracked open.'

'Uh-oh.'

'Yeah. The photo underneath hers fell out too. There they were, wife and girlfriend lying side by side on the kitchen floor. My worst nightmare.'

'Shit, what did she do?'

'Nothing at first. Just stared at the other picture.'

'Ya twat. What the hell were you thinking?'

'Stupid, I know. But I was always so careful to swap the photos over before I'd come home. Anyway, then she chased me around the house.'

'You're joking.'

'Swear to God. Had to hide in the bathroom till she went to work.'

'Ha ha.'

'Seriously. Rang me at lunch and told me to clear out before she got home. What time is it now?'

'I'd say around five, five-fifteen. I can take over now if you like.'

'No, I'll finish out my shift, thanks.'

'So, that was that?'

'For like three weeks. Then she took me back.'

'Wow.'

'Yeah. But ... Vicki's biggest fault was her taste in men.'

'You didn't. Not again?'

'I was a shit.'

'Same woman?'

'No, a new one.'

'Was it worth it?'

'S'pose it depends. If Vicki hadn't divorced me, I'd never have met my Nic.'

'But still ...'

'I know. How about you and Meme?'

'We're fine. Hey, let me make you some breakfast before you get hangry.'

Paul had watched Phil boil water day after day, but never before had he heard it bubble. This morning it hissed. Was this another side effect of hallucinations, sound seeming amplified? Even after Phil poured it into the packets, he could still hear it. He shook his head. God, he needed sleep.

'Maybe you should eat first, skipper, here you go.'

'Thanks, mate.'

'Wait,' said Phil, 'did you hear that?'

'What?'

Phil scanned the horizon. 'Hissing.'

'You hear it too?'

Both men sat still and listened.

Whisssh.

'Oh my God, Paul, look.'

'What? Where?'

'There. Look. It's a whale.'

Paul abandoned his breakfast. So many rowers had talked about their amazing experience of seeing a whale in the wild, but there was no guarantee.

'Wow, wow. It's like right there.' Paul could see the black shape under the water only five metres away. Its head emerged and its big black eye seemed to be looking at them as if to say, 'Who is making all that noise slapping oars in my ocean?' Another mushroom of water sprayed behind it.

'Oh my God, there's two of them.'

The first one submerged its head again, but its long back seemed to glide past the boat for an eternity. Such fluid movement, so powerful. Paul was filled with a mixed sense of awe and quiet caution. He and Phil were the visitors. Either whale only had to surface directly underneath them or breach on top of them to smash poor *Didi* into a million pieces. As the long form passed in front of them, it arched its back and started

304

its dive. The tail rose high into the air and the magnificent creature slipped soundlessly beneath the waves. The second one followed.

Neither Paul nor Phil spoke. The longer they held their silence the longer they could embrace the awe-inspiring moment and banish the mundanities of their daily lives. Salt sores and sleepless nights seemed insignificant in the grand scheme of nature. These minor hardships were worth enduring to be able to experience such a privileged encounter. They had witnessed one of the greatest creatures that roamed the oceans. How could they not be moved?

Paul wished those who thought global warming was a hoax, or ocean pollution unimportant, could observe this special moment. Maybe they'd be inspired to work to protect the environment. He hoped mankind would step up before the damage became so great it could not be reversed. Before these animals were lost forever.

Chapter 54

28 January 2020

996 miles to go

Phil was enjoying his time on the oars. Ever since they'd seen the whales a week earlier, he'd been on the lookout for more. Today was one of those rare pleasant days: the sun was shining, the wind was behind them and the seas were moderate for the Atlantic. He'd been thinking about where he and Meme would live after they sold the apartment. He did like one house in particular. Imagining all the ways he could transform it from a house into a home helped pass many hours. Although chances were it would be sold by the time he got back. He heard a ping from the cabin. A moment later Paul held out the phone.

'It's for you.'

'Okay, I'll get it after my shift.'

Paul looked straight at him. 'I think you should read it now.'

Phil stopped rowing and took the phone. It was from Meme.

I have decided we should separate.

And another one: *I love you, but I am not in love with you.*

Four texts in all: *I believe we can be good business partners.*

I want us to work professionally and respect each other going forward.

Phil sat there, the oars stowed, his hands holding the phone. He read them again. And again. But the words never changed.

I love you, but I am not in love with you.

He couldn't breathe. He felt the corners of his vision closing in. He heard Paul's voice as though he was speaking through cotton wool.

'Do you want to get off the oars?'

'No.'

'I think you need to, mate.'

But Phil was afraid to sit still. He passed back the phone and picked up the oars. His mind filled with every image he had ever stored of Meme: their first date, the day he told her he loved her, the day she said she would leave the US and live with him in England, the engagement ring on her finger, her smile, the way she tossed her hair, their wedding night. All the love she gave his children, especially Tom. How they'd grown the business together, how she was running it by herself because he wanted to take three months off. All the support she gave him on every challenge, driving support vehicles, uploading social media. She was so proud of him and all the money he raised for charity. Although at one point she joked that maybe when this one was over, he could make her his charity for a while. But above all he thought about her beauty, inside and out. How could he ever live without her?

If he didn't get out of his head it would explode. He had to talk it out. He rowed, he talked, Paul listened. Everything came blurting out, all the questions, the doubts, the fears.

'I love her so much.'

'I know.'

'I have to call her.'

But Phil also worried whether that would push her further away. Meme had once said that if you have a beautiful bird in a cage, you should open the door and let it fly. Is that what she had done? Was she so desperate to fly she had opened the door herself?

'When was the last time you talked?'

'Been a few days. But that's what she prefers. Whenever I'm away she always says I call too often.'

Phil stopped rowing. 'Can I see the phone again?'

Phil scrolled through the last ten texts from Meme, looking for clues. Oh God, he should have noticed. After the one he'd sent about their plans to retire together in America, she'd stopped adding xx kisses.

When his shift was over, he dialled her number. Her phone rang out. He tried again later, and again. By nightfall she still hadn't answered.

'What should I do? Should I chase her?'

An hour later another text came in: *Don't try to contact me, I am not well.*

Oh God. He had heard that before. She used to tell him that his personality and energy would suffocate her to the point of making her feel ill. She could read his spikes in energy, like when he came home from the gym late at night, bouncing around like a two-year-old. When the white noise became too much for her, she'd have to leave the room.

Had his personality been eating away at her like a cancer all this time?

Chapter 55

28 January 2020

996 miles to go

Paul had dreamed about the finish line for years. They were two-thirds of the way there, but how could he enjoy it now when the man he'd shared the journey with was devastated?

When their main satphone had pinged earlier, he hadn't recognised the number. They'd agreed that whoever was in the cabin would read the first line to see who it was for. This time he wished he hadn't. The words sat heavy, reminding him of how desperate he'd felt when Nic had asked him not to call again. When he'd reached out, phone in hand, and Phil had leaned in to take it from him, he felt like he was handing over a baton of trauma in a relay race. Now the pain was Phil's.

Unlike Paul's technique for coping, which was to go to his 'fuck you' place, he knew Phil preferred to find his 'happy place'. For him, that was images of Meme – how she looked, laughed, made him feel. How was Phil going to cope now?

Paul remembered Christmas Day and felt his pain. But this was worse. This wasn't about miscommunication over mistaken phone numbers, or Phil's wife being sad without him. If anything, it seemed the woman Phil loved had grown happier without him.

Didi was drifting, riding the swells by herself.

'I can't imagine life without her.'

'I know, mate.'

Phil was staring straight through him when he said: 'To be honest, I just want to jump over the side and put an end to it. I don't want to live if I can't be with her.'

Paul managed to stay quiet and let him talk, but it wasn't the kind of comment he wanted to hear from his rowing partner when they were almost a thousand miles from land. The Atlantic had proven herself to be temperamental at best, enraged at worst. But how could he console Phil? He reached out to take the phone.

'Let me put this on charge for you.'

Phil took up the oars again and put the blades in the water. Paul watched him closely. Although Phil made an effort to row, there was no intensity to his work. The danger of him jumping overboard was real. Paul was relieved when the shift was over and it was his turn on deck. The pain he usually felt during the first ten minutes back in the seat seemed insignificant compared to Phil's frustration when he couldn't get a signal. When the satellites lined up and he did get through, the call went to voicemail. Twice.

'I just want to talk to her.'

The fifth time it went unanswered, Phil said, 'I don't think she wants to talk to me.'

'Perhaps she's just giving you time to get used to the idea.'

'I just want answers.'

He had a point. Maybe this was Meme's way of giving him a kick up the backside to make him work harder on their relationship, but he didn't think so. Phil did need to talk to her. And for the good of the boat, Paul needed Phil to talk to her too.

'I'm going to text her. I'll tell her I'm not angry, I just want to talk.'

If that was what Phil looked like when he wasn't angry, Paul didn't want to see him lose his temper.

'I need her to know I love her and I want a chance to make it better. I can be whoever she wants me to be.'

310

Paul watched him punch his message into the phone. How could anyone express their thoughts and feelings into a screen that only displayed 200 characters at a time? On the plus side, Phil was in the cabin, which took a little pressure off. Only the sounds of the ocean covered the human silence that had descended on the boat. Paul continued to row. He felt guilty, and it wasn't a feeling he liked. If he hadn't asked him to be his team-mate, Phil would've been home in Newcastle and maybe this wouldn't have happened. What could he do about it now? He peered into the cabin. Phil was lying on his back.

'Are you asleep, mate?'

'No.'

'Okay.' *Here goes*, thought Paul. 'Call Ian. We'll get you picked up so you can go home and sort this all out.'

There, that should help ease Paul's guilt. It would be a big ask for him and *Didi* to finish the race by themselves, but he had to put the idea out there.

'What an amazing offer, thank you, skip.'

'Whatever you need.'

'As much as I want to be at home right now, I can't let you down. Even Meme would think less of me. So, thanks, but no thanks.'

Paul stood there a moment looking at Phil, wondering if he meant it.

'We're going to see this through, together.'

'Okay, mate. If you are sure.'

'Sure.'

'Try and get some rest.'

Paul closed the hatch and returned to the oars. The bird was back. Paul had started to think of it as an omen. If it stuck around, it meant things were good at home; if it landed and took off straight away, chances were that Nic was pissed off with him too. Yikes. He hadn't even thought about what Nic might say if he had rowed the last leg solo. Thank goodness

Phil had agreed to stay. The bird rode the bow for at least half an hour.

After dinner, it was Paul's turn to rest but he was still concerned about Phil's mental state.

'Are you going to be okay on deck by yourself tonight?'

'Yeah.'

'It's mild enough, I could sleep with the cabin door open.'

'I'm fine.'

'Okay, but it'll be really annoying if you are not on the boat when I get up.'

Phil managed a sliver of a smile. 'I'm okay.'

'Look, mate, even if I am asleep and you need to chat, wake me.'

'Don't worry, I'm past that. I think it was just the shock talking.'

When Paul came on deck at 8am he was relieved to see Phil rowing away.

'Okay, skipper, I've had a few hours to think.'

'Great.'

'She'll expect me to be angry, but I won't be. I'll just ask her for her reasons.'

Paul knew he should say nothing, just listen. He'd witnessed a friend of his consoling a bloke after a break-up, saying things like he'd be better off without her, only for his friend to find himself minus his best mate when the couple kissed and made up. No way he was making that mistake.

Chapter 56

30 January 2020

940 miles to go

Phil had spent the last 48 hours wondering why Meme had not waited until he came home to tell him. Was she afraid she would change her mind? It crushed him to think that living with him was what had made her ill. Yet he knew she still cared about him. Why else would she still want to work with him?

The phone pinged. Another text.

Can I call you?

Phil didn't reply but called her instead.

'Hi, Meme, how are you?'

'I'm okay, how about you?'

'Okay, I suppose, considering.'

'I know. But you understand why I have to do this, don't you?'

'I do and I don't. I'm heartbroken that you feel I've been so difficult to live with that it's affecting your health.'

'I've been telling you, Phil, the *noise* is killing me. It's only when you are gone, I feel I can breathe. I need to get better.'

'And I want you to get better, too. I love you.'

'I know you do. I love you too, but I just can't live with you any more.'

'I'm so sorry, I wish I had listened more carefully. I feel awful that you believe I have hurt your health.'

'I know.'

'So, what can I do?' He heard Meme take a breath.

'I'm moving in with Chris. Brittany is coming over from the States. She's going to live with us too.'

'What? When was all this decided?'

'I need my family around me, Phil.'

'You're leaving before I get home?'

'Yes. I can't stay.'

'Meme?'

'I just can't, Phil.'

It was as though she had hit him again. He couldn't picture home without her.

'Phil?'

He'd lost her. What was the point in coming home?

'I still want to work with you, though, we make a good team.'

That was true, but could he bear it?

'Phil?'

'My battery is dying. Can I call you again tomorrow?'

Paul knew Phil had the resilience to pull through, but he'd wanted to help him find it. During the afternoon, he tried to raise Phil's spirits. When none of his subtle approaches worked, he decided to go for the jugular.

'Remind me why you're rowing an ocean?'

'For Tom.'

'Right. Imagine how proud he'll feel when he sees you arriving in Antigua.'

'He'll love it,' said Phil.

'Compared to all the other challenges you've done, this one is off the charts.'

'Yeah,' said Phil, 'but I never thought that when this one is over, I'd be facing an even bigger one back home.'

'It's Thursday.'

'I know.'

'Are you going to tell him?'

'Not yet. Meme and I have agreed to wait until I'm back.'

'Makes sense. It's almost time. Why don't you go in and call him?'

Phil stood up. Although much of their physical contact on the boat was high-fives and back-slaps, this time, when they were about to pass each other, Paul reached out and drew Phil into a hug. He held him for a moment while *Didi* gently rocked them.

'Thanks, Paul.'

'I'm here for you, mate.'

'You know something?' Phil paused at the cabin hatch. 'I think she did the right thing.'

'What d'you mean?'

'Telling me now.'

'Oh.'

'I can't imagine what it would've been like to arrive home on a high, have her pick me up at the airport, drive me to the apartment and say … what? "By the way, I am not coming in with you, I live somewhere else now."'

'You have a point there.'

'At least this way, I have time to get used to the idea.' He climbed into the cabin and punched Tom's number. Paul heard the smile in his voice when he said: 'How's my bestest pal?'

As the days passed the phone kept pinging. Now that they had completed over 2,000 miles, messages of encouragement had started pouring in.

Well done, mates.

You're almost there.

Paul smiled at that last one. With over 800 nautical miles to go, they still had to row more than the length of Britain.

One message stood out from the rest. The travel agency was not going to sponsor the Hopkinses or Pughs to come to Antigua. Plane tickets were too expensive for either family to purchase on their own. When Paul and Phil eventually completed their crossing of the Atlantic, there'd be no one waiting to greet them in Antigua.

315

Chapter 57

4 February 2020

710 miles to go

Another midnight and time for Paul to get back on the oars for his five-hour stint. The travel agency deal had been a long shot, and as the days had gone by it had become too late for Nic to schedule time off anyway. Once they got to Antigua, he and Phil would still be busy with the post-race inspection, so even if they could have afforded the flight, she and James would have been hanging around waiting for him to finish prepping the boat to be shipped home. The idea of the two of them going on holiday after he got back was better and would give him the chance to show her how much he loved her.

As he got dressed, he thought about how Phil was starting to accept his new situation. The more he and Meme had communicated and figured out the logistics of what would happen next, the more Phil's heartache seemed to dim. He was already talking about moving on and even dating again. Paul no longer fretted about him.

He was more concerned about the weather. As they'd crept closer to the Caribbean, the squalls had intensified. Tropical rain stabbed at their bare legs. Their clothes were sodden, which made the salt sores on their genitals and backsides even more painful.

When he opened the hatch, he could see he was in for another long, miserable night on the oars.

'How are you doing, mate?'

'Hanging.'

The footwell was full of water, presumably rain and sea. As they started the handover, Paul thought he saw something move near the side of Phil's foot.

'Did you drop something?'

'Don't think so.'

Paul flicked on his head torch. Then he saw it, sloshing back and forth. 'Oh no, it's our bird.' It was soaked through, its dark feathers stuck together. 'We have to help it.'

'Let's get it out of the weather so it can dry off,' said Phil.

'How about under the overhang by the cabin?'

Phil curled some spare rope to form a makeshift nest and placed the bird on top. 'Looks like you'll have company tonight.'

'Yeah, see you in the morning.'

'Night.'

A couple of hours into Paul's shift, the rain eased a little. He kept thinking about the bird. He and Phil had been so focused on their own survival that it was a welcome change to concentrate on this little creature. He vowed to do everything he could to keep it safe and get it back in the air. Its partner was probably waiting for it to return, just like Nic was back in England worrying about him.

'No pressure, bird. I need to see you fly again.'

As the day broke, the clouds ganged up on the sun and kept it from shining. But at least the rain had stopped. When Phil emerged, instead of the usual exchange about the conditions, the GPS readings, and miles to go, he asked: 'How's the bird?'

'Still here, mate, she hasn't budged all night. I think she's still breathing.'

'Good.' Phil looked at the little drowned lump. 'What do you think we should do?'

'Maybe she's thirsty?'

'How about I use this cap?'

'Great idea.'

Phil poured a few drops of water into the cap of his water bottle and placed it beside the bird. 'What about food, what could we give her to eat?'

'No idea.'

Phil cracked a smile.

'What?' asked Paul.

'Look at us, two old men in the middle of the ocean trying to figure out how to save a bird.'

'Yeah. Do you remember what it felt like when you were a parent for the first time?'

'Yep. The kids didn't come with an instruction manual either,' said Phil.

'Exactly. We'll figure it out.'

'Do you want to be mum or dad?'

Paul gave Phil a thump in the bicep.

As the afternoon progressed the sun burned its way through the grey. The bird took a tentative step out from the rope nest. She pecked at her feathers, trying to separate them from each other. After a few minutes' effort she gave up, hopped back to the rope and settled down again.

'Take it easy, bird,' Paul said, remembering only too well the first time he had tried to get out of bed by himself after his brain haemorrhage. 'Physio's a bitch.'

'Any requests for dinner?' Phil asked.

'Highest calories, I'm starving.'

'You've got it.'

Any philosophical dinner conversation was put on hold; tonight, the only topic was how they might feed the bird.

Before Phil finished his last spoonful, he paused. 'Do you think she would eat carbonara?'

'No.'

'Why not?'

'She's not Italian.'

After dinner, Phil said he was going to stretch out in the cabin. It made Paul laugh. They both said it all the time, 'I'm off to stretch out a bit,' which they both knew was code for a nap. When or how they had decided they couldn't man up and say they needed to sleep was a mystery. Before Phil left, he topped up the water in the cap. The bird still hadn't eaten anything. Paul knew if she was going to fly, it would have to be soon, while she still had some reserves.

As soon as the deck was quiet again the bird hopped out of the nest and made her way down the inside of the boat, on to one of the lockers near Paul. She cleaned her feathers, then stretched her wings. She reminded Paul of an old-fashioned prop plane testing its engines before flight. The bird flapped hard a couple of times, then paused as if calculating if she had enough lift yet. Apparently not. She ran through the routine again but still no luck. She gave up and hopped back to the nest.

The light was fading, stealing the sun's heat with it. No more drying out today. Paul was worried about her being stuck on board another night. Considering it was cold enough for him to wear his fleece, maybe she would need warmth too. He picked the bird up, popped her in the pocket on his upper left chest and zipped it up. He could feel her squirming about, trying to get comfortable. Maybe his heartbeat would settle her down. He opened the zip again and she poked out her head. And there she stayed, like a marsupial in her mother's pouch.

Paul felt he had company as he rowed through the night. It was as if she was standing watch with him. By 4.30 in the morning he reckoned she must be dry. As much as he was enjoying her company, he didn't want to wait too long. He took her out and put her down on the same spot where she had been testing her wings earlier. She went through the motions again, only she looked stronger this time. Maybe he should help her, throw her up in the air? But what if he threw her up and she fell into the water? She'd be breakfast for goodness knows who. So, should he throw her or not? But if he waited ... Paul had spent years making life-or-death decisions, sending his firefighters into burning buildings, rescue teams into swollen rivers, and here he was more worried and indecisive about the fate of one small bird. Maybe Phil would want to see her take off? No. Sleep was like winning the lottery, he wouldn't deprive him of one minute. Light was creeping skyward on the eastern horizon.

'Right, bird, you and me, pal, it's now or never.'

He picked her up again. She didn't fret, but sat quietly in his hands. He steadied himself, felt the rhythm of the waves. He would have to pick the perfect moment to make sure neither he nor the bird went over the side.

'Ready?'

He held her up and with a *whoosh* threw her high above the centre of the boat. Her wings flapped hard but then she dropped from the air like a stone.

Oh, God, what had he done? She wasn't ready.

But before she hit the bottom of the boat, her wings flared and stopped her descent. She flapped again, maintaining position just above the deck. Seconds passed. Paul pulled on the oars to create an airstream. She rose a foot, hovered. Flap, flap. Slightly higher. Then she was above his head, three feet forward and two feet higher. Now she was clear of the boat, her small body silhouetting against the early dawn.

'Fly bird, fly.'

And then she was gone.

Chapter 58

5 February 2020

648 miles to go

Phil had slept well, as well as could be expected on a bucking boat riding the ocean. He'd enjoyed the last two days looking after the bird and was happy to learn she'd flown. Despite the constant noise of wind and waves, the boat seemed quieter now that she'd gone.

Their second battery was now failing too; in the last five days it had dropped from holding a 60 per cent charge down to 40 per cent. Phil had spent most of the day trying to make water, but after several hours had only produced a half-litre.

'Maybe we could try the hand pump,' Paul said.

'Great idea.'

'Do you want to take the oars for a minute and I'll give it a go?'

'Sure.'

Paul retrieved the pump from the locker and assembled it. Trying to connect the hoses to the water maker in the cramped space where the desalination system was housed would have been better suited to a contortionist.

'Bet you wish you had an extra joint between your wrist and elbow right about now.'

'Yeah, never a big fan of yoga,' said Paul. 'Hang on, I think I've got it.' He began to pump by hand. 'Maybe this will work.'

It did, but Paul was producing more sweat than water. At this rate they wouldn't have enough to rehydrate their meals, never mind their bodies.

'It seems crazy to think we have the 300 bottles of fresh Eco For Life water stored in the keel,' said Phil.

'For ballast and emergencies,' Paul reminded him.

'I think this constitutes an emergency, skipper.'

Paul wiped his forehead in his sleeve. 'You're right. Go ahead and give Ian a call.'

The satellites must have thought it was an emergency also because the call went straight through.

'Hi, Ian.'

'Hi, Phil, you both okay? You're the one crew that calls in every day. When I haven't heard from you by noon I start to worry.'

'We're fine, thanks, Ian, but our power situation is getting worse. One battery is dead and the other is running down.'

'Have you cut back on non-essential draws?'

'Yeah, but water is an issue. Paul has already tried using the hand pump.'

'Good. These things can happen. Sounds like you've done your best so far.'

Phil crossed his fingers. 'Do you think we could use some of the fresh ballast water?'

'Let's see, you've about 600 miles to go and you have 150 litres on board. Yes, I'd say you should be okay to start using it.'

'Are you sure there are no penalties?'

'No, not at all.'

'Oh, that's a relief.'

'How are the salt sores?'

'Bad. Especially our genitals. Fresh water is about the only thing that helps.'

'I know. Worst part of the row. Listen, we want you to stay safe and healthy. You should have enough wet rations to get you the rest of the way so don't even bother with the water maker any more, just use the fresh.'

'Fantastic.' Phil gave Paul a thumbs up. 'Ian says we can use the wet rations too.'

'Thanks a million, Ian,' yelled Paul.

'Just don't forget to refill the bottles with seawater and replace them in the keel for ballast.'

'Sure.'

'Okay, guys, good luck. See you in Antigua.'

Within seconds of Ian hanging up, Phil had the phone back on charge and was unscrewing the hatch cover to one of the lockers running down the centre of the boat. He pulled out six bottles of water, handed one to Paul and gulped the other.

'God, that tastes better than beer,' said Paul.

'So soft, wow. Can't believe we'd forgotten what real fresh water tastes like.'

'Uh-huh.' Paul was barely listening. He'd taken off his shorts and was pouring the second half of the bottle on his balls. 'Forget gold, that's just pure silk.'

'Velvet,' said Phil, doing the same.

The two men sat there enjoying the momentary reprieve from pain, neither one rowing.

'I think *Didi* is blushing.'

Paul grinned, then looked around and up. 'Do you think the satellites can see us?'

'Don't care if they do,' said Phil, waving his bare bum at the sky.

'Me neither.'

'We're hardly likely to make Page 3 anyway.'

'You have a point there, mate,' said Paul.

'Where? Here?' Phil said, pointing at his business and grinning like a schoolboy.

Laughter snuck up on the pair of them and took a hold of their bellies till their sides were sore and Paul had started to snort.

Dinner was a gourmet affair. Instead of using the chemical sachet to heat the wet rations, Phil emptied a couple of packets of Thai curry and mixed rice into the Jetboil and stirred.

'God, that smells good,' said Paul.

'Shall I eat first?'

'Yes, chef, go ahead.'

Phil sat in his usual spot by the cabin hatch. Paul continued to row.

'What'll we talk about?'

Between the bird and the water maker, they'd forgotten to pick a topic earlier.

'How about your work with the fire service?'

'What about it?'

'Well, I imagine it was quite the adrenaline rush most of the time but what was your least favourite part?'

'The damn budget cuts. We were supposed to be in the business of saving lives, but that only worked when we could get there on time. It seemed to me that every year the government cut funding a little bit more. People died, people who should have lived. Made me so angry. I fought changes wherever I could but what can you do? It just wasn't right.'

'Yeah, don't get me started on budget cuts. Tom's funding was down eight per cent last year. You know what really pisses me off?'

'Tell me.'

'The bloody inequality of it all. You have all these large corporations with their fancy tax lawyers who pay hardly anything into the coffers and then there's people like Tom whose quality of life is directly dependent on the funding his facility receives.'

'It's not right.'

'Downright stealing if you ask me. The haves taking it from the have-nots.'

'Yes, especially the multinationals who house their head offices in countries that demand the least amount of tax.'

'And the ridiculous salaries.'

'What's the difference whether they have four or five million? How much money does one person need?'

Phil finished his meal and swapped places.

'Another gorgeous sunset tonight,' said Paul.

'Sure is. Bon appétit.'

'Thanks, mate. Oh, this is delicious.'

'Isn't it? Have you given any thought to what's next when this is all over?'

'Not really. It's been my focus for so long. It will be weird.'

'Will you go back to work?'

'Not to the fire service anyway, that's done, but it might be nice to pick up something part-time. Add a little cash to the bank account.'

'I think you'd make a great carer.'

'Me? Why do you say that?'

'Think about it. You've worked in the service profession your whole life. And what about your volunteer work with Nic's programme, the adults with learning disabilities?'

'That's just one night a week. Nic and I have been doing that for years. It's fun, great to see a smile on their faces at the end of the evening.'

'See, you remind me of Emily, you care.'

'Give you a laugh. Last year someone asked us how much we got paid for volunteering.'

'There you go. Some people only do things for the money. Don't get me wrong, professional carers should be paid a good wage, but, in my opinion, not enough people in the profession actually care. You know, the company that services Tom's facility is always looking for good people.'

'Hmm.'

'You should think about it.'

Chapter 59

9 February 2020

449 miles to go

Paul had been on his nightshift row for almost three hours when he saw a lighted channel marker buoy in the distance slightly off to his left. How could that be? They were in the middle of the ocean, with thousands of fathoms beneath them. He didn't remember passing it, and logic told him there were no buoys out here anyway. But it looked just like the yellow one they'd bumped into when leaving La Gomera. Was he hallucinating again? He smacked his face and took another look. It was still there, but slightly bigger, which didn't make sense since he was rowing further away from it. The larger it got the more it spread out in a semi-circle. The water beneath it lit up. He stopped, and watched, gobsmacked. He realised he was observing something he had never seen in his life before. Ever. The full moon rising from the sea. The higher it got, the rounder it became until it turned into a huge yellow disc sitting on the horizon. Then, as if Poseidon had given permission, the ocean released it to fly skyward.

He dipped the oars again and pulled. With every stroke, *Didi*'s topside became a little whiter until she and the waves around her were completely lit up. With the moon aloft, Paul felt like an actor standing on stage in the middle of a follow spot, a light that kept him company for the rest of his shift. After almost 60 days as an ocean-going nomad, he could still be surprised and thrilled at seeing an everyday occurrence in the natural world through the innocence and wonder of a fresh perspective.

After his 5am to 8am nap, he suggested they call Carl to check what time it would rise this evening so that Phil, too, could treasure the experience.

'Lovely idea, thanks, skip. How's your breakfast?'

'Gourmet.'

It wasn't quite dining at the Ritz, but the addition of fresh bottled water and wet rations made a gigantic difference. Curried beans, spaghetti rings and beef stroganoff had never tasted so good. This morning's delicacy included sausage and beans.

'Are you saving that bit for later?' Phil asked, pointing at the runaway bean now lodged in Paul's fully-grown grey and auburn beard.

'I might be.' Paul laughed, picking it out. 'Have a good rest.'

'Thanks.'

When Phil disappeared into the cabin, Paul shuffled his bum around the rowing seat, looking for the one position that didn't aggravate the recently developed boil near his hip bone. Once he found it, he counted his strokes. If he could pull 200 before a wave knocked him off, his mind would have enough time to wander and he could forget the pain for a while. He hadn't rowed more than 50 metres before the AIS alarm started screeching and adrenaline spiked his arteries. He felt like he was back at the station on high alert, ready to face whatever emergency the printer would spit out. But out here, a ship, or whatever had set off the AIS, was more a threat to his and Phil's safety than any five-alarm fire. Apart from lightning, his biggest fear was being run over by another vessel. They'd seen a few since the French sailboat. You could hardly call them ships, more like floating cities, but most of them had been far enough away not to pose a threat.

'Coming,' said Phil, climbing out, binoculars in hand.

From Paul's position, low on deck, his view forward and aft was partially blocked by the cabins. Through the binoculars, Phil scanned the water all around them, from close in, all the way out to the horizon – 360°. Nothing. He made another pass.

'There,' he said, 'she's behind us.'

'How big?'

'Lost her. No, got her again. I'd estimate she's about four or five miles off.'

'Okay,' said Paul. 'Can you get a fix on her?'

Phil braced against the cabin bulkhead. 'She's lined up between our VHF antenna and the AIS.'

'Great. Keep a lookout.' At least now they had a proper line of sight on her. Paul put the oars back in the water. There was no point in losing forward momentum. He kept his compass heading and waited to hear Phil say the ship had moved from between their two aerials to either port or starboard, so he could relax knowing that she was on a different course to theirs. But for the next five minutes Phil said nothing. When he did speak, they were not the words Paul wanted to hear.

'Do you want to take a look at this, skipper?'

Paul slipped out of the foot straps, stood up and took the binoculars from Phil. Instead of a dot, he could clearly see the bow of a vessel and white horses breaking either side.

'Shit. That's close. Looks like a tanker.'

'Yeah,' said Phil, 'she hasn't moved off her heading.'

Paul got back in the rowing seat. 'Keep an eye on her.' Even though he knew there was no way he could outrun the ship, he rowed harder.

'Is she moving?'

'No.'

As Paul rowed, Phil called out an update every 30 seconds, but always the same thing: 'She's gaining. Still on our course.'

The AIS alarm kept beeping; Paul kept rowing, his sleep-deprived brain unable to think of what else to do.

'Make sure the VHF is on channel 16 in case they call.'

Phil reached into the cabin and turned up the volume. Nothing. 'Still gaining. Still on a collision course.'

'Surely they can see us by now?'

'They're not looking for a 20-foot boat out here. Shouldn't we try and hail them, skipper?'

'Duh.' Thank God at least Phil was thinking clearly. 'Pass me the mic.'

It wasn't the first time Paul wished they'd had more money for a more sophisticated AIS that would give them the name of the ship to call. Instead, he hailed: 'Calling all stations, all stations, this is *Dream It, Do It, Dream It, Do It*, on channel one six, over.'

He waited the two minutes for a response. Nothing. He tried again.

'Why aren't they responding? They should be monitoring 16, but let's try the commercial shipping channel.'

'Good idea.' Phil reached into the cabin and turned the dial to channel 13.

Paul hailed again. Still nothing.

'She's closing the gap, skipper. Maybe try the hand-held VHF, make sure we are transmitting?'

Paul hailed again and heard his own voice on their main radio. 'They should be receiving us.' Paul tried to think of other options. 'Get the signalling mirror, maybe they'll see that?'

'Not enough sun.'

'Okay, okay … the white flare then.'

Phil grabbed the signalling flare from the locker.

'Okay, keep it ready. We need to time it.' Paul tried the radio again and again, his voice more urgent each time. Silence. 'Right, Phil, let's make sure everything is fastened down.'

It was something to do. But almost everything on deck was permanently secured in case a rogue wave would wash it overboard. As Phil tied down the second set of oars, Paul secured the other rowing seat. He couldn't help wondering about the size of the Atlantic. There was plenty of room for everyone. What were the chances of a tanker and a rowboat colliding at sea? If this monster hit them, it wouldn't really matter whether shit was tied down or not.

'Phil, check your life jacket straps are cinched.'

Paul started rowing again. Phil kept watch, updating him that she was still gaining and on a collision course. But Paul already knew that. The tanker was so close now he could see its cranes from where he sat. If it didn't turn, they were either going to be capsized by a massive backwash or splintered. Some say it's impossible to be hit head-on by a vessel this size, as the volume of its bow wake would push them forward and they'd bounce down the side of the ship, but Paul wasn't in the mood to test that theory.

'One thousand metres, skipper.'

It was time for the flare.

'Wait,' said Phil, 'I think she is moving. No. No, she's back in the antennas.'

'She's rolling.' Paul could see it too. Something wasn't right. A vessel that size should not be pitching from side to side in calm seas.

'All stations, all stations, this is *Dream It, Do It* off your bow. Repeat, we're in a rowboat in front of you and cannot take evasive action.'

'Eight hundred metres, skipper.'

Paul took the flare out of its container. The ship continued to rock.

'I can't see anyone on the bridge,' said Phil.

'Fuck.'

The sudden crack of static from their radio made them both yelp as though they'd been shot. Then a voice, an Asian accent: 'It's safe. We see you.'

Nothing more.

'What the—' said Paul.

It seemed an eternity before he heard Phil say, 'Their bow is moving.'

Paul watched, not trusting it wasn't just the roll.

'It's definitely moving. They're changing course, skipper, they're going to take us on the port side.'

As the vessel drew level with *Didi*, it looked like a large city and blocked out the sun. Paul thought he could see two figures in the wheelhouse. 'What is wrong with you fuckers?' he screamed at them. Pointless, he knew. His voice would be swallowed up by the waves, but at least yelling helped discharge some of his adrenaline.

Phil filled his lungs to capacity. 'Well, skipper, I suppose that's what you call a near miss.'

'Watch out, here comes the wake.'

The two of them hunkered low in the boat and grasped the railings. *Didi* rode the first one broadside and slalomed down the back of it, and the next, and each one after that until they diminished back to the size of normal Atlantic rollers.

It was well after sunset before Paul started to relax a little. He kept replaying the incident in his mind, especially that one radio transmission: 'It's safe. We see you.'

Safe for whom? Not two men in a rowboat, that was for sure. Why did the vessel not respond on the VHF? And when someone did, why did he not communicate using proper radio procedure? Who were these people and why was the vessel rolling? He might never know the answer. For years, Paul had been telling people his biggest fear on this challenge would be fear of failure. Today, that changed. Nothing had made him feel more vulnerable out here than the sight of that tanker bearing down on them.

As the days passed, the fear of a repeat incident dwindled and the pain from salt sores and boils took centre stage again. Twenty-nine of the 35 boats had already arrived in Antigua. Paul became fixated on the GPS, watching the countdown of miles to go. How he longed to see three digits become two.

'Phil, Phil, look,' he called on 16 February, day 67. 'Have you ever seen two more handsome numbers in your life?'

Phil grinned. 'Best looking pair of nines ever.'

Paul wanted to believe the worst was over but knew they still had to battle the current that flowed past the hidden entrance to English Harbour. If they missed the opening, they would be swept south of Antigua, with no way of rowing back. They talked about strategy. Since the foot steering had been broken in the first storms, usually only one could row while the other steered by hand. Paul was stronger on the oars but Phil wanted to row across the finish. As they had always done across 3,000 miles of ocean, they came up with a solution that would work for both of them. Paul would pull them across the current, Phil would steer. Once in safe water, they would swap and Phil could bring them across the line.

Chapter 60

20 February 2020

30 miles to go

Paul had visualised crossing the finish line countless times. Through four years of sacrifice and training, and every moment of pain he'd suffered out here on the ocean, he'd remained focused on the euphoria he expected to feel when he stepped ashore. Today would be the day. Last night he'd slept like a child keeping one eye open for Santa.

He climbed out of the cabin, hoping to see land, but the clouds that touched the horizon hid the prize. Once he got through the pain of the first ten minutes on the oars, his mind wandered. Who would welcome them in? Presumably Carsten, Ian, the rest of the staff, and maybe a few locals might be about. Most of the teams they'd hung out with in La Gomera, including Lars and his gang, were long gone. How he wished Nic was coming. Maybe she'd used the credit card and flown in to surprise him? It would be the fulfilment of his dreams. *Come on, Paul, that's not going to happen.* She'd told him on his last call she'd booked their holiday to Tenerife in March. He was looking forward to having the time to reconnect and promised there'd be no talk of boats, fundraisers or work.

He checked over his shoulder. Still no sign of land. The phone rang — it was one of the race officials with the weather report.

'Okay, thanks.' Phil hung up. 'Winds are north-east 22 knots. Cloudy all day but no rain forecast.'

'Makes a change.'

'Yeah. Get this. Carsten's in the air at the moment. He's been off island since Atlantic One arrived last week. When he left, they weren't expecting us till the day after tomorrow. Now they think we'll be there between 11pm and 2am.'

Paul smiled and continued rowing. 11pm? Maybe they were right, but they didn't know Paul Hopkins.

'What's that?' said Phil, pointing south-west.

Without breaking rhythm, Paul glanced over. The haze had burned off. 'Antigua!' Paul cried, pulling even harder on the oars. 'It's bloody well Antigua.'

'Woohoo!'

At 2pm they still had eight miles to go, but Phil started to tidy the deck. As battered as *Didi* was, they wanted to look their best crossing the line. An hour later, the phone rang again. This time it was Ian.

'What are you guys doing?'

'Finishing?' said Phil.

'You're doing *four knots*.'

'Yep, Paul wants to get in.'

'Do you think you can keep that pace?'

Phil pretended Paul hadn't heard.

'Ian wants to know if you can keep up this pace, skipper.'

'Tell him he'll see us sooner than they think.'

'Guess what?' said Phil, after he hung up. 'Carsten's plane hasn't landed yet. If we keep this pace, we'll get there before him.'

'So?'

'It's funny. Ian said the airline captain has agreed to let Carsten off the plane first. He'll be expedited through customs, and there'll be a car waiting to rush him across the island. Now who's royalty?'

'Carsten?'

'No, numpty, us.'

While the challenge was called a race, Paul had only been concerned about completing the row. Phil was right, it was amusing to think they were racing Carsten to the finish.

At 4pm the phone rang again.

'Lads, you're too far out,' said Ian. 'That current will kill you. Get in close to the east side of the island and hug the coastline all the way to the south.'

'Okay.'

'Otherwise, you'll miss it.'

'Got it, thanks,' said Phil.

'Right, mate, steer us in,' said Paul.

'Okay. I'm watching out for those rocks.'

Paul heard a launch boat speeding their way. Within minutes it pulled alongside. Charlotte, the communications officer who produced the livestream videos of each team's arrival, waved: 'Hi, Paul, hi, Phil.'

'Get in closer to the island,' shouted Adly, the official race photographer.

'How far out are we, Phil?'

'Three quarters of a mile.'

'Steer us in.'

Phil pulled on the hand steering.

'Whoa,' said Paul, feeling the boat turn back out to sea. 'What are you doing?'

'Sorry, skip.'

It wasn't the first time either of them had made the mistake of pulling the wrong line but out there they'd had miles of ocean to correct the error.

'Closer, guys, you're going to miss it.'

As Phil pulled on the other line, Paul rowed hard on one side only. They turned, but the current pushed.

'Harder, row harder.'

Paul pulled.

'Harder!'

With his back to land, Paul gauged the situation from the tension around him. Even Phil had joined the shouting.

'C'mon, skip, real food. Hot shower.'

'Harder or you'll miss it.'

Paul was not going to come this far and fail now. He felt every muscle in his back, his shoulders, his legs, as though they were a football team with one goal in mind. The strength of pulling lifted him off the seat each time.

'I'll buy you a beer if you row harder,' Adly promised.

Paul noticed Charlotte had not started filming. Was she afraid to get footage of them failing? If they got swept south, they'd wash up in Guadeloupe. They'd miss the finish and have to pay to get the boat back to Antigua so she could be shipped to the UK. No way Paul was letting that happen. Besides, he didn't speak a word of French.

'Think about that dry bed,' said Phil.

'Two beers.'

'How far, Phil?'

'Em … 'bout three-quarters.'

'What? Still?'

He was putting his heart, his soul, his *everything* into each stroke, but making little progress.

'Three beers,' yelled the photographer.

He pulled again.

'Aim for the rocks,' the local captain called out.

'Maybe only 1,000 metres now, skip.'

Paul made the calculation: 1,000 metres, 250 strokes. Did he have another 250 strokes in him? His muscles burned; his throat was on fire.

'Anything,' Adly shouted. 'I'll get you *anything* you want.'

Shit, thought Paul, he was rowing as hard as he could. *How desperate is the situation?*

'Aim at the rocks.'

'Where are you aiming, Phil?'

'Harbour entrance.'

'For fuck's sake,' Paul yelled, 'they're telling us to aim at the rocks, so aim at the fucking rocks.'

Paul kept counting off strokes; he'd done about 70 of the 250. He was desperate to see Charlotte pick up her camera, but he no longer looked around, just pulled. He thought about all those teachers who had called him stupid. 120 strokes left. He thought about the schoolkids they'd inspired. 100. About all the supporters who'd donated to their charities and signed the boat. 80 strokes. Carl and Zoe, the volunteers who rowed a million metres, Meme. About Sean and Jamie and James, what would they think of their dad if he failed? 60. Nic, he wanted Nic to be proud of him. He couldn't live with himself if he let them all down. And Phil, without Phil he wouldn't have come this close. 20.

Then, just when he thought he had nothing left to give, Paul felt the change. The current had eased; he'd found safe water. Charlotte raised her camera.

'Ladies and gentlemen, welcome to the Talisker Whisky Atlantic Challenge. You're watching the live shot of Atlantic Dream Challenge arriving in Antigua.'

'Well done, skipper, you did it,' said Phil.

'Thanks, mate.' Paul's body screamed as he clambered off the seat. He stood, braced himself against the cabin bulkhead and took up the steering lines.

'Okay, Phil, your turn. Let's finish this.'

Phil picked up the oars and pulled.

To Paul's left, an old fort stood on the cliffs, marking the entrance to the harbour. There must have been 20 or more people waving. To his right, dozens of sailboats and trawlers bobbed on anchor, and on their bows more sailors waved. Ahead, a red and a green buoy marked the entrance to the channel and the finish line. All they had to do now was row between them. Paul pulled on the steering to line them up.

'Four more strokes, Phil.'

The moment *Didi* skimmed between the buoys they heard the crack and whizz of a flare going off at the fort. That was it – they'd crossed the finish line. Instantly, the sound of the sea was drowned out by the blast of horns, hooters and whistles. Everywhere they looked, sailors and yachtsmen were cheering them home.

Charlotte called out, 'Light your flares, guys, this is your moment.'

The media boat sped up and began to circle them, Charlotte's video camera rolling all the time. Through her lens, their families, friends, co-workers and anyone who'd signed their boat and supported the Fire Fighters Charity and Tiny Lives could watch the spectacle live.

Paul and Phil each lit a hand-held flare and stood face to face. Arms stretched out, flares up, their jubilant faces were illuminated by the red glow. Paul locked eyes with Phil, Phil with Paul. Although they were surrounded by well-wishers, they were alone together inside this moment, the moment that captured the heart of their journey. Every song, every movie score that had ever been composed to highlight the enormous capacity of the human spirit played through their minds. No matter what the future held for either of them, this shared experience had formed an unbreakable bond that would connect them forever.

When the flares burned their last, Phil dunked them in a bucket of seawater and sat back down. 'Now what?'

'We still have to row to the dock,' Paul laughed.

'Let's steer by oar and row together.'

Cameras still rolling, thousands watching on the internet, the two of them eased into their rowing seats and pulled. Slowly. This felt like a victory lap of an Olympic stadium and they wanted to savour the feeling. From every superyacht, to every tiny inflatable, the horns and whistles kept sounding, people still cheered and shouted congratulations in a variety of languages. It didn't matter who they were or where anyone was from, Paul felt he and Phil now belonged to this brotherhood of seagoers. They had taken on the ocean and won. The chronic pain Paul had endured traversing the Atlantic was gone; the intense pain crossing the current, also gone. All he felt now was a warm glow of satisfaction. He had put himself to the ultimate test and survived.

They thought they'd seen every well-wisher, and absorbed every drop of adulation, but then they rowed around the bow of a yacht which had been blocking their view of Nelson's Dockyard. Knowing that their wives, friends and family would not be there to greet them, they expected to see only a few race officials. Instead, the quay was thronged. Who were all these people?

They heard Carsten's voice over the PA system. He had beaten them to it after all.

'Ladies and gentlemen, in a time of 70 days, 9 hours and 11 minutes, Atlantic Dream Challenge, Paul Hopkins and Phil Pugh, welcome to Antigua.'

Didi touched the dock.

Champagne sprayed over their heads. Someone thrust a banner into their hands. Paul took one end, Phil the other. Cameras and phones flashed in their faces, snapping the image: *We Rowed the Atlantic.*

Then came time to step ashore.

Paul reached out to take Carsten's hand, the man who'd said he would be the last one to wish them farewell in La Gomera and the first to welcome them ashore. But it was not just a symbolic hand that Carsten held out, because as soon as Paul put his second foot on the quay he wobbled. He'd known it might take time to regain his land legs, but he had no idea how unbalanced he would feel. The next man to grab him was none other than Ian Couch, but now Paul saw a different Ian, not the nemesis he had conjured but the man whose primary objective all along had been to keep them safe. This Ian knew the struggle they'd been through and in his eyes, Paul could see his respect. Other than Nic, he could not have chosen a better person to be the first to welcome him with a hug.

He looked back at Phil who was being congratulated by Fraser and Ros. What a perfect partner he had been and what a team they had become. Paul couldn't imagine having done the race with anyone else.

Charlotte began reading messages of congratulations as they streamed live.

'One from Rod: *Tell Dad and Paul we're sorry we can't be there, huge congratulations to them. The good thing about not being there in person is that we can't smell you.*'

Phil roared with laughter.

'Monica Hopkins says: *So proud of you, Paul, love Mum.*'

'Thanks, Charlotte, my mum is now a silver surfer and has watched every boat come in. So, hello, Mum, I'm safe. Hope Dad would be proud.'

'Another one for Phil: *Are you still sane, or has Paul driven you bonkers?*'

'I was never sane to start with,' said Phil, 'so it hasn't got any worse. And we're still friends.'

'Aw, that's lovely to hear,' said Charlotte.

As Carsten beckoned them to the podium, Paul wobbled some more, but before he could fall over, Ian had an arm around his waist. He climbed on to the podium and found his way to the corner where he could hold the rail with both hands. Water, he was desperate for water. Ros gave him a bottle, which he almost drained in one go.

Carsten handed Phil the mic and asked what it felt like to step on dry land after 70 days.

'We were thinking about it for days,' said Phil, 'but today, when we had the countdown from 30 miles, we actually wanted to start again. No. Seriously, it's great to be here, we didn't know what to expect.' He looked around the dock at all the unfamiliar faces. 'Thank you all for being here, for coming out to support us, and all the people who signed our boat, they have been with us all the way, all the schools in Newcastle, thank you, great to be here.'

He passed the mic to Paul.

'As well as everyone Phil has mentioned, we have to thank our families who have allowed us the time to come and do this. It's not every wife or girlfriend or family who would support you doing something as mad as this, especially over Christmas. It's been emotional, it's been immense, just an awesome challenge.'

'Phil, tell us a few of the highlights.'

'Well, we're in mixed company, so I'd better be careful. We shared an awful lot. Obviously living in close quarters, we learned a lot about each other. The scariest things happened at night. One night I had about three tonnes of water deposit itself on top of me, but that boat ...' He paused and pointed at *Didi* on the dock. 'She's a wooden boat and has never capsized, and with three tonnes of water in her she just stood there and went on.'

'The other scary thing was having to wake up Paul in the morning to get him on the oars. He's not the nicest thing to see. Some of you have seen the ad for Snickers. Well, if Paul is hungry when he wakes up ... let's just say he's a bit of a bitch.'

All the onlookers laughed. Paul did too.

'Paul, what about you, the highlights?'

Paul paused and drank some more water. How could he communicate what the journey had meant?

'Em ... the highlights for me? Seeing the wildlife and the scenery. We've seen some amazing creatures in their own habitat where they should be, so that was an absolute treasure. And the night sky. To row in the night-time without a cloud in the sky and just look up and see the stars makes you realise we're just a small part of this immense universe and we should be more grateful to be where we are. For me personally, it was quite an emotional thing. My father passed away three years ago on New Year's Eve and we've named a star after him, so when I was rowing on New Year's Eve, I could look up and know my dad, the star, was there.'

The crowd issued a collective, 'Aw.'

Carsten asked: 'Would you ever do it again?'

'No,' said Phil. 'Once is enough. But I would certainly say to anyone who's got a desire to step out into the wild, enjoy what Paul has described, and want to take ownership of their future, it's a great adventure, a great challenge. Sign up.'

'And Paul?'

'People go around the world looking for challenges, don't they? Climb Everest, do all sorts of things. But if you want the ultimate challenge – row the Atlantic. It's not just a physical endurance challenge, it's emotional. It's ... you go to places you never thought you would go. People say you think a lot, you've got the time. I'm 55 years old and I've just started thinking.' He looked at Phil. 'But obviously I suck at it.'

The crowd laughed.

'So, ladies and gentlemen,' said Carsten, 'let's hear it for Atlantic Dream Challenge. Hip hip ...'

And all the people Paul and Phil had never met shouted, 'Hooray.'

PART 3

Chapter 61

21 February 2020

Antigua – 1 day after the challenge

It was 4am and Paul was wide awake. In the other bed, Phil's face was illuminated by the pale blue light from his phone. Even if they hadn't been trying to save money, it seemed natural to share. But neither of them bothered speaking; it had all been said.

Artefacts around the fancy hotel room gave it a colonial feel, a reminder of the British navy from days gone by and how Nelson's Dockyard got its name. Compared to *Didi*'s cramped cabin, the space was luxurious, the bed a cloud of cotton wool. And yet, when he stared at the ceiling, which was at least six feet above his head, rather than one, it made Paul feel weirdly vulnerable. Gone was their tiny cocoon, their wide-open ocean garden. There was no movement rocking him to sleep, no waves banging on the hull. They were back in 'normal', where people lived with walls and doors. Re-entry to life on land would take some time.

After the welcome ceremony yesterday, and a brief medical check-up, Carsten had led them to a round table set up on the lawn outside the restaurant downstairs. Oh, how soft the cushioned seat had felt beneath his bum. He'd swallowed the welcome fruit punch in one gulp, then savoured the crispness of the ice-cold lime soda that followed. The burger and chips had hugged the inside of his tummy like an old friend.

As soon as he'd finished, he called Nic.

'Congratulations, Paul, we were all watching you arrive.'

'Thanks love, it's amazing. You should see all these boats, and everyone is so friendly. We've been invited to dinner tomorrow night on one of the yachts.'

'That's nice. Hope you get some rest.'

'Still a bit wobbly, but it will get better. Can't wait to see you.'

When they'd walked across the lawn to check in, Paul had thought his legs were getting accustomed to land but when he'd stood in that glorious shower last night the room had begun to sway. Something about the hot water cascading down his face made him feel as though the ocean still rolled beneath his feet. He lathered the soap and scrubbed at the months of salt that clung to his skin. As he washed, each area of his body brought a new discovery. His arms, which had been so big last December, now felt like twigs. Gone was the fat that had housed his neck, he could feel his collarbones and every one of his ribs. He shouldn't have been surprised. The official post-race weigh-in had told him he'd lost 19 kilos in 70 days.

His buttocks felt like the dark side of the moon, pitted and uneven. Beneath the surface, more boils threatened to erupt. How much damage had he done? As he stepped out of the shower, he grabbed the towel rail to steady the sway. With one hand he cleared the steam from the mirror and gasped. It was the first time he'd seen his face in 70 days. Who was that person looking back? The head was sunspotted and bald, the beard thick and unkempt, but beneath it all was a gaunt face that held nothing of the familiar. He looked more closely. In the eyes he could see the man who had accomplished what he'd set out to do, a man who had pushed through physical pain and emotional turmoil, a man who had fulfilled his dream. If the flares up moment had been a triumph for the team, this one was just for Paul.

He'd spent most of his life believing he was indestructible, putting his life in danger to save others. Dying in the line of duty would have been noble. Even if the brain haemorrhage had killed him, he'd have seen it as an act of God. But during the row, he learned how he'd never really respected his mortality or how his death would affect others. If it had gone wrong out there, how would Nic have coped? He remembered the look on her face when she'd stood beside his hospital bed, having already lost her father to a brain illness, and the fear she might lose Paul too. And yet, because he wanted to achieve something that he thought would make others admire him, he had willingly put himself at risk, and her security in jeopardy. She had not asked for this, neither had his kids or grandkids.

Now, as he lay there looking at the ceiling, he appreciated what the Atlantic had taught him. He would approach the rest of his life with a different understanding of what was important and how his decisions affected those he loved. He would be a better husband, father, friend. He would listen more attentively. He was not immortal and would die someday, but until that day came, he would pay attention, create special moments out of the ordinary, and cherish every breath as the gift it was.

In the morning, after a night of sporadic sleep, dressed in his tee-shirt and shorts that had been laundered overnight, he and Phil fortified themselves with a full English breakfast and the long-craved pot of tea. They still had to face the unpleasant task of emptying every one of *Didi*'s lockers, and face Ian one more time for the final post-race inspection. What neither of them expected was how long it would take to get from the hotel restaurant to the dock some 100 metres away. Every step they took, locals and tourists stopped them to talk, to ask questions, to congratulate them again. The wild and bearded look made them instantly recognisable as the new celebrities on the block.

Phil left to buy some cleaning supplies. Paul opened the cabin hatch; he was taken aback by the smell and the size. How had he and Phil lived in that space for over two months?

He began the ugly task of opening lockers and pulling kit out on to the wharf. They would have to prove they had not jettisoned anything overboard to make the boat lighter, nor polluted the ocean with a single bag of rubbish. The stench was overwhelming. Their mattress cushion, which had remained wet for months, stunk of mildew, while empty meal packets no longer held the scent of food. Every one of the 300 bottles of ballast water had to be loaded on to the dock, separated in rows of fresh and those refilled with seawater. He had barely begun when he heard a voice say: 'I see you're not ready for the inspection.'

Paul looked up and saw Ian and Ros, clipboards in hand.

'Sorry, mate, we've been trying, but everyone wants to talk.'

'It happens,' said Ian. 'How are you feeling today?'

'Still on cloud nine, not sure if I have come to terms with it all.'

'Don't worry, Paul, you will. And the experience will change your life in so many different ways. Anyway, take your time, we'll come back in a couple of hours.'

Paul watched in disbelief as Ian sauntered off.

Not only did Ian come back in the afternoon, but he and Ros helped them offload the rest of the bottled water. The post-race inspection was as thorough as those before, but felt far more relaxed as all four Atlantic-rowing alumni chatted about the journey. Paul recognised that if he had been less defensive before, and had been open to seeing Ian's protocols as helpful, it could have saved him a lot of anger and frustration. Life lesson number 967: check.

Chapter 62

24 February 2020

Antigua – 4 days after the challenge

For Phil, relaxing into this style of 'island time' at Nelson's Dockyard was a welcome change. The inspection got done when it got done. Meals were served when the food was ready and people stopped to chat whenever. After cleaning *Didi* and preparing her to be shipped back to the UK, he and Paul spent the rest of the weekend walking through this UNESCO World Heritage Site, admiring the original eighteenth-century stonework and renovated buildings from days gone by, chatting to sailors, yachtsmen and sun-kissed tourists. As they walked the dock, they passed every type of vessel, from modest to uber-luxurious, and the owners who ranged from middle class to the super-rich.

'It's a different world, isn't it?' he said to Paul. 'That one must be 40 metres.'

'Yes, mate, and the one at the end has more staff than the entire brigade at Byker. But you know what? A rising tide floats all boats.'

'Even our little *Didi*.'

'Small boat, big heart.'

While the few days had been a wonderful break after the pressure of the row, Phil was ready to go home, whatever home was now going to look like. It was time to face his next challenge. Given the pace of life on Antigua, he was pleased to see the taxi arrive on Monday morning at 10am sharp. A big, tall local man got out and shook their hands.

'Hi, I'm Bernard,' he said, his face dimpled by the largest smile. 'You must be Phil and Paul. Congratulations, my friends told me about your trip.'

'Thank you.'

He loaded their small duffels into the boot. 'That's all you have?'

'Yeah, not much to show for three months' worth of travelling, huh?'

Bernard let out a healthy laugh. 'Ready?'

'Ready,' said Phil, and climbed into the white van after Paul.

'First time in Antigua?'

'Yes,' said Phil.

'What have you seen so far?'

'The harbour.'

Bernard grinned. 'That happens to all you people arriving by sea. Welcome. Now I will show you my home.'

He drove on the left, a reminder that Antigua had been under British rule for 350 years.

'You will see the length of my country on the way to the airport.'

As they left the harbour, he chatted about his family, his young daughter and how she liked to ride with him after school. Phil had rarely seen anyone smile or laugh as much as Bernard. Even the tiniest things made him chuckle. It was contagious.

'So where are you flying to, today?'

'Newcastle, England, via New York and London.'

'Oh my,' said Bernard. 'That's a very long, tiring journey for you.'

Phil and Paul laughed. And laughed. Bernard joined in.

'Not really,' said Phil, 'when you consider it ...' he tried to get the words out but couldn't stop laughing. ' ... when it took us 70 days ... and we'll ...'

Paul tried to hold his belly to help. '... we'll be home in ...'

'... less than 26 hours,' Phil finished.

As Bernard drove up the road that twisted and climbed up the hill, he was still laughing.

'See down there,' he said, 'that's Falmouth, the other harbour.'

A much larger inlet, it was filled with hundreds of sailboats tied to mooring balls. Along the docks, more super-shiny yachts reflected the morning sun. As soon as the road turned inland the contrast was stark. Here the houses were simple buildings, painted in random pastel colours of pink, mint green, yellow, pale blue. Chickens ran about the gardens and open drains flanked the road. Children played barefoot in the street.

During the 45-minute drive, winding through the heart of the country, they passed village after identical village. On the approach to V.C. Bird International Airport, named in honour of the first prime minister elected after Antigua and Barbuda gained its independence, the road widened into a highway, and a very modern terminal came into view.

The journey reminded Phil of all the nights their dinner conversation had turned to the inequality in the world, and how society had failed. In less than an hour they had emerged from Nelson's Dockyard, where maritime history had been meticulously preserved, passed some of the wealthiest modern-day vessels of the uber-rich, and crossed into the interior, where the impoverished resided. Such a capsule of disparity. It wasn't right; it wasn't fair. How could some have so much and others so little?

After take-off from JFK Airport, while Paul listened to music, Phil stared out the window at the Atlantic below. From this vantage point, thousands of feet above, the ocean looked vast and forbidding. When the sun set, it looked even more scary. It was hard to imagine that they'd been out there by themselves in the dark, night after night.

But down there he and Paul, two different people, with different mindsets, had settled in like two cogs turning together with a single purpose. They had confidence in their abilities and in each other. It left no room for the petty squabbles the outside world assumed they'd have. When Paul had been single-minded, Phil had presented options. When he had needed rest, Paul had powered through. And when one of them was stressed, the other's calmness calmed them. They had exposed their vulnerabilities to each other. They were a team that had co-existed in another world, the natural world, and the bond that was formed between them would never be broken.

The moment before they left La Gomera, when he'd placed the St Christopher medal on the bow, Phil firmly believed they would be safe. Throughout their journey, it was like a beacon leading them west, and it became the conduit through which he could talk to the gods of the sea and *Didi*. He remembered on nights when Paul was sleeping and the wind and waves were frightening, he would hunker down beneath her gunwales, feel her love and protection, and be reassured she would take them to Antigua. St Christopher became so corroded with salt and unrecognisable as a medal any more but still it carried them home. He had left it in place, right where it had sat for 3,000 miles, to ensure *Didi*'s safe return to the UK.

Chapter 63

25 February 2020

UK – 5 days after the challenge

From the day he had put the first oar in the water in La Gomera, Paul had imagined his homecoming. It would be like something out of Hollywood. There would be crowds at the airport welcoming them, cheering their achievements, but he would see none of them. The crowd would part and there she would be – Nic. They would run towards each other. He would gather her up and swing her around. They would hug and never let go. Every ache and pain in his body would melt away. He would have proved himself to the world and she would know that he loved her with all his heart. All the sacrifices he'd made and the hardship she'd endured would be behind them, their lives would go from strength to strength.

'Ladies and gentlemen, the captain has turned on the seatbelt sign in preparation for landing.'

Beside him Phil flicked through the airline magazine.

'How are you doing, mate?'

Phil took off his glasses. 'Okay. The hardest thing will be walking through those doors and seeing who's there.'

'Meme coming?'

'Originally, I asked her not to. We weren't sure how either of us would react, but we've talked about it a lot. This is bigger than us and she deserves to be part of it. She did so much to support us.'

'She sure did.'

'But I'm having someone else drive me to the apartment. It would be too hard on both of us.'

'Can't imagine, mate. But you're stronger than you were four weeks ago.'

'Yeah, life goes on. I'll always love her and support her in whatever way she will let me. And her kids. I'll always be there for Brittany and Chris too.'

'Good for you, mate.'

'Excuse me, sir,' the flight attendant said to Phil, 'could you please raise the shade?'

'Sorry.' The sudden glare from the winter clouds made them both squint. 'Well, Toto, we're not in Antigua any more.'

Paul continued to look over Phil's shoulder until he felt the wheels touch the tarmac at Newcastle Airport. It would have been cheaper to fly from Heathrow to Manchester but Paul wanted the symbolism of completing the circle. So much had changed since Nic had dropped him off on that cold December morning almost three months ago.

'Thank you for flying British Airways today. Welcome to Newcastle, you may now disembark.'

Paul jumped up into the aisle and retrieved their hand luggage. 'Well, Phil, this is it.'

'Yeah, skipper, you're going to miss me tucking you in tonight.'

Paul laughed. 'You're cute but ...'

'Eighty-seven nights been enough for you?'

It was hard to believe it'd been that long since he'd wrapped his arms around Nic; only half an hour to go now. He was still smiling at the idea as they sailed through the arrivals hall and the doors slid open into the waiting area. He searched the crowd. Not one familiar face. No one. His stomach churned.

'Phil! Hi, Phil.'

A friend from one of Phil's business groups made her way up to them. Paul nodded at her but felt absolutely gutted. It was his own fault. He should never have let his imagination run away like that, creating a scene that could only lead to disappointment.

He should have taken into account that it was a midweek, daytime arrival. It was hardly likely that Newcastle would have come to a standstill to welcome home two middle-aged men. It wasn't as if they were rock stars or gold medallists. Yet, surely some of their followers would have been there to greet them. And where was Nic?

'Maybe they're waiting at international arrivals?' Phil suggested.

'Let's hope.'

It seemed a long walk to the other side of the airport. From 20 metres back, Paul spotted Phil's family. 'Look, Phil, there's Tom.'

Phil waved at Tom.

'Dad, Dad.'

As Phil reached his family the hugs and congratulations began. Meme was quick to embrace him and kiss him on the cheek.

'How are you?' she asked.

'I'm okay.'

'How was the flight?'

'A lot quicker than rowing.'

Meme laughed.

Paul could tell how tough it must be for both of them, trying to feel their way through this moment with everyone watching. How many of them knew? Tom's smile was so big hopefully no one noticed.

Phil got down on his hunkers. 'How's my bestest pal?'

'Great, Dad. I liked the phone calls. We had lots.'

'Yes, we did, Tom, yes we did.'

'Let me introduce you to Veronica.'

'Hi, Veronica.' Phil rose to greet Tom's support worker. 'I'm Tom's—'

'No, Dad, I'm introducing you. Veronica, this is my dad, he's been away a long time.'

'But I'm back now,' said Phil. 'Come on, let me have one of those big special Tom hugs.'

As lovely as it was to watch, Paul still scanned the group, looking for her. He started to recognise some faces, friends, supporters; then, finally, there she was. Nic saw him, but she didn't move towards him. People slapped him on the back, shook his hand, but he kept looking at her, and the distant air about her.

'Hi sweetheart,' he said. 'I've missed you. I am so glad to be home.'

He reached out and put his arms around her but she shied away from him, almost turning her back as if she was a child who had been warned about a stranger trying to touch her.

'I'm glad you're back,' she said.

Others poured in on top of him, jostling for handshakes, back-slaps and hugs.

'Well done, mate.'

'Congratulations.'

'We knew you could do it.'

Paul went through the motions, his smile fixed. All he could think about was Nic. Why was she so distant?

'Over here, Paul, Phil.'

Like someone on the red carpet, Paul posed for photos.

'What was it like?'

'How's your bum?'

The crowd laughed. The state of his bum had been the focus of many a conversation but the physical pain was starting to fade. Memories like whale sightings, the birds, the sunsets were what he wanted to talk about. He managed to get close enough to Nic to hold her hand for a brief second. He still couldn't understand her demeanour. They'd talked every night since he'd arrived in Antigua and she'd seemed thrilled he was almost home.

The crowd began to drift away and both families headed for the car park. Paul stopped to embrace Phil.

'Speak to you later, mate.'

'See ya, Paul.'

As he watched Phil walk away, Paul felt a strange sense of loss. The journey was really over. No matter who he would talk to in the days or weeks ahead, there would only be one person who would understand exactly what he had been through.

He didn't envy Phil and the changes he was about to face, but at least Phil knew where he stood. With Nic holding back, Paul had no idea what was in store for him. If she'd told him in advance that she was giving their neighbour, Diego, a lift home from the airport, he would have been disappointed to have their first possible private moments invaded, but given the way Nic was acting around him, he was glad of the distraction. As she drove through Nuns Moor, Paul chatted with him over his shoulder.

'Thanks for looking out for Nic while I was gone, Diego.'

'No bother, so what was it like?'

'Hard to put into words.'

'Yeah. My heart was in my mouth most of the time. No clue what it must have been like for you.'

Paul stole a glance at Nic. Whether she noticed or not she didn't show it. He had expected the silence from her on the way to the airport three months ago, but not now. He was so sure she would have been relieved that it was all over and glad to have him back. It was so confusing.

'I'll leave you to it,' Diego said as she pulled into their driveway.

'Thanks, mate.'

'And welcome home again. I'm sure you're going to love what Nic has done with the place.'

Paul was sure he would too. Several times when he'd been away before, Nic would take the opportunity to improve the décor. He walked into the lounge, now painted grey and mustard. Not his cup of tea but: 'Wow, I love it.'

But it wasn't the new paint on the wall he wanted to talk about.

'Nic, why are we not okay?'

'Get upstairs …' she said.

Paul had been longing for this moment. The idea of being back in bed with her had motivated him through some tough days at sea. But something about her tone led him to believe she wasn't feeling romantic. What kind of game was she playing?

'… and shave that bloody beard off.'

Paul fingered the three-inch-long beard. While in Antigua it had been their ticket to recognition of what they had achieved. He'd hoped to keep it for a few more days so that his mates in England could see the look of someone who had suffered hardship, not the same old clean-faced Paul, who might as well have been off gallivanting on an extended cruise.

'If you want to come anywhere near me, it has to go.'

With that, Nic turned and headed to the kitchen, throwing a 'Do you want a cup of tea?' over her shoulder. Tea? Was she giving him time to figure out whether he wanted to keep the beard and delay their reunion or was she just taunting him to see if the promises he made to put her first were empty? *Fuck tea.* He took the stairs three at a time.

He ran the clippers across his face as though shearing a sheep. If the beard was the only thing standing in the way of making love with his wife, then off with it. Clumps dropped into the sink.

As he had that first night in Antigua, he stared at his reflection. It was like watching Michelangelo carve something out of stone; little by little, Paul was being revealed to himself – a man who had a story to tell. He chose a brand-new razor to shave away the stubble. He ran his hand over his cheek, smooth as a baby's bum. Nothing like *his* actual bum, which would take weeks for the scars to heal. He took a final look in the mirror and hoped the man in front of him was someone Nic still loved.

Coming down the stairs, he wondered if it was just the beard, or if there was something else. He waited in the lounge, she arrived through from the kitchen. For a moment they stood six feet apart looking at each other. Then the edge of her mouth turned up, the birth of a smile. It crept up to her eyes. Recognition. She crossed to him, raised her arms and embraced him fully for the first time.

Paul held her tight, not wanting to let her go. The smell of her, the familiar touch, he was home, home where he wanted to be.

'Shall we go upstairs?' she asked, not waiting for his answer.

He had envisioned it for months, but being with her again was gentler, more loving that he could have dreamed. He delighted in the soft curves of her body next to his, her gentle touch, the intense connection he felt as they lay next to each other in the afterglow. He put his arm out, she nestled into his chest.

'I got such a shock when I saw you.' Nic ran her hand across his belly. 'You looked so skinny.'

'But you'd watched me arrive in Antigua.'

'Yes, but it was different seeing you in person. The beard, the bones, everything was different. The only thing I recognised was your voice.'

Paul kissed the top of her head. His beloved Nic. He could see it clearly now, where he had gone wrong in the past. He wanted to tell her but he knew that words meant nothing to her. She used to say: 'Promises are like pie crust, easily broken.'

Why had he never listened? He was listening now. Actions were what counted. He would have to show her how much he loved her and how he was now choosing her as his number one priority.

At teatime James came home from work and threw his arms around his father.

'Dad, so great to see you, sorry I couldn't come to the airport.'

'Not a problem, so happy to see you.'

'I'm so proud of you.'

'Thanks, son.'

'I never doubted it for a second. You remember when I was a kid you always told me we were different from other people ...'

'Yeah?'

'... that we were made of stronger stuff, we were indestructible and nothing could beat us?'

'I remember.' He was glad his son had inherited the Hopkins strength and determination but as to their indestructibility ... well, he might have to amend that message. 'So, how did you behave for your mum while I was gone?'

'Good.'

'Glad to hear it.'

The calls and messages had started pouring in. Everyone wanted to see him, but Nic had a few days off, so he made them wait.

After she went back to work, he met up with his station manager, Dave Linsley.

'Well, mate, you said you would do it and you did.'

'Thanks, and for keeping me up to date with Forest's results. Little things like that meant the world to me out there.'

'No bother. Swing by the station. The lads would love to see you.'

'Will do.'

But first he owed Zoe a visit. He rang her bell, and immediately the door flew open and Zoe grabbed him into a hug.

'Hops. I'm so glad to see you. Jeff's still at work, he's going to be mad that he missed you. Come in, come in.'

In the kitchen, she put the kettle on.

'I asked Carl to come over.'

'Great.'

'Before he arrives, I want to apologise.'

'For what?'

'I'm so sorry I ever doubted you.'

'Don't be silly.'

'You said you would do it and you did. I'm sorry.'

'You were right. We were underprepared.'

'But you did it.'

'It was more luck than judgement.'

'Nothing gets in your way, Hops. You've never failed to achieve what you set out to do. I admire your determination so much.'

Paul smiled. 'Oh, if you only knew the half of it. How close we came to failing. And you had predicted it. I'm the one who should say sorry for not listening to your advice.'

Zoe went to answer the door. What a great friend she had been to him. Even though she had been so worried about the race, his lack of training and the less than new equipment, she'd still supported them at every fundraiser. Her gift of the two head torches had been invaluable. The breakfast bars she'd given them had lifted his mood many a morning. And she was apologising to him? Crazy, loveable girl. What a friend.

'Hey, hey, hey, skipper.'

Carl breezed in behind Zoe. Paul stood up for a bear hug.

'So great to see you. Look at you.'

Zoe and Carl listened intently as Paul recounted stories from the ocean, particularly how tough the last half mile really was.

'Amazing,' said Carl. 'It was so incredible to see you crossing that finish line.'

'Your updates really helped keep us on course. Thank Jeff for me too, Zoe. Don't know what we would have done without you guys.'

Carl clapped him on the back. 'You're welcome, Hops. We had fun keeping track.'

Paul knew that these two mates also deserved some of the low points too. He told them about Christmas Day, the call with Nic and how desperate he felt.

'Hearing your voice, and Katrina's and Poppy's, on Boxing Day lifted me from a very dark place, Carl.'

Over the next few days, the newness of Paul being home started to wear off and conversations between himself and Nic revealed more of what life had been like for her in his absence. Yes, she was proud of him, yes, she knew he could do it, but what she didn't know nor couldn't understand was: why? Why had he deserted her?

'You left me to deal with an 18-year-old by myself.'

'I'm sorry.'

'From the moment you left on your little holiday, he was a nightmare. Wouldn't do a thing I asked. Thinks he knows bloody everything.'

Paul closed his eyes, and inhaled slowly. The one thing he'd asked James to do while he was gone was to behave for his mum. The more Nic told him what she had to deal with, the more he could feel his achievements tarnish.

'Why did you leave me?'

Now that he was starting to see things from Nic's point of view, he didn't have an answer. He wanted to reach out and touch her hand, tell her he was sorry for being selfish and promise to make it up to her, but he knew that wouldn't work with Nic.

Betty whined. Nic leaned forward to get up.

'You stay, love, I'll take her.'

Paul could feel Nic's eyes on him and felt ashamed that she looked surprised at his offer. For years he'd sat back and watched her take the dog out twice a day, no matter the weather. He hoped she would give him the chance to show her he had changed. Baby steps.

The next morning, and every morning after that, he got up early, walked the dog, brought her coffee in bed, and tidied the kitchen after breakfast. He kept looking for opportunities to show her how much she meant to him. The more he did, the more he realised how much she had done to support him over the years and how little he had done for her. It was sobering. He had proved he could row an ocean. Now he had to prove he deserved Nic's love.

Chapter 64

7 March 2020

Newcastle – 17 days after the challenge

At 2.30 in the morning, Meme's phone call woke Phil with a start.

'Hello.'

'Phil, I've lost some feeling on my left side.'

'What?' Phil sat up. 'What happened?'

'I think it's a stroke.'

'Oh God.'

Two things Phil knew about Meme: she was not a hypochondriac and she was a trained nurse. If she thought she was having a stroke, she probably was. The shock almost sent him into a panic but he needed to stay calm. She needed immediate care. She lived a mile from the hospital but he was a 30-minute drive away.

'Is Chris in the house?'

'Uh-huh.'

'Can you wake him? Tell him to drive you to A&E right now.'

'Okay. I'll call when I know.'

Phil stared at the phone and rocked back and forth. Please be okay, Meme, please be okay. He couldn't lose her. He may have lost her as a wife but she was still his best friend.

He lay down and tried to meditate, to slow his breathing. But every few minutes he checked his phone for a missed call, a text from Chris. Anything. He had never felt more alone.

In the days since his return, he had been going from business appointments to network meetings feeling like a castaway dressed in a suit. Everyone wanted to talk about the Atlantic Challenge, the highs and the lows, and he was happy to regale them with his stories from the sea. At work, life felt normal. He and Meme worked together as though nothing had changed. But at night, her absence as his wife was magnified. Compared to the six-foot cabin he'd lived in with Paul, the apartment, which had been a cosy home for the two of them, now felt as grand as a palace, but it was a palace without its queen. He would wander from bedroom to bathroom, kitchen to lounge, always expecting to find her in the next room. Life felt empty. Even Morgan was gone.

He checked his phone again. 4am. No word. Chris's phone went to voicemail. He wished he could call Tom, hear his laugh. It was wonderful to be able to talk to him on the phone every day now and connect with him in person again. Tom would always have a joke for him and a string of questions. But, if Phil was honest, he could see that even Tom had been changed by the challenge and the length of his father's absence. Last Thursday, he hadn't got upset when it was time for Phil to leave. Yesterday, Tom had asked him to ring back later because he was introducing Emily to a lady who was visiting the facility. During the last three months, supported and surrounded by family and friends, Tom had learned to cope without Phil's constant presence and was no longer focused solely on the relationship with his dad. Although Tom was 32 and had lived in a care facility for years, to Phil, the shift made it feel like his eldest son had just left home and gone off to college. His beautiful baby boy, who had defied doctors and lived, had not only survived his absence, but had matured. Phil could not have been prouder. Now, his job was to listen to what the Atlantic wind had told him and release *his* dependency on Tom so that their relationship could shift from that of parent/child to one of mutual respect between familial adults.

Phil closed his eyes and prayed. God bless my family, my friends, my co-workers. And please, God, please let Meme be okay.

Please let Meme be okay.

Please let Meme be okay.

Sometime after 6am he drifted off to sleep.

Later that morning, the call came. Meme had indeed suffered a transient ischaemic attack, a TIA. Thankfully, she'd regained the use of her muscles and so far, showed no sign of lasting damage. She was discharged the same day with orders to adjust her diet and eliminate stress and pressure from her life.

Listening to her, Phil's heart was overwhelmed with both relief and sadness. He loved her so much he knew that he had to do whatever he could to support her recovery. As heart-breaking as it was, that could only mean one thing. No matter his feelings, his wants, his needs, he had to remove the door of the bird cage completely and let her go so she could spread her wings and truly fly.

Chapter 65

8 March 2020

Tenerife – 18 days after the challenge

Eleven days after he'd arrived home, Paul was once again headed to the airport, only this time Nic was coming with him. He couldn't wait for the week's holiday in Tenerife, to rekindle their love and continue showing her how much he cared.

It seemed Nic was really looking forward to it too. She had splurged on booking the VIP lounge at the airport, his first time experiencing such a treat. He was up and down to the bar like a yoyo on a string, taking advantage of all the free food on offer. What a change from battling the crowds and noise in the departure lounge. Yes, they deserved to spend their money on this kind of luxury. The holiday was off to a great start.

Landing in Tenerife was like déjà vu, but this time it was his beautiful wife sitting beside him, not Phil, and he wasn't about to board a ferry to La Gomera. Instead, they transferred to the opposite side of the island and checked into the all-inclusive BLUESEA Puerto Resort. Paul couldn't help noticing that the bed alone was bigger than the entire cabin he and Phil had shared. But enough thinking backwards, time to live in the moment and be fully present with Nic.

In the dining room, Paul pulled out her chair. Remembering her favourite, he asked: 'Would you like a piña colada?'

'Yes, please.'

He passed the buffet and saw an array of fresh fish. *Good, she'll love that.* The barman was friendly and spoke perfect English. As Paul crossed back to their table, he couldn't help but admire Nic. She looked so beautiful sitting there, the sun catching her hair.

'Here you go, sweetheart.' He sat down and raised his glass. 'To you, to us. Let's have a great week.'

She didn't hold up her glass. 'It's not quite as simple as that, Paul.'

'Huh?'

'By the end of this week I will let you know if I still want to be married to you or not.'

Paul was still in shock when he opened the curtains the next morning. Nic's statement had hit him in the chest like a wrecking ball. He was on trial, his marriage on probation. So many questions ran through his mind. Why now? Why wait until they were on holiday? But he was too scared to ask, in case the answers killed all hope before it began. He knew some of the conversations they'd had in the last few days had taken a bit of a shine off his homecoming, but this latest had flung his life into darkness. In contrast, Nic seemed more relaxed. After all the times she'd played second violin, it was now her orchestra to conduct.

Okay, Paul. Breathe.

He was relieved to see blue skies and sunshine. Nic loved the sun. It would give her a lift. He made the coffee and brought it to her in bed.

'Here you go, love.'

'Thanks, love.'

Breakfast was served in the same restaurant. To Paul it felt like revisiting the scene of the crime, but he had six more days to prove himself. He would do everything to save his marriage. He brought their juices to the table, then queued at the omelette station and brought back her favourite.

They finished in time to find a good spot by the pool to sunbathe, cool off, and relax. How long had it been since they'd been on holiday together? Years. He'd always been so busy with the challenge, she'd gone off with her girlfriends instead. Nic settled in to read her book. Paul brought her a cocktail, then took himself off to the gym for some light training. The workout room was empty, which gave him the mental space to think about her declaration.

On reflection, he was glad she'd spoken her truth, though he'd have preferred if it hadn't been in the form of an ultimatum. But he realised she must have felt it necessary to take such a stand, to make sure she'd been heard. Clearly, she was still processing her emotions – and, what was scarier, her options.

He didn't doubt she had the moral high ground; she'd suffered through the last four years just as much as he had, but it hadn't been because of a dream she'd wanted to achieve. It was because he'd dragged her unwillingly into his. He shuddered to think how close he was to losing her for good. Was a week going to be long enough to show her how much he'd changed?

For the rest of the day, his mind churned through all he could do to show her his love. He fetched and carried, told her how beautiful she looked and eliminated all talk about the ocean, Phil, *Didi*, salt sores and any of his fears.

Over dinner, he listened as though they were on their first date and, whenever possible, steered the conversation to some of their happiest memories and plans for some fun trips in the future.

'Fancy a stroll?'

'Sure.'

As the week wore on, evening walks along the promenade became a ritual. They would enjoy the warm air and setting sun and find a nice bar for an after-dinner drink. Ignoring the football playing on wall TVs, he would keep his focus on her.

She seemed to appreciate the effort. As each night passed, he felt her warming. Their conversations became more hopeful and Paul's confidence began to grow.

He told her how Phil thought he'd make a good support worker, and could connect him with some headhunters.

'I was thinking it'd be lovely to earn some extra cash so we could enjoy more holidays like this, what do you think?'

'I think you have to be careful.'

'How do you mean?'

'There are a lot of companies like that who talk a good game but don't provide the best care.'

Given her background in the medical profession, Paul paid attention to what she had to say.

'Knowing you, you'd struggle working for someone who provided poor quality care and—'

'Keeping my mouth shut?'

'Yeah.'

Paul smiled. His wife knew him well. But it was worth giving it a go. He hoped it would give him the same satisfaction as working with the fire service had, the feeling he was making a positive difference in another person's life. Worst-case scenario, if it didn't, he could walk away. He would still have his pension and Nic's wage. If, of course …

Paul's seven days were up. How the week had flown. He took extra care to shower and change before heading down for their final dinner. She looked amazing, suntanned, and a little more relaxed. He pushed the button for the lift and dared to hope the ride back up to the room would feel as happy and romantic as the ride down. He steered her towards a lovely table in the corner, which would offer some privacy for their conversation. He brought the drinks, set them down and came back from the carvery with beef for himself and fish for her. He raised his glass.

'Cheers. How's the fish?'

'Lovely, thanks.'

Two mouthfuls in. *Here goes*, he thought. 'Well, love, it's been a great week. I think you know I really want to be with you, I want us to be together.'

He waited. Took a swig of water. Readjusted his cutlery. How long should he let the silence hang? Should he push for an answer? His whole future was riding on what she said next.

'Yes, I want us to be together.'

Paul put down the fork he had been strangling and picked up his glass, smiling: 'To us.'

As they boarded the bus to take them to the airport the next day, Paul felt he was coming home from his honeymoon.

'How many parties do you think James will have had while we were away?' Nic asked.

'Let's hope he listened this time. Believe me, I will have a good sit-down with him when I get home. We need to get him back on track before he derails his life.' Just as his father had done for him.

Across the aisle, a couple stared at their mobiles. The man looked up and asked Paul: 'Who are you with?'

'EasyJet.'

'Our flight is cancelled.'

'Oh, how come?'

A voice behind Paul answered. 'Ours too. Spain is on lockdown.'

'Really?'

'No flights allowed in, mate.'

Paul checked his phone. *Flight delayed.* Well, that could be okay, right? 'Let's not worry till we get there,' he told Nic.

The airport was in chaos. Lines of people with no one in charge. Paul and Nic made their way to the easyJet office and were horrified to see the queue snaking off around the corner. Several people were wearing face masks. *To each their own*, thought Paul. He had heard something about a virus but was not sufficiently stressed about it to wear a mask.

If three hours on the rowboat had been slow going, it had nothing on three hours standing in the airport queue surrounded by a stressed-out crowd. Paul felt sorry for the families with young cranky children, and if the backpackers were anything like he was in his youth, they would probably be penniless by this stage of their holiday. That said, even though he had money in his pocket, there was nowhere to spend it. Shops, bars, restaurants were all closed. Then he heard that sickening sound of clanking metal as the staff pulled the shutters down on the check-in desk, with more than a hundred people still in front of him.

Staff made their way down the line, handing out scraps of paper.

'What's this for?' Paul asked.

'All our flights are cancelled. This hotel has rooms. Go there and try to book a flight with anyone you can.'

Outside, throngs waited for the bus. Hoping to beat the rush for rooms, Paul hailed a taxi.

'It's bad, man,' the driver said. 'So many sick people on the mainland.'

'But our flight is going straight to the UK.'

'No planes coming into Tenerife, though. Government has shut the border. Some of them had to turn around in the air and go back to England.'

Paul turned to Nic. 'Hopefully it will only be for one night and we can get home tomorrow.'

The driver dropped them a hundred yards from the lobby, where they joined the back of the long queue. Uniformed maintenance workers and housekeepers scurried past them, clearly trying to prep as many rooms as possible. Paul and Nic shuffled forward every time someone up front got checked in. After 30 minutes, they were feeling a little more optimistic as they crossed through the lobby doors. However, the line came to a standstill with ten more couples in front of them. Every receptionist was on the phone. He didn't need to speak

Spanish to understand that they had run out of rooms and were trying to find other hotels that could accommodate the crowd.

Another piece of paper with the name of another hotel was thrust into his hand.

'Right. Looks like it's up to us,' he said to Nic.

Outside, more and more people were arriving from the airport, so they were fortunate to grab a taxi right away. By the time they reached the second hotel it was dark, but mercifully, they got a room. For the first time all week, he turned on the TV. The one English channel reported the gravity of the virus.

'Well, I suppose we'd better make the most of it. Hungry, love?'

'Yes, let's go down for dinner.'

On the way into the restaurant, a couple passed them wearing masks and goggles.

Bit of overkill, Paul thought, but he slathered on the sanitiser just the same. There was only one topic of conversation among those queuing by the buffet counter – how to get home.

The man in front of Paul asked him if he had secured another flight.

'Not yet, mate, just got here.'

'Better hurry, the prices are going up by the hour.'

'Thanks.'

He brought the starters over to Nic, who had found a nice table out of the way. He was happy to remain far from the sense of panic that cut the air.

For the rest of the evening, they searched for flights home. No sooner would a flight become available than it would be booked out. There was talk of repatriation charters that might be allowed to land in a few days, but in the meantime, they were stuck. If he were to look on the positive side, at least the test was over, Nic wanted to be with him. He couldn't imagine what it would have been like if she'd made up her mind to leave him; now fate had intervened to bind them together.

373

The following morning, Paul woke to the sound of someone shouting through a loudhailer. He opened the curtains and stepped on to the balcony. The sight was astonishing. Shops were shuttered. Military vehicles rolled through the streets. Soldiers were stopping tourists. The messages were repeated in English: 'Stay in your hotel, stay in your home.'

A helicopter buzzed overhead.

'Morning, love,' Nic joined him.

'Look at this.'

Down below, clad in face masks, hotel staff were asking guests to return to their rooms. Within minutes they had cordoned off the pool with red and white hazard tape.

'It's like something out of a movie,' he said. 'Or World War II.'

'Pretty view, though,' said Nic.

Until that moment, Paul hadn't taken in the complete vista. They'd been given a room with an ocean view. He looked to the west and saw it.

'Oh, wow.'

Nic followed his gaze. 'Is that——?'

'Yes.'

What were the chances? How strange it was to find himself here, stuck in a hotel he wasn't supposed to be in, with this particular view of La Gomera. He had come full circle. Paul used to say things like 'it's a small world', but that was before he'd set off in a 20-foot boat. Was it only four months since he and Phil had taken that ferry ride to the starting line? He remembered the excitement, the anticipation, the pride in having made it that far. Looking at the island now, he couldn't believe just how naïve he'd been, how little either of them had understood what they would face — not just the physical pain they'd have to endure, the fears they'd have to overcome, but what the race would cost them. The adventure had killed Phil's marriage and brought his own to the very edge.

374

But he'd had to go do it to find out. To discover the joy of dolphins in the wild, the night sky without light pollution from land, the recesses of his thinking mind, and the revelation of who he really was, his purpose in life and his role in society. Now, when he looked out over the water, he wasn't afraid of what was beyond that line in the ocean. He had been to the horizon and rowed past it.

He looked at Nic, his wife, his love, the woman he had pledged to protect and cherish for the rest of his life.

She read from her phone. 'It's been officially declared as a pandemic.'

Shit. While he'd been focused on rekindling their love, he'd paid little attention to the news. How was he going to keep her safe from an invisible enemy?

'This is serious, Nic. Maybe we shouldn't even be trying to cram on to a plane full of germs?'

'What choice do we have if we want to get home? We can't stay here forever.'

'There could be another way,' said Paul, watching the ferry leave for La Gomera.

Nic followed his gaze. 'No.'

'What?'

'Paul Christopher Hopkins, no.'

Paul smiled. 'I could, you know.'

'Yes, I believe you. But I will say this only once – I am not getting in a 20-foot boat so you can row me home.'

Epilogue

30 June 2021

Newcastle upon Tyne

Paul strolled through the gardens of a gated community outside the city centre, checked the address on his phone and confirmed he was at the right building. He looked up at the south-facing apartment on the second floor and called out: 'Ahoy there, matey!' He waited. A few minutes later, Phil appeared on the balcony.

'A-ha!' Phil said with a laugh.

'What's so funny?'

'Turns out you were wrong; people *do* come to see me when I appear on my balcony.'

Paul looked over his shoulder. 'Nah, just me mate. You still can't compete with the queen. But maybe I should call you Juliet?'

'You're certainly no Romeo.'

'Nic might disagree with you there, mate. Anyway, how are you feeling?'

Phil put a hand on his chest and took a shallow breath. 'Not bad for a man who's just survived quadruple heart bypass surgery, I suppose.'

'Indeed.'

Had Phil experienced that innocuous symptom of pain in his teeth and jaw while they'd been in the middle of the Atlantic Ocean, he would have been dead by now.

'Sorry, they wouldn't let me visit you in hospital, but it's great to see you now, even just like this.'

'Yeah, believe me, it's great to be seen.'

'How much longer do you have to self-isolate?'

'Another two days.'

'Do you think you'll feel up to coming on Saturday?'

'Wouldn't miss it.'

It had been 16 months since they'd stepped ashore in Antigua, and oh, how their lives had changed. After a week's delay in Tenerife, Paul and Nic had returned to Newcastle like newly-weds, more in love and more deeply committed to each other than they'd been for years. Paul had taken a part-time job as a caregiver and also temped at a funeral home. In the autumn, he returned to the emergency services and became an ambulance driver, working on the front lines during the pandemic. Now they were both fully vaccinated, the pair of them were planning their next holiday together – a December trip to Bavaria to enjoy the Christmas markets. Nic delighted in telling her friends: 'He's like a new man, and now he even walks the dog.'

Phil and Meme, on the other hand, separated but remained best friends. Meme recovered from the mini-stroke without any permanent damage and was living with her son and daughter and her new greyhound, Hotep. Phil managed to sell their original apartment to a cash buyer who took on the issue of getting the cladding sorted. At work, he and Meme continued to run and grow their telecommunications company together. Their business was doing so well that Meme had hired a new assistant. When she retires, she plans to move back to the United States.

Phil's relationship with Tom had changed too. He was still calling him almost every day, but on his Monday and Thursday visits he no longer took physical care of his son's bathroom and bedtime routine, but left that to the professionals instead. Now they would spend time chatting, or going for a beer together – activities more in keeping with what a father and adult son might do rather than a child dependent on his parent. Their jokes remain as corny as ever.

A month after Paul and Phil had returned to the UK, *Didi* arrived back by ship. Due to the travel restrictions imposed as a result of Covid-19, the boat sat in the yard at Rannoch Adventure for six months. In September 2020, Paul was finally allowed to drive down to collect her. Once again, Nic accompanied him. The day couldn't have been more different than when he'd spent 12 hours packing the boat and driving through the night. Paul was filled with so many emotions. He felt like he was driving to the airport to pick up an old friend and was looking forward to seeing her again. The mood in the car was light-hearted and he was enjoying the conversation about Christmas. By the time they got to Essex, Nic had completed all her online shopping for gifts.

When he pulled into Rannoch, he could see the long line of fancy, similar-looking boats. To him, they seemed bland. In the middle of the yard, though, bursting with personality and bruises, was *Didi*. When she'd arrived in Antigua she'd looked run down but now, having been abandoned all summer, she looked derelict. Most of the signatures had faded; the rust stains, not so much. But when Paul climbed aboard he got that same feeling he'd get when he'd return to his mum and dad's house – a sense of coming home. He opened the cabin. If the sight hadn't been a reminder of their voyage, the smell of damp certainly was. *Didi* needed some love. He wanted to sit there, talk to her, apologise for not coming to fetch her sooner, but he gave himself a nip and jumped off.

'Right,' he said, 'let's get you hooked up and on the road.'

Before leaving on the return journey, Paul thanked the staff and asked them to pass on his details in case anyone came looking for a second-hand boat. He'd almost secured a buyer back in March, but the deal had fallen through because TWAC changed the entry rules, making wooden boats ineligible for the 2021 race and beyond.

In the meantime, until they could sell her, Phil had arranged to have her stored at the Azure Garden Centre in Cramlington, about 15km north of Newcastle. When Paul parked the trailer, chocked the wheels, and drove away that September evening, he felt like he had dropped a child off for her first day at school.

On 12 December 2020, in the midst of the global pandemic, another 21 boats set off across the Atlantic. While those teams were at sea, the rest of the world was also learning what it was like to live in isolation for months at a time.

By the spring of 2021 Paul and Phil were in negotiations with another potential buyer, but before the deal could be completed, the lad found a cheaper boat elsewhere. Paul repainted the hull, replaced the deck lockers. Even after the upgrades, he still worried *Didi* might be marooned on land for the rest of her days.

But, this Saturday, all that was about to change. A young man by the name of Adam had signed up for the 2023 GB Row – a race that would start on the River Thames in London and circumnavigate Britain. Wooden boats were allowed.

'Okay, mate,' Paul called up to Phil on his balcony. 'I've got to head off.'

'Thanks for coming. What time Saturday?'

'Two o'clock.'

'See you there.'

When Paul left, Phil walked back into the apartment, and sat down. He was tired, but it was a different fatigue than he'd suffered before the op. During the winter, it had started to take him three or so days to recover after one of his weekend swims in the sea. The brain freeze was normal, the pain in his jaw probably not. But without any sign of chest pain, or other symptoms he associated with angina, he'd no idea his heart was only getting 20 per cent of its oxygen needs. It wasn't until a few months later, when he started feeling extremely tired after exertion, or by 4pm every afternoon, and experienced a mild tightening in his chest, that he sought medical attention. After a CT scan, he'd learned how lucky he'd been, that not only had he escaped a fatal cardiac infarction, but that his heart had not been permanently damaged. However, he required immediate surgery and would not be allowed home until it was performed. Phil couldn't believe it at first. He'd played sport all his life, exercised, ate a healthy diet, but he was to learn that many an athlete suffered a similar fate. Their hearts could quickly go from 45 beats per minute to 180, forcing more blood around the body, sometimes dislodging plaque along the way.

Due to Covid-19, the hospital restricted visitors, but because of Meme's 28 years as an ICU nurse, she was allowed to sit with him in recovery. When he was coming out of the anaesthetic, he could hear her say: 'It's okay, darling, just relax.'

He felt her hand on his shoulder. 'Lie back, now, you're okay.'

Her voice felt like a warm blanket, protecting him. She was his angel, and he knew she would always be there for him, as he would for her. They were soulmates, just not ones that could live together.

On Saturday, 3 July, Paul got to the garden centre at 1.30pm. The previous night, he'd loaded the car with all the spare equipment he'd agreed to pass on as part of the sale. As he'd handled each piece of kit, he'd been reminded of poignant moments on the ocean: the day he tried to make water with the emergency pump, the time he scrambled up the rope ladder when he thought he was being chased by sharks – every item had a tale to tell and now they'd all belong to someone else. For months he'd wanted to sell the boat, and be able to donate more money to their charities, but now that the moment had come to hand *Didi* over, he felt reluctant to let her go. She'd been part of his life for five years now. Secretly, he wished he could do it all again, only better. When Adam had told him that he was struggling to find a team-mate, he was tempted, especially now that GB Row were claiming their race to be the world's toughest row because of the need to navigate busy shipping channels and handle drastic tidal changes at various points around Britain. But Paul had managed to say no.

He parked the car next to *Didi* and loaded the kit on board for the last time. He'd just finished attaching the light bar to the trailer when Meme drove up. She walked around to the passenger side and opened the door. Paul watched Phil push himself out of the seat without using his arms, something he'd been advised to do until such time as his sternum had knitted back together.

Paul checked his watch. It was 1.59pm. For once, Phil was bang on time.

'Well, well, well,' said Paul, 'did that surgeon accidentally install a pacemaker while he was in there?'

Phil grinned. 'Good one, skipper. I'll save that for Tom.' Phil walked slowly towards *Didi*.

'Wow, Paul, you've done a great job getting her ready. So sorry I couldn't help.'

'No bother, mate, just glad you're okay.'

'Never better.'

A black four-wheel SUV arrived and two men got out. One of them introduced himself as Adam's dad, and the other was a friend of his.

'So, can you show us what's what?'

The sky was getting darker, just like Paul's mood. He wanted this to be over with, like ripping off a plaster. Having to spend time showing them all the kit, and how *Didi* functioned, felt like pulling it off millimetre by millimetre, memory by memory. When they hooked her on to the SUV, Paul felt dangerously close to crying.

Meme came to his rescue: 'Paul, why don't I get a photo of you and Phil with *Didi* before she goes?'

'Thanks.'

Paul and Phil posed either side of her bow and gave her a kiss. Meme captured the moment before the first drops started to fall. Meme took her camera back to the car.

'I suppose we'd better get going,' said Adam's dad.

'Yeah, sure.'

The two men hopped in the SUV and started to drive off. The ground was uneven and *Didi* pitched and rolled as though she was on the ocean. Paul and Phil stood there waving, oblivious to the rain pouring down on top of them, until *Didi* disappeared around the bend.

'And then she was gone.' Paul choked back the tears that loomed.

'She had the heart of a lion.'

'Yeah.'

Phil turned to Paul. 'Did you tell them not to change her name?'

'I forgot.'

'Don't worry, she probably won't let them.'

They stood there a while longer, missing their friend, the one who had been the true heartbeat of their voyage.

'So, Phil, what's next for you?'

'Physio, and some light training in the near future. But. For my seventieth birthday, in 2024, I'm going to America to hike the Appalachian Trail, from Georgia to Maine.'

'Really? How long is that going to take?'

'About five months. Want to come?'

Desire for adventure welled up in Paul, and for just an instant, he felt himself teetering on a cliff edge. But the row across the Atlantic Ocean had changed his outlook on life, forever. He didn't need to prove himself any more, nor did he need to hear his dad whisper on the wind that his place was at home either. Paul stood tall, comfortable in his skin. Above all else, he cherished the love he and Nic had rekindled, and he refused to risk anything that might threaten it again.

He rested a hand on Phil's shoulder. 'Yeah, no. Sorry, mate. I'll be cutting the grass that summer.'

Author's Note
Niamh McAnally

Life offers us millions of moments. From the mundane to the extraordinary, the familiar to the exotic. Many of them pass us by, so wrapped up are we in blinkered routine. But, if you keep your eyes open and listen with your soul, you will be ready to witness one of those magical moments, a moment that will be forever seared on your retina and engraved on your heart.

And so it was, on 20 February 2020, at 5.30pm Atlantic Standard Time, that my husband, Gary Krieger, and I happened to be in the right place at the right time with an open-minded intention – to capture a moment of glory for someone else.

We had been sitting in the cockpit of our sailboat home, *Freed Spirit*, berthed at Nelson's Dockyard, the UNESCO World Heritage Site situated on the southern coast of Antigua. This historic venue, that had once housed members of the British Royal Navy and Admiral Nelson of the Battle of Trafalgar fame, is habitually alive with activity. True to tradition, it is still a working harbour that attracts many a mariner looking for shelter or in need of ship repairs. But tourists also throng the paved walkways to photograph history. A museum tells stories to the curious. Respectfully restored hotels offer luxury accommodations to holiday-makers, and charming restaurants propose chilled libations for the thirsty.

Gary and I had spent the winter months sailing north through the Caribbean islands from Grenada. Ordinarily, we would anchor offshore, or tie up to a mooring ball in the harbour. But we had been invited to give a talk at one of John Kretschmer's sailing classes on what it was like to live and cruise full-time on a sailboat. As an author, and renowned sailing instructor, John's classes on land, and aboard his famous yacht, *Quetzal*, draw 'students' from all over America and beyond. We were honoured by the invitation and looking forward to sharing our experiences with those wishing to sail away.

We were finishing a late lunch when we noticed people walking towards a podium at the end of the dock. I had never heard of ocean rowing until the day before, when I'd seen an old wooden rowboat on display in the dockyard. I couldn't fathom the idea that someone had rowed it across the Atlantic Ocean. While I had worked as a scuba instructor in the Florida Keys for several years, and had lived aboard *Freed Spirit* since 2016, my longest open water passage had been a horrendous ten days beating into high wind and seas on our voyage from the Bahamas to Puerto Rico. I wasn't in a hurry to experience that again. So, I couldn't imagine what these rowers must go through, and was thrilled to learn that two men from the UK were about to row ashore. Rumour had it that they had no family on island to greet them.

Rather than wait with the growing crowd ashore, where the actual finish line was obscured from view, we decided to jump in our dinghy and drive to the mouth of the harbour to cheer them in. Beyond the reef marking the edge of the inlet, the seas were rough. I pulled my Canon camera out of our dry-bag and through the zoom lens scanned the horizon.

'Can you see anything?' Gary asked.

'Just the Atlantic Campaigns media boat flying the Antiguan flag. And lots of swell. Wait, what's that? Can you circle back?'

Gary manoeuvred the dinghy to keep us facing out to sea. I clicked and enlarged the image in playback. No. Just an inflatable boat, bigger than ours, carrying two of the race officials who'd passed us earlier. We waited. Bobbed around. And waited some more.

'As soon as we see them cross the finish,' I said, 'let's hurry back so we can join the greeting party as they step ashore.'

'Sure,' said Gary.

'Only, not too fast, we don't want to upset them with our wake.'

Gary laughed. 'They've survived massive Atlantic rollers in a rowboat, I don't think the wavelet our outboard spits up is likely to put them off their stroke.'

Trying to swallow my mother hen, I returned to my camera lens.

'Oh my God. I think that's them.'

'What? Where?'

'Left of the media boat. I think I see a dot.'

But then it disappeared. The light was fading. Did I imagine it? No. It rose into frame on top of the next swell. I clicked again.

'It's them, it's gotta be them! Woohoo!'

I kept clicking, my camera sounding more professional than I did. My stomach heaved; my hands shook. Through my zoom lens I watched them swap places, one stood by the cabin, the other rowed. We were just to the west of the red and green channel markers when they crossed the line and the cannon fired and the horns and whistles blew. I'd never heard such a cacophony. Everyone waved and cheered. The men waved back. Beside me, Gary whooped and hollered and whooped some more, his face beaming with delight. Instead, my words were scarce, but my tears abundant.

And then the moment came. The moment I knew that would live in my memory forever. They stood up and lit their flares. The media and TWAC boats circled them. Outside the white water ring they churned up, Gary motored us in the opposite direction. *Click, click, click.* My eye was glued to the viewfinder capturing this incredible scene. *Click, click, click.* Then, on the very next pass, the Antiguan flag crossed left of frame, the white flare burned to the right. Red sparks reflected on the water below casting a sunset over the rowboat and silent oars. And there, in the centre, suspended in triumph, were the two men we would come to know as Paul and Phil.

CLICK.

'Oh. My. God.' I said. 'I think we've got *the* shot!'

Gary nodded. In our non-verbal way of communicating that comes from living 24/7 on a 40-foot boat, he read my thoughts and peeled us away. We scrambled to tie up in time and ran down the dock just as the rowboat came into sight for the excited crowd.

After the welcome ceremony was over and Paul and Phil were sitting down to their first meal outside the restaurant, we wandered over and introduced ourselves. They were incredibly gracious, answering all sorts of questions. Since they had no friends or family in Antigua, we invited them to dinner on *Freed Spirit* for the following night.

During the day I wondered what to prepare for what would be their first home-cooked meal. We wanted to treat them to whatever they wanted but also didn't want to make it too rich lest their tummies would need time to adjust. Since they'd managed to stomach a hamburger the night before, steak and salad seemed the way to go.

We spent a lovely evening chatting and learning all about them. When I showed Paul the photograph we'd taken of their *flares up* moment, he was moved to tears. For him it summed up not just the 70 days at sea but the four-year struggle it had taken to get there. Once they learned I was a writer, we discussed the idea of this book. I told them I wasn't interested in writing about how to row an ocean, but if they were willing to dig deep to the emotional reasons of *why* they rowed that ocean, and how it had impacted them and their families, then I was all in. Paul's response was: 'I always knew we would find someone to help us on this journey — I just never thought it would be at the end.'

Acknowledgements

A note from Phil Pugh

I am deeply grateful to Meme Pugh. Thank you for all your love and support throughout our marriage. You've always been there for me, supported me throughout all these crazy challenges and kept our business running smoothly during my absences. When I woke up from heart surgery there you were, soothing me. I treasure our continued friendship.

To Rod and Alex, thank you for accompanying me on the earlier challenges and for your continued support. Tom, your patience with me and understanding that I could call only twice a week from the ocean made all the difference.

We knew the Talisker Whisky Atlantic Challenge would take a toll on our bodies. Paul and I are indebted to our personal trainer, Martin Whitaker of OneTake Fitness, who donated so much of his time to help get us into the physical condition required to keep rowing no matter what the ocean threw at us.

Special thanks to all the local companies who supported us: Driftwood Ltd, Satcom Global, PureGym, the Gate, Succorfish, Azure Charitable Enterprises, North Tyneside Council, NE1 and Tariq Albassam, Excelsior Academy, MOTIF Pictures, SJP Wealth Management and Mark Beverley, BBC Newcastle, Spice FM, and Port of Tyne Authority. We'd also like to thank all the members of the North Tyneside gyms who supported our fundraising events. Without all of you, we'd never have made it to the starting line.

When we finally arrived in Antigua, we were welcomed by so many strangers, two of whom invited us to dinner on their boat. Gary and Niamh, thank you for your hospitality and Niamh for all the work you have put in to writing our story and pushing us to think about the real reasons we chose to take on the World's Toughest Row.

To Paul, what an opportunity you gave me to row an ocean with you. I couldn't imagine a more fitting end to my five years of challenges. We complemented each other's skills, compensated for our weaknesses and made a great team. I will never forget our time at sea. Friends for life, mate.

And to *Didi*, you really are a dream boat. For 70 days you were our home and protector, especially the night the torpedo wave threatened to drown us all. But we trusted you and you delivered us safely to Antigua. May you continue to ride the ocean swells for years to come.

Acknowledgements

A note from Paul Hopkins

I would like to thank my wife, Nic, for putting up with me through all the years of planning and the row itself. I understand now how difficult it was for you, especially when I was away for Christmas. Nic, I love you.

To my mum, my children Sean, Jamie and James, thank you for believing in me and supporting me on this challenge. I'd also like to thank my dad for all he did to help shape me into the man I am today. I wish he had lived long enough to see us cross the finish line.

To Dave Linsley, thank you for letting us store *Didi* on station while we worked to get her ready for inspection.

Carl Latimer, your help with course plotting and weather updates while we were at sea was invaluable, not to mention how comforting it was that you were always available at the end of the phone. Thank you, Jeff Neasham, for your land-based support and especially to Zoe Neasham for your thoughtfulness, and, of course, introducing me to Phil.

To the army of supporters who helped us with fundraising and attended our events, thank you, and especially to the children from Hadrian Primary School for the fantastic Christmas carol concert that brought both me and Phil to tears.

Phil and I are especially grateful to the 3,000 people who signed the boat. Your faith in us helped spur us on during the difficult days. And to all our 'dot watchers' – it wasn't until we returned that we learned just how many of you were cheering us on. Thank you for all your messages on Facebook. We never realised just how many people's lives we had touched.

To everyone at Atlantic Campaigns, thank you for all your support. I'd especially like to thank Ian Couch. Despite my initial grumpiness, I completely understand you were doing your job, and because of your attention to detail you kept us and all the other teams safe.

Sincere thanks to Niamh and Gary. Niamh, you've worked on this book way longer than it took us to row an ocean. What an amazing job you've done. We're thrilled with how you told our story and getting it to print is just out of this world. Gary, we appreciate how you've supported this project from the beginning and knowing how much Nic gave up spending time with me, I can imagine how much time you missed out on with your new bride.

Finally, other than Nic, the person I would like to thank the most is Phil. If it wasn't for you, mate, I would probably never have rowed the Atlantic. You stepped in when I needed someone the most and you never once let me down. Thank you for helping me achieve one of the greatest challenges of my life.

Acknowledgements

A note from Niamh McAnally

Paul and Phil, thank you for trusting me to write your story, for allowing me to push you to dig deeper emotionally and spiritually and unearth the real reasons you undertook this challenge.

It has taken me two years of research and interviews, writing and editing, but it has been a labour of love because I still get goosebumps remembering that moment in Antigua when you held your flares up.

To Nic and Meme, thank you for your support and for graciously allowing me to delve into your personal lives in order to show how the challenge impacted you and your marriages. You are the heroines of this story. Rod and Alex, thanks for chatting with me about your dad and your brother, Tom.

Many thanks to everyone at Atlantic Campaigns, especially Carsten Olsen and Ian Couch for taking the time to answer all my questions both in person and online. Thank you, Laura, Lia and Nikki for co-ordinating those communications. Carsten, I greatly appreciate your permission to reproduce photographs from the race.

To Roger Haines, the man who built *Didi* with his own hands and was the first person to row her across the Atlantic, thank you for helping me understand how the boat was constructed. You named her well.

Dave Linsley, I appreciate the time you spent educating me on the workings of the fire station and Paul's career as a firefighter.

From the first draft of my memoir, *Following Sunshine,* to the final draft of *Flares Up: A Story Bigger than the Atlantic,* my editor and agent, Brian Langan of Storyline Literary Agency, has been my rock. Brian, you have taught me so much about the publishing industry and the craft of writing. Your feedback is always perceptive and on point. All my work is better because of your input. In addition, your gentle delivery and excellent communication makes it a joy to work with you.

To Jane Camillin, and everyone on the Pitch Publishing team including Alex, Dean, Graham, and Rob, thank you for believing in this project and bringing Paul and Phil's story to bookshelves around the world. Special thanks to Laura Wolfe for organising the publicity and to Duncan Olner of Olner Sport Media for incorporating my photographs into his wonderful cover design.

To Academy Award-winning actor, Jeremy Irons, I am honoured and grateful for your inspiring contribution to this book. Thank you for writing the foreword. As an avid sailor yourself, you have a natural respect for the sea and a great appreciation for the plight mariners often face.

Every writer needs a tribe and I am blessed to be the founding member of Zoomwriters International. Thank you to Ben Tufnell, Billy Green, Catherine Johnstone, Conor McAnally, Emy Lucassen, Lisa 'Lily' Orban, Nina Smith, Sandy Foster, and Wendy Williams, all of whom I met via Curtis Brown Creative's writing school. The ten of us are geographically spread across the globe but we meet online once a month to hold each other accountable to our goals, offer constructive feedback and celebrate each of our successes, no matter how big or small.

To Hilary Fannin, thank you for your mentorship and friendship. Your comments are always insightful.

To my beta readers and cheerleaders: Maria Sanger, Monika Tur, Meloney and Don Roy, thank you for your encouragement. Special thanks to my seafaring friends, Roy Campbell and Tayce Wakefield, who offered Gary and me shelter on land during the pandemic. Much of this book was written in their home.

I'm blessed to have the support of both the McAnally and Krieger families. Your encouragement means so much to me, especially the grandchildren who always ask: 'How's your book coming along? When can we read it?' It's wonderful to finally be able to say — 'Here it is!'

To Gary, from the moment I gave you one of my short stories to read you have believed in my ability, invested in my aspirations, and created space for me to write. Whether on land or sea, the best part of my writing day is reading sections aloud to you. You listen with your heart. It's gratifying when a paragraph makes you laugh or you shed a tear. Thank you for your wisdom, for your kindness in how you critique, and above all for the joy, love, and laughter you bring to my life.

And to you, our reader, thank you for coming on this journey. I hope my efforts in bringing you Paul and Phil's story have inspired you in some small way to push through challenges you may face, achieve goals you set for yourself, and to live your greatest life.